THE CORPORATE
MECHANIC

THE ANALYTICAL STRATEGIST'S GUIDE

Jacques Magliolo

THE CORPORATE
MECHANIC

THE ANALYTICAL STRATEGIST'S GUIDE

Jacques Magliolo

The Corporate Mechanic
The analytical strategist's guide

First published 2007

Juta & Co.
Mercury Crescent
Wetton, 7780
Cape Town, South Africa

ISBN: 978-0-702-17282-3

Typeset in 9.5/15 ITC Stone Informal

Project Manager: Sarah O'Neill
Editor: Sandy Shepherd
Indexer: Ethné Clarke
Typesetter: WaterBerry Designs
Cover designer: WaterBerry Designs
Printed in South Africa by Creda Communications

'Business is like an automobile.

It won't run by itself, except downhill.'

Henry Ford

DEDICATION

To my daughter, Marina Alix Magliolo

:: CONTENTS ::

PART II: THE STRATEGIC ANALYST DIVISION

PART III: THE WORK OF A STRATEGIST

:: PREFACE ::

This book, like the previous six books and everything else I've written in the past 11 years, is simply a work in progress.

It is a culmination of experience I've gained since entering stockbroking, but – more specifically – since I started up a corporate finance and research consultancy in July 2000. So, this is my unfinished inventory of knowledge and ideas at a particular point. There is no doubt that by the time I finish *The Corporate Mechanic*, I will have had new insights which will probably be included in future books. Such is the nature of writing – and of learning.

My first book, *Share Analysis & Company Forecasting*, was published in 1995. It represented a combination of concepts I had been thinking about for five years. Similarly, the books, research papers and journals that followed were based on an accumulation of my thoughts.

Share Analysis & Company Forecasting was a consequence of a series of articles I wrote as a columnist for Independent Newspapers in Johannesburg. One reader, who called me after the series on company analysis had been completed, made a pertinent comment. This caller, the managing director of a large JSE-listed company, said: 'Do you know how many of my board of directors simply do not know what factors analysts look at when assessing companies?'

This highlighted a critical issue. If board members do not know the driving force behind share price movements, then there is a need to educate not only those individuals but also corporations on business sense. This was again highlighted the following year when I was working for a venture capital firm. I was commissioned to write a business plan for a petroleum company. After an exhaustive search, I could not find a single book about business plans or even methodologies, written for the South African market. This led to my writing *The Business Plan: A Manual for South African Entrepreneurs* in 1996.

I spent the following six years back in stockbroking. I was approached to set up an equities research division, which ultimately lead to my securing the position of director and partner for the local stockbroker. During this period, South Africa went through an amazing number of corporate finance changes that culminated in a financial services Big Bang. The old boys' club had finally been disbanded, allowing banks and other financial services enterprises to own or start up their own stockbroking firms. No sooner had this occurred than the trading floor was disbanded and, almost simultaneously, the emerging market crashed. These events highlighted the phenomenal growth of global markets and the use of the Internet as a work tool.

Two new challenges had emerged: a need to educate the public on portfolio management (which I dealt with in *The Millionaire Portfolio*, 2002), and new global corporate trends taking hold of world markets (this resulted in the publication of *Jungle Tactics: Global Research, Investment & Portfolio Strategy*, 2003, now a South African MBA textbook).

But new and more complex challenges were surfacing, both in First World economies and in emerging markets. Around the world the growing threat of terror attacks, wars and xenophobia was taking root, while in South Africa black empowerment, higher consumer demand and strong economic, political and business trends were becoming evident of a potential bull run. The new decade also brought online trading to investors. The failure of the development capital market and venture capital market brought home inefficiencies and highlighted the need to restructure the way in which small market capitalisation companies listed on exchanges were handled.

These challenges ultimately piloted the launch of the Alternative Exchange (AltX). The lack of corporate and investor understanding of this Exchange directed me to write a book explaining the need, requirements and corporate and legal issues involved in listing on such exchanges in both the UK and South Africa. *A Guide to AltX* was published in 2004.

The global stock market bull run during the following years and the growth of online trading meant that there was a hunger among investors to take hold of their own stock investments. I met the need for a book on stockbroking strategies for the individual in *Become Your Own Stockbroker*, 2005.

Yet the bull market took place not only in the share arena. Rather, it became even more prevalent in the corporate field, with the growing demand for business plans, due diligence and industry analysis. And so I have written *The Corporate Mechanic*.

This book is distinctive in several ways. First and foremost, *The Corporate Mechanic* is a book for corporate managers and general readers, whether at university or business level. It is concerned with application and strategy, and aims to be practical and easy to implement.

The book is a new approach to strategy, combining the skills of corporate finance companies with direct and long-term corporate needs. But it could not have been written without an extensive grounding in actual business situations. I have been able to test and refine my ideas about organisational design and teamwork, as well as to conceive new ideas, in both long-term consulting engagements and conferences. In all, my consulting, writing and lectures have each enriched the other to culminate in *The Corporate Mechanic*.

Enjoy, and contact me if you have any query.

Jacques Magliolo

bci@magliolo.com
www.magliolo.com

October 2006

PART I:

PRACTICAL ISSUES

CHAPTER 1

THE IMPORTANCE OF STRATEGY

The field of corporate strategy has come under immense scrutiny over the past 20 years and in particular since 1997, when emerging markets crashed and changed the way companies conduct business. There is no doubt that continually shifting trends have repeatedly hit the global economy, to the point that many theorists and market and industry experts have even come to question the viability of strategic thinking.

Why, they ask, should you have a strategy when that strategy is continually changing?

Experience has shown that companies that follow trends ultimately never become winners, whereas those that have well-thought-out strategies in place find that they tend to become leaders in their field. Business owners who have the foresight to have strategic plans in motion will find it much easier to change the direction of an existing strategy than to start one from scratch. Strategy is essential for every organisation, large or small, public or private, service or manufacturing.

The introduction of complex strategy systems in the 1980s and 1990s was a step in the right direction. However, there is still some way to go before the use of strategy by South African companies becomes the norm rather than the exception.

GETTING THE APPROACH RIGHT

Many smaller businesses in South Africa believe that strategy simply means focusing on the company's core skills and products. Then, once they have achieved a level of comfort in the process of identifying their firm's core competencies, they develop a mission statement to make sure that the workers keep focused on doing what they were already doing.

In reality, strategy is never that simple.

Contrary to popular belief, strategy may have nothing to do with a firm's core competencies. Indeed, companies that base their strategic plan on the firm's historic competencies often find themselves in trouble when global markets change or they become the target of a hostile takeover. In the first instance, the company may find that it has started losing market share to the point where it can no longer compete. In a sudden corporate change (as in the second instance), the company cannot focus on anything other than the corporate issue at hand.

These sorts of problems may be one of the reasons why some consider the field of strategy itself to be in trouble.

Many questions have been raised by the apparent failure of strategic planning in the South African corporate sector. While researching and writing *Jungle Tactics* in 1997, I had to stop when emerging markets suddenly took a tumble. It seemed a lack of strategy was responsible for the failure of many firms to take action during that turbulent time. The book took another three years to complete as research and additional findings added new scope to the book.

A conclusion I drew from my research was that companies that continually develop and execute a good strategy are significantly more profitable than those that do not. My analysis of failed companies clearly revealed that their failure was caused by their poor ability to determine the changing needs of their target markets. Corporate strategy is clearly the key to sustainable profitability in the new global economy.

Managers need to understand what does not work for firms, as well as what does. The field of strategy has encountered problems not because corporate strategy itself has failed, but because the wrong approach to strategy has been employed. Ultimately, strategy is simply the foundation of the future profitability of firms. Managers who understand this will be much better prepared to lead the global organisation in the early 21st century – a time of change, constant volatility and uncertainty.

MANAGEMENT FRAMES

During the past three years, I have repeatedly found managers confused about the difference between decision-making processes and strategy that enables them to make informed decisions. What many managers use are actually management frames, and not strategy.

According to Marvin L. Minsky, 'A frame is a stable, coherent cognitive structure that organizes and simplifies the complex reality that a manager operates in. Many frames reside in memory and are usually evoked or triggered automatically. The terms "frame" and "framing" have their origin in cognitive science and artificial intelligence (AI), and refer to the mental representations that allow humans to perceive, interpret, judge, choose, and act.'

There are three types of frames:

• Problem frames: used to generate solutions

• Decision frames: used to choose among clear alternatives

• Thinking frames: structures based on years of experience.

Frames, thus, are decisive in determining the way in which managers view the world. Not only are managers not sensitive to the cognitive frames that form the basis of their perceptions and decisions, they are ignorant of the systematic methods of using these frames and the skills of reframing.

The aim of using frames is to make things simpler and to help focus attention on the issues deemed to be most relevant. This helps in coming to quick decisions more efficiently by avoiding dispersed attention. Since frames are embedded in our minds, they determine the information that is attended to and that which is ignored. Whenever a person experiences something new, he or she tries to match the patterns with past experiences. This pattern-matching is crucial to taking quick action in situations that are contextually similar. Mental structures and processes like pattern-matching thus help in connecting events, elements and so on, thereby structuring our thinking.

But relying on pattern-matching is not appropriate in a rapidly changing global environment. There is hence a need for managers to be aware that the same frames may be potential troublemakers.

> **Example 1.1**
>
> Adopting the wrong frames can prove disastrous for companies. Encyclopaedia Britannica had framed itself as a book publishing company. In 1989, it had sales of R627 million. Five years later, its sales had fallen by 53%. This reversal was due to its incorrect framing. Its competitors had developed CD-ROM versions that were more interesting, less expensive and easier to use. But Britannica persisted with only the original, printed version. And by the time the company realised that a knowledge and information business frame was more appropriate, they were left with little resources to exploit the electronic media. Getting locked into the wrong frame can thus have disastrous financial implications for a company.

Another pitfall to be avoided is to rely excessively on a frame that once delivered spectacular results in a certain place or at a certain time. Frames have to be commensurate with the context, the place and the time of decision-making. The business environment has to be scanned for the right cues for strategic decision-making.

Framing traps

Frames simplify issues. But excessive simplification leads to distortion. Many important things may be kept in the shadows by frames. Frames also result in the setting up of mental boundaries leading to the preclusion of important options. For example, a manager's domestic frame may miss out on global expansion. Improper yardsticks and reference points may also be set up due to frames.

Distortions may cause communication problems within a company. This might be the result of people with different functional backgrounds or cultures having different frames. Business literature refers to the effects of frames on thinking as 'mental traps'. A number of these traps are especially harmful for any company.

- **Frame blindness:** It is risky to be unaware of our frames. When a manager looks at the world through only one mental window he or she fails to see the views presented by the other windows. This may lead to the use of outdated, or even the wrong frames. And the manager may not even be aware of the errors being so committed. This is called frame blindness.

- **The illusion of completeness:** Since most managers are unaware of the operation of frames they tend to believe that they have the complete picture. This is the illusion of completeness and the root cause of incorrect decision-making. There is nothing like a complete frame. Each frame highlights and hides different aspects of any situation. Hence it is important to assess the fit of a frame and identify its gaps and limitations.

- **Overconfidence:** People have a tendency to overestimate what they know. This makes them overvalue their frames and undervalue the relevance of the frames possessed by others. This overconfidence can be detrimental to organisational success.

- **Frame conflict:** Conflict arises due to the presence of various frames and their assertion due to overconfidence. Such frame conflicts may lead to hostility, or even to the casting of aspersions about competence. It is important that all the managers of a company get together and develop a more robust frame that has representation of a few relevant elements of each individual frame. Cross-functional teams can help overcome frame conflict. They may even help identify potential sources of such conflict, thereby preventing their occurrence.

Managers must aim at avoiding such traps. It is possible for them to consciously control their frames and use them to their advantage, using the following three key steps.

- **Frame audit to see the frame:** If a frame is invisible, it cannot be managed. Frame audits help in surfacing your own or your organisation's frame or frames, understanding the frames of others and gaining appreciation of newly emerging frames.

- **Surface your frames:** This is achieved by presenting frames visually. Using interviews, focus groups and discussions helps in representing mental models on paper. System dynamics modelling is also being used for surfacing frames.

- **Identify and change inadequate frames:** It is difficult to identify a poor frame since our frames filter out what we see and create an illusion of completeness. Nevertheless, it is important to constantly challenge our frames.

To ascertain whether frames are effective, ask the following questions.

- Does your frame prompt you to ask the right questions most of the time?
- Have you tested or challenged your frame, or have others tried to do so?
- Does your frame help you resolve tough issues decisively?
- Is your frame easily communicated to and understood by others?

- Do key stakeholders accept your frame as a guide to joint action?
- Is your frame sufficiently simple (without being too simple)?
- Is your frame adaptable to change?
- Does your frame generate solutions that achieve the desired results?
- What are some notable failures of your frame? Where did it lead you astray?
- In which cases did your frame allow you to see the forest for the trees?
- What are some of the deeper assumptions that underlie your frame?
- What is the origin of these assumptions in your past experience?
- How do the frames of those you admire differ from your own?
- How have you improved your framing skills over time?

There are a number of tactics that can be used to effectively challenge frames.

- **Observe the symptoms of frame misfit:** Some of these symptoms are poor results, violations of expectations and inconsistencies. It is important to keep in mind the possibility of a frame being wrong. Experimentation with opposing frames helps.

- **Question your reference points:** Determine from where your or your company's reference points stem.

- **Recognise your key assumptions:** Many of your assumptions may be explicit. But there may be quite a few which lie below the surface. Understanding all assumptions helps recognise how attention is directed and how/what information is filtered. Changing assumptions may lead to changed courses of action.

- **Master techniques for reframing:** Surfacing of frames and identification of weaknesses is the first step. It is necessary to synthesise and create new frames. Selecting the right frame for the situation is crucial. You cannot afford to fall back on habit or conventions while choosing a frame.

- **Use multiple frames:** Experimentation with different frames and an analysis of the solutions for each is called for. It is important that you gain new perspectives by placing yourself in different environments. Thinking about how others would frame the same problem is a good idea. When people with various backgrounds are together, a lot of good perspectives emerge, alternative frames are developed, and even existing frames can be stretched.

- **Look for ways to align frames**: Frame blindness must be guarded against by looking for and exploiting opportunities to align your frames with those of others.

- **Change metaphors to regain control of a frame**: The use of descriptive imagery or strong analogies leads to framing. Your frame will be guided by such external prods. It is better to change the metaphor, under the attack of outside suggestions, and see what happens to the problem. Challenging with alternative images will help you to regain control over a frame and achieve the best perspective on a problem.

- **Challenge others' reference points**: Shifting of others' reference points by adding new dimensions will help you to take control of a frame.

- **Stretch a frame**: It is easier for you to stretch others' frames to the appropriate extent, than to change them completely.

- **Build new frames for new situations**: New situations and contexts require new frames. Stay clear from the temptation to rehash the same old frames in changed business environments.

- **Speak to others' frames**: Opposition to your perspective can be brought down by aligning your message with others' frames. Deep dialogue between organisational stakeholders must be encouraged.

Reframing requires the willingness and ability to live with discomfort for a while. You must seek out opposing, divergent views and instead of considering them as criticisms, use them constructively for reframing. Also bear in mind that people have an emotional commitment to their frames. They require a sufficiently long time to adapt.

Since complex issues cannot be tackled through a single frame, senior managers must ensure that the frames used in such cases are appropriate and robust. Complex decisions should be evaluated using a variety of alternative frames. Finally, keep in mind the difference between managers and leaders. Managers operate within existing frames and execute. On the other hand, leaders have thinking, questioning minds. They provoke new ideas, operate across frames, and constantly keep reframing. Challenging old frames and envisioning new ones are the hallmarks of a leader.

A CHANGING WORLD

Many managers, diverted by the daily battle with mediocre issues, often fail to realise that their principal task has changed during the past decade, from short-term trading to long-term planning. At one time, to be a successful manager you had to be a capable trader and able to make sound, intuitive decisions based on past experience. Then, the practitioners of scientific management began to concentrate on operational efficiency and devised many valuable management techniques for their purpose. Today, good management means leading a business enterprise through successive radical changes, out of obsolete activities and into new opportunities, in order to keep pace with accelerating technology and shifting social and economic forces.

As business author Peter Drucker has continually pointed out, managers need to concentrate more on effectiveness (doing the right things) than on efficiency (doing things right). Management has become much more difficult than ever before. It demands an ability to recognise the forces of change and to establish a favourable climate for introducing change, despite the normal resistance of people.

Unfortunately, too frequently senior managers close their minds to change or give lip service to long-range planning of change. There are perhaps two reasons for this:

- **Failure to accept the inevitability of change.** Anyone can easily recognise and accept the changes that have occurred during the past 10 and 15 years. The flaw is in thinking that such changes will not affect the future or that somehow the latest change is the final change and there will be no more.

- **Failure to comprehend the accelerating rate of change.** This shortcoming is perhaps due to the heavy proportion of senior management jobs being occupied by administrators rather than innovators, ie people whose inclinations are to operate the business tidily for today rather than to imagine what tomorrow might bring. This is where the communication of analytical reports and media public relations (PR) comes into play.

Whether or not top managers are receptive to change, they are continuously under pressure to do something, either to move in some new direction or to halt movement in another direction. The problem is often one of time. But if the manager does not have the time to plan change, then he or she should hire someone who will be the specialist in planning and monitoring strategy, undertaking reports and communicating with the shareholders.

The inevitability of change, the reactions it provokes and the accompanying pressures, present a serious dilemma to top management. First, there is the danger of doing nothing or of discounting the forces at work. Second, there is the problem of changing too quickly or without the resources needed to succeed. The path of progress is littered with the skeletons of pioneers who failed to appreciate the enormity of their task. Statistics in South Africa suggest that six out of 10 new ventures fail because of a lack of planning, resources and skills.

To make matters more confusing, managers who do want to adopt strategic methods to enhance profitability and protect against future market changes find that strategy itself is in a state of confusion. With the emergence of multiple (and, indeed, contradictory) strategic models representing various approaches, it is vital for today's strategist to be conversant with all strategic approaches.

Regardless of which course is adopted, no matter how well the plans are made and implemented, the risks are great and the stakes are high. However, if the manager has completed the research and analysis, followed by due diligence with due care, there is no reason why failure should even be considered. Implementation should be a matter of course.

PROFIT NEEDS PLANNING

Business planning is a process of:

- Assessing the company's position and the opportunities and threats it faces
- Setting goals, establishing priorities and developing strategies
- Making plans for each business activity
- Ensuring that plans are carried out.

It is a complete and continuous process directed towards improving business results. It is a systematic and logical process that does not have to be scientific to ensure the success of an enterprise.

It deals with the questions:

- Where are we going?
- How are we going to get there?
- How are we going to remain successful when we get there?

It calls for dynamic, imaginative thinking. It means probing the future. It requires an attitude of flexibility and the capacity to change. It calls for making long- and short-range plans and implementing them in thorough programmes designed for specific needs. The objective is to put the company into a leadership position in three respects: product, profit, growth. In the final analysis, these business results are expressed in terms of profit.

Profit is not by any means the only objective of the business, but it is an essential one, and therefore merits emphasis.

Over the past 15 years, I have found that most corporate owners recognise that a modern business enterprise has a variety of responsibilities, including those to its shareholders, customers and employees, to the community and to government. These responsibilities, however, can be met only by a profitable business. A business that fails to make a profit, or barely avoids a loss, will be unable to fulfil its responsibilities, and will often cease to exist. The crucial measure of effective performance in business, therefore, is profit, which is really a measure of how well the business performs economically. It is also the way that shareholders see a company.

In an environment of competition and change, continuing profit is dependant on both improving what exists and developing new opportunities. The amount of profit is largely contingent on how effectively and efficiently resources are used. Resources are inevitably limited – all demands for manpower, money and plant can never be satisfied. A key part of business planning lies in determining how resources should be allocated to secure the best long-term results. It forces corporate owners to choose alternatives and to convey these reasons to the investing public.

Managers have always planned. However, methods that were successful in the past will not necessarily be suitable for meeting the challenges in the future. The accelerating rate of change is making today's products and services rapidly obsolete. The financial implications of major decisions, both in magnitude and degree of risk, are becoming greater. Decisions must therefore be based on a full assessment of what the future is likely to bring and of alternative courses of action.

STRATEGIC APPROACHES

There are countless books on strategy, business policy and other methods to increase profit. While some may take a slightly different approach in minor areas, they are generally all the same. Until recently, almost all the articles written on the topic had as their foundation the same basic assumptions and all suggest that consultants who are specialists in their field should be hired to undertake specific projects. For instance, if you need a due diligence report, hire an accounting firm to undertake a financial audit and attorneys to assess contracts, patents and copyrights.

There does not seem to be a school of thought on strategy that suggests that all corporate deals can be handled by an internal division that is also independent. This is the nature of *The Corporate Mechanic*.

The various 'schools of thought' in the field of corporate strategy are based on common foundations and assumptions that managers need strategy either to find solutions for problems when they occur or solutions for problems that may occur in the future. There are no models that combine the following:

- **Methods to find solutions and eliminate existing problems**: these are tackled through *troubleshooting techniques*.
- **Methods to prevent new problems from occurring**: these are resolved through *analytical processes*.
- **Methods to strategise for future possible changes (global trends) and to assess specific corporate issues** (such as mergers and acquisitions): these are resolved through *research* and *due diligence*.

In this book I show that you can combine the above in a system I call The Chairman's Office, detailed in Chapter 4.

Strategic approaches can be categorised using the following terms:

- Complex-historic (emergence)
- Complex-futuristic (predictive modelling)
- Simple-historic (self-confirming theories)
- Simple-futuristic (extrapolation).

Every strategic approach, or model, can be studied quite effectively by using these descriptive terminologies. The following is a brief overview:

Complex-historic: This approach assumes that the competitive environment is highly complex and therefore uncertain. This means that the emerging or future business environment could be volatile or chaotic or both. The idea of an emerging market is based on the concept that the global business environment is nearly the same as the natural environment. That is, it is highly complex and constantly adapting in an organic manner. Most analysts who subscribe to this view suggest that it is impossible to predict the future, so there is no need to try. As a result, these strategists focus on the present.

Furthermore, there is an assumption that the organisation can 'self-organise'. This system ignores the fact that many managers do not like change and, therefore, will avoid making necessary alterations to their business structures to account for changing consumer demands.

Complex-futuristic: This approach focuses on understanding the long-term future (10 years ahead, or more) as a complex system, but ignores the shorter-term future, such as changing trends in the next five years. Analysis suggests that there are a number of contradictions within this model and therefore strategists tend to use a hybrid model, combining this approach with the simple-historic, as outlined below.

Simple-historic: This system focuses primarily on the organisation and its current resources. Here the theorist generally begins a strategic quest with the assumption that the world will continue to buy whatever product or service the firm currently produces.

In this system, there is an assumption that the firm will leverage existing resources in the future. Some analysts have called the complex-futuristic and simple-historic approaches 'self-confirming theories', because they focus on continuing historic competencies.

Simple-futuristic: This approach involves a linear extension of present (historic) trends into the future. If the firm's revenues have been growing at 20% per year and the firm has consistently achieved after-tax profits equal to 12% of sales, the simple-futuristic strategist would assume that those relationships will be stable in the future. Regardless of what many companies say they do in the area of corporate strategy, many continue to use this approach as the foundation of their strategic plan. In its simplest form it is called 'budgeting'.

So, which of the multitude of strategic approaches should strategists adopt? Essentially, the strategic approach a firm adopts should have everything to do with the future performance of the firm. In fact, in South Africa it often has everything to do with the very survival of the firm. The strategic system used must be about profit and performance. A good understanding of all four generic strategic models will help managers discover the effective strategic approach that will lead their own firm to a future of maximum corporate profit. In addition, it is important to determine the cost of an error in predicting future profits, as outlined by the following example:

Example 1.2: Cost of prediction errors

There is always a cost involved in failing to predict a certain variable accurately. The cost of the prediction error can be substantial, depending on the circumstances. For example, failure to make an accurate projection of sales could result in poor production planning, too much or too little labour versus capital, thereby causing potentially huge financial losses.

How is it calculated?

The cost of the prediction error is basically the contribution or profit lost because of an inaccurate prediction. It can be measured in terms of lost sales, disgruntled customers and idle machines.

Assume that a company has been selling, for R1.00 each, a toy doll that has a cost of R0.60. The fixed cost is R300. The company cannot return any unsold dolls. It has predicted sales of 2000 units. However, unforeseen competition has reduced sales to 1500 units. The cost of its prediction error (that is, its failure to predict demand) is calculated as follows.

The net income as a function of units sold is equal to the number of units (calculated by price minus cost) minus fixed cost.

- **Initial predicted net income:** 2000 units × (R1.00 - R0.60) - R300 fixed cost = R500.00
- **Actual net income:** 1500 units × (R1.00 - R0.60) - R300 = R300.00
- **Actual revenue:** 1500 × R1.00 = R1500.00
- **Total cost of product:** 2000 × R0.60 = R1200.00

It cost the firm R1200 to produce the goods. Add fixed costs to that of R300 and you get a break-even. No profit was made. Therefore, what is the **actual predictive cost?**

Cost of prediction error	=	net income	-	fixed costs
	=	0	-	R300
	=			R300

It is important to be able to determine the cost of the prediction error in order to minimise the potential detrimental effect on future profitability of the company. Prediction relates to sales, expenses and purchases. Research has to be thorough to avoid such errors. Note that the error is not the difference between predicted

>>

net income and actual net income. And, imagine if the amounts above were in the millions. To make an error of R300 is simply nonsensical to even consider, but an error worth R300 million?

WHAT DOES STRATEGY INVOLVE?

Strategy involves analysing possible scenarios to the following questions:

- Where are we now and how did we get here?
- What did we do well, or badly, to arrive at our current position?
- What business are we in?
- Will this remain the same, or will we need to change our business? If so, to what?
- What factors (internal and external) will, or can, have a telling impact on what we do in the future?

These questions are principally about the first phase of formulating a strategy.

As I have stated earlier, one criticism levelled at strategic planning is that the future is too uncertain to predict. The pace of change today no longer allows us to plan 15, 10 or even five years ahead. The five questions raised above are no longer to be asked every two, three or five years, but continually. The strategic process should, in addition, be flexible enough to anticipate and embrace change, instead of resisting or repelling it.

WHERE STRATEGY FITS

How does strategy relate to planning and managing change? Quite simply, strategy comes first, and nothing can really start in earnest in a business until the strategy is in place. Strategy involves forming a path for the organisation to follow that will lead to products or services that customers will want. In an existing business this will usually mean some kind of new departure for the business, requiring the manager to implement various new tactics or sub-strategies. These tactics are usually set out in the component parts of the business plan.

Here, however, lie some of the fundamental reasons for many companies not having strategic departments. There seems to be a misconception that once strategy has been implemented, it is no longer the major priority. Therefore, management theorise, there is no need for the company to continue to pay for the privilege of having a department that isn't effective.

In the structure I call The Chairman's Office, the strategic department is apart from the daily running operations of the firm. It is independent, but holds a prominent position with the managing director and chairman.

As all organisations are different, no two strategies are the same. We all have different strengths and weaknesses, we all spot different opportunities in different ways, and we all want to achieve maximum profits. These can only be achieved with sound and effective strategy.

THE KEY CHARACTERISTICS OF STRATEGY

- The formulation and execution of strategy is uniquely affected by external opportunities, internal strengths and constraints, the organisation culture and the value system of the company, or in the case of a merger, the dominant company.
- It is an essential element of strategic investment and entrepreneurial management.
- It is involved in the development of the long-term objectives of the firm or share portfolio.
- It can and should be deliberately determined and specifically articulated.
- Its implementation can and should be managed.

As a basic tool of strategic management, a competent strategic plan should specify:

- The market priorities used for the allocation of resources or the securities assets.
- The assumptions used to determine priorities.
- The changes necessary to capitalise on the market opportunities.
- The timetable for change.

The strategic plan should provide the point of reference for measuring deviations from:

- Expected environmental conditions
- Expected progress in implementing change.

The strategic plan should describe:

- The objective of the company and assign growth objectives and investment priorities to strategic served markets. These growth objectives should form the basis of a commitment to the desired business mix (asset allocation) to achieve the long-term objectives of the organisation.
- The implementation needed to achieve the desired market position.
- The desired changes in business variables.

Strategic management of a business takes place on several levels: the corporate level, the given strategic business level, the sectors of individual businesses. Successful strategic plans are coherent and integrate all three levels to prevent conflict. The preferred market sector is the starting point for strategy development. The organisational structure may affect the responsibilities for making changes in key variables, but the nature of most changes will be the same. The organisation or portfolio structure is a variable under the control of the entrepreneur, corporate owner or manager, or investor.

How will future changes affect the business? Has the analytical work identified future opportunities and is it prepared to cope with the threats that such changes will present? Corporation casualties are high in South Africa and are likely to increase in future. Although it is usually tougher for a smaller business to survive, size is actually no assurance of continued profitability. Nor has anyone yet devised a magic formula that can guarantee prosperity. Theodore Levitt, from the American Business Association, put it clearly in 1960 when he wrote:

> There is no such thing as a growth industry. There are only companies organised and operated to create and capitalise on growth opportunities. Industries that assume themselves to be riding some automatic growth escalator invariably descend into stagnation. The history of every dead and dying "growth" industry shows a self-deceiving cycle of a bountiful expansion and undetected decay.
>
> (John E Richardson, Annual Editions Marketing 06/07)

While there are many reasons for a business to fail, here are four conditions that managers could take as a guarantee that their business is decaying:

1. The belief that growth is assured by an expanding and more affluent population.
2. The belief that there is no competitive substitute for the company's major product.

3. Too much faith in mass production and in the advantages of rapidly declining unit costs as output rises.

4. Preoccupation with a product that lends itself to carefully controlled scientific experimentation, improvement and manufacturing cost reduction.

CHARACTERISTICS OF SUCCESSFUL STRATEGIES

Back in the late 1980s, I headed a study of over 90 companies that had a successful history of profit growth after listing. These five common characteristics were highlighted:

-   Organised programmes to seek and promote new business opportunities.
-   Organised research and due diligence in potential growth markets.
-   Courageous and energetic management, willing to take carefully considered risks based on good understanding and information.
-   Proven competitive abilities to succeed in their new ventures.
-   Continued and updated information to clients, investors and staff.

Investors attach considerable importance to such factors. Other studies made of companies whose shares are traded on main boards (larger market caps) concluded that those with high price earnings multiples possessed similar characteristics:

-   Cohesive business direction, research and other information easily accessible to staff, investors and clients.
-   Operations in growth markets.
-   Above-average return on equity.
-   Recognised end products.
-   Leadership position in these fields.
-   Record of new product development.

With change coming so quickly and constantly, these factors will become even more vital in the future for any company wishing to improve its position. Indeed, they are prerequisites for survival.

Strategy developed at the corporate level must, therefore, be related to and integrated with strategy development at the individual business level to produce a coherent, integrated, corporate strategy that prescribes the key changes in the business, the resources required and the capabilities needed. These are then implemented.

The same linkage should apply between the individual business segment level and the various market sectors.

THE STRATEGIST

The person preparing a strategy has to have several things in mind when taking on this role.

- To make an organisation stand out from the competition
- To have a significant impact on the company's market share
- To capture the imagination and commitment of the entire workforce
- To establish strategies that are consistent, so that staff and customers identify with what is being delivered, but flexible so that the strategy can exploit change and adapt to such changes
- To be responsive to market and environmental conditions and not merely led by them
- Never to be only theoretical but rather to be focused so that the strategy is clear, defined and understandable to staff and customers, but not cast in stone.

In preparation, the strategist has to know that he or she can answer the following questions.

- **How well do you really understand markets, research, corporate finance?** How much money does the company need to grow, for working capital, fixed assets and marketing costs? How will prices, volumes and costs change over the next three years?
- **What is 'risk financing'?** What type of financing is best for growth?
- **What do investors look for in small businesses?** How do you assess a business environment and a firm's internal processes? How much is the company worth?
- **What kind of management do investors look for?** How strong is the management team? Can the team be improved to stay competitive?
- **Can you draft an effective investment proposal?** What should you put in a proposal and what should you leave out?
- **Can you raise funds?** How to prepare for your first meeting with a potential investor. How to plan and deliver a successful investor presentation.

- Negotiation skills: What will be the key areas of negotiation? The typical stages of a negotiation.

- How to assess offers and close a deal: What is due diligence and how can you prepare for it? What's required for successful investor relations?

WHY PLANNING FOR THE FUTURE IS CRUCIAL

Staggering changes have occurred in South Africa in the last 15 years and future changes are forecast to be as dramatic during the next three decades, locally and globally. In addition, changes are accelerating in every direction and in every environmental sphere. This will affect the production and distribution of goods through the development of new materials, power sources and automated equipment. There will be a significant impact on working hours, leisure time, educational requirements, longevity, government services and ultimately every aspect of an individual's private and working life. In turn, businesses will also be affected. Therefore, while it is professional to have strategies, if these are not implemented, or if such strategies (and the resultant action) are not conveyed to the investment community and general public, the entire process of research through to implementation has just been an expensive waste of time.

CHAPTER 2

STRATEGIC TECHNIQUES

Strategists find that various businesses often require different approaches to identifying problems and thus solutions. For instance, a valuation of a tobacco farm will be very different to conducting due diligence on a furniture company or drafting a prospectus to list on an exchange. In addition, businesses that are experiencing financial problems complicate the corporate process. In other words, different corporate problems often require different strategies.

IDENTIFYING THE PROBLEM

The financial performance of any business can be assessed using three well-known concepts: profitability, liquidity and solvency.

Profitability is the most important determinant of long-term business performance. Profit in an economic sense is the return to management (and operator labour in the case of a farm) and equity. In the long run, the farm manager must earn a competitive return on these contributed resources if the business is to continue. In the short run, the farmer must earn sufficient returns to at least pay for variable costs. If this is not possible, then some short-term response to minimise losses will be necessary. Profit can be measured with an income statement at the farm or enterprise level. In addition, there are a number of financial measures or ratios that can provide further insight into a corporation's profitability.

Liquidity, or cash flow, refers to the ability of the business to meet its cash obligations within a specific time period. Profitability and liquidity are related concepts, but are by no means equivalent. Unlike profit, cash flow includes loan principal payments and proceeds from liquidated assets. Cash flow does not include profitability factors such as depreciation, the value of inventory changes or capital gains and losses. Liquidity is best measured with cash flow statements or budgets.

Solvency refers to the ability of the business to secure debt or withstand adverse conditions. Solvency is synonymous with net worth or owner equity. Owner equity serves as a source of security for acquiring debt capital. Or it can simply serve as a potential credit source, a credit reserve to allow borrowing for unexpected events. Finally, solvency indicates the risk-bearing ability or capacity of the business. Solvency is measured using a balance sheet.

ANALYTICAL TOOLS

There is a host of ratios referring directly to project and strategy that can be used as tools to determine and calculate profitability, liquidity and solvency. While imperfect in their own ways, the following methods can help tremendously in quieting the chaos, surveying the available options and then collecting and evaluating the information you need to choose the best course of action.

- **Ratio Analysis:** There are literally hundreds of ratios available to determine any aspect of business, corporate analysis and accounting/financial strength or performance. In *The Corporate Mechanic* we use ratios that focus on strategic analysis. These are as follows:

  - The *Profitability Index*, which differentiates the net present values of competing proposals to determine profitability.

  - *'Pressing' current liabilities* and *'patient' current liabilities* analysis to determine the flexibility that a company has in paying certain debt, ie its liquidity.

  - *Leverage ratios* and financial leverage to determine solvency.

The more common ratios are as follows:

- **Pareto Analysis:** Often known as The 80/20 Rule, Pareto helps you locate where you can derive the greatest benefit by expending the least relative effort (or cost or resources).

- **Paired Comparison:** This involves composing a table that pits each option directly against each other option. You then weight each for relative importance. It's a fast way to plough through what would otherwise be a huge mess to evaluate.

- **Decision Trees:** This system is used to build a set of 'what-ifs' based on a tree of possible options, assigning the estimated value, costs or savings associated with each choice.

- **Force Field:** You identify all the forces for and against a theoretical change, weighted for the amount of force exerted by each 'side'. This technique can be used for sensitive political decisions. It may also help in mitigating risk and knowing where best to allocate resources and influence.

- **Six Thinking Hats:** A technique which appears in Edward de Bono's book, *Six Thinking Hats*, it is a method for seeing an issue from all perspectives by forcing yourself and your team to adopt different 'thinking hats' that reflect opposing points of view (analytical, positive, negative, creative, etc.).

- **Cost-benefit:** This is a well-known system, used to estimate costs and benefits and determine the delta (the rate of change of a price with respect to changes in the price of the underlying asset). As ever, be sure to account for all the costs of a change.

DECISION-MAKING TECHNIQUES

The techniques in this chapter help the strategist make the best decisions possible with the information he or she has available. With these tools he or she will be able to determine various aspects of a business, map out the likely consequences of decisions, work out the importance of individual factors and choose the best course of action to take.

For instance, to work out the most important changes to make in a business, the strategist would use Pareto Analysis, but to evaluate the relative importance of different options he or she would use Paired Comparison Analysis. This method is used in selecting between good options, whereas choosing between options by projecting likely outcomes is best analysed through Decision Trees.

Force Field Analysis can be used to investigate the pressures for and against change. Looking at a decision from all points of view is well documented in Six Thinking Hats, which is enhanced by Cost-benefit Analysis to see whether a change is actually worth making. In addition, Ratio Analysis enables a strategist to use the company's financial statements to determine whether a company has achieved a reasonable level of profits, liquidity or its solvency rate. He or she can do this quickly and efficiently. The industry score methodology is also quick and uses ratios to determine whether a company is in an 'attractive' industry or not. This last methodology can also be used to assess the industry of competing companies.

Ratio Analysis

Profitability index

The profitability index is used to differentiate the net present values of competing proposals. It compares the initial cash investment to the discounted value of future net cash inflows. This index is used by strategists to rank projects in order of attractiveness.

fig 2.1 :: profitability index calculation

	Ratios	Calculation of ratio
Common usage	• Profit margins	(Any profit figure ÷ turnover) × 100
	• Return on shareholders' equity	(Attributable profits ÷ shareholders' funds) × 100
	• Return on net assets	(Attributable profits ÷ net assets) × 100
	• Return on capital employed	(Operating income ÷ capital employed) × 100

Formula: Profitability index = Present value of cash inflows divided by present value of cash outflow.

Rule of thumb: Strategists would accept a proposal with a profitability index **equal to or greater than 1.** If the index is less than 1, the company is losing money on the proposal.

Warning: A higher profitability index does not always coincide with the project with the higher net present value. Thus, the important characteristic of this ratio is that it eliminates the distorting effect of company size.

The following examples are based on actual projects.

Example 2.1

Assume that the following information has been obtained in relation to two proposals:

Figures in R'000	Proposal A	Proposal B
Initial investment	100,000	10,000
Present value of cash inflows	500,000	90,000

The profitability indices are then:

- Proposal A: R500,000 divided by R100,000 = 5
- Proposal B: R90,000 divided by R10,000 = 9

The net present value of Proposal A is R400,000 and that of Proposal B is R80,000. Based on net present value, Proposal A appears better than Proposal B. However, this would be an incorrect conclusion, because a budget constraint exists. The profitability index should be used in evaluating proposals when budget constraints exist. In this case, Proposal B's profitability index of 9 far surpasses Proposal A's index of 5.

The result is that Proposal B should be selected over Proposal A.

Example 2.2

A contingent proposal is one that requires acceptance of another, related proposal. Hence, the proposals must be looked at together and a profitability index should be computed for the group, as indicated below.

Project	Investment	Present value	Profit Index calculation		Index
A	70,000	112,000	112,000 ÷	70,000	1.6
B	100,000	145,000	145,000 ÷	100,000	1.45
C	110,000	126,500	126,500 ÷	110,000	1.15
D	60,000	79,000	79,000 ÷	60,000	1.32
E	40,000	38,000	38,000 ÷	40,000	0.95
F	80,000	95,000	95,000 ÷	80,000	1.19

The budget constraint is R250,000. Projects A, B and D should be selected, as indicated by the following calculations. Start the calculation by using the top three indices.

>>

- Investment: R70,000 + R100,000 + R60,000 = R230,000
- Present value: R112,000 + R145,000 + R79,000 = R336,000
- The net present value is R336,000 - R230,000 = R106,000

Example 2.3

Consider the following proposals:

	Proposal A	Proposal B
Present value of cash outflow	160,000	210,000
Present value of cash inflow	60,000	40,000
Total	220,000	250,000

The combined profitability index is then: R250,000 ÷ R220,000 = 1.14

Pressing and patient current liability ratio

Pressing current to patient current liabilities is a ratio that describes the degree of flexibility a company has with regards to meeting its debt payment:

- **Pressing liabilities** are those that must be paid without excuse, such as taxes and loans payable.

- **Patient liabilities** are those that offer some flexibility when corporate financial difficulties exist (eg, accounts payable). For example, in times of corporate financial difficulty, the supplier may postpone or even modify the amount of the debt.

fig 2.2 :: pressing and patient current liability ratio analysis

	Ratios	Calculation of ratio
Common usage	• Current asset ratio	Current assets ÷ current liabilities
	• Quick ratio (acid test)	(Current assets - stock) ÷ current liabilities
	• Stock to working capital ratio	(Stock ÷ net current assets) × 100
	• Defensive interval ratio	Defensive assets ÷ projected daily operating expenses

Formula: Pressing current liabilities divided by patient current liabilities

Example 2.4

Assume that a company's current liabilities are made up of the following:

	2005 (R)	2006 (R)
Accounts payable	400,000	500,000
Taxes payable	50,000	60,000
Bank overdraft payable	200,000	220,000
Short-term loans	50,000	60,000

Pressing debt to patient debt is:

2005:	(50,000 + 200,000 + 50,000) divided by 400,000	= 0.75
2006:	(60,000 + 220,000 + 60,000) divided by 500,000	= 0.97

A higher ratio of *pressing* to *patient* short-term debt in 2006 indicates that the company's liquidity is at greater risk.

Leverage ratios

Leverage ratios reveal the extent of debt within a company's capital structure and the company's ability to pay the debt. Financial leverage results from the company's use of debt financing, financial leases and preferred stock.

Leverage-ratio information is derived from a company's balance sheet and is used by strategists to determine the solvency of a company and of that company in relation to competitors.

fig 2.3 :: leverage ratio calculation

	Ratios	Calculation of ratio
Common usage	• General solvency check	(Fixed assets + investments + current assets) × [long-term loans + current liabilities]) × 100

The following are leverage ratios commonly used in analysing a company's financial position:

- **Ratio 1: Gearing** (also called debt to equity ratio). This is calculated by dividing total liabilities by total shareholders' equity. The usefulness of the gearing ratio is enhanced if securities are valued at their year-end market value rather than book value. If year-end values are not representative, average market prices can be used.

- **Ratio 2**: Capital structure ratio. This is calculated by dividing average long-term debt by long-term debt plus owners' equity.

- **Ratio 3**: Owners' equity includes the owners' investment (primarily capital stock) plus retained earnings. It is calculated by dividing owners' equity by borrowed capital.

The financial leverage index is equal to the return on common equity divided by return on total assets. The financial leverage ratio is equal to total assets divided by ordinary shareholders' equity.

Example 2.5

A partial balance sheet for a company follows:

Long-term liabilities	R500,000
Total liabilities	R700,000
Shareholders' equity	R300,000
Cash flow provided from operations	R100,000

The company's ratios are compared to average norms taken from competitors:

	Calculation	Company index	Average norm
Long-term debt to shareholders' equity	500,000 ÷ 300,000	1.67	0.8
Cash flow to long-term liabilities	100,000 ÷ 500,000	0.2	0.3
Total liabilities to shareholders' equity	700,000 ÷ 300,000	2.33	1.5

After comparing the company's ratios to industry norms, it is clear that the firm's solvency is worse than its competitors. The company has a much greater extent of total debt and long-term liabilities in its capital structure and has lower cash flow to cover its debt.

Pareto Analysis

Pareto Analysis is a very simple technique that helps you choose the most effective changes to make. It uses the idea that by doing 20% of the work you can generate 80% of the advantage of doing the entire job. This analysis is a formal technique for finding the changes that will give the biggest benefits. It is useful where many possible courses of action are competing for your attention.

Write out a list of the changes you could make. If you have a long list, group it into related changes. Then score the items or groups. The scoring method you use depends on the sort of problem you are trying to solve. For example, if you are trying to improve profitability, you would score options on the basis of the profit each group might generate. If you are trying to improve customer satisfaction, you might score on the basis of the number of complaints eliminated by each change.

The first change to tackle is the one that has the highest score. This one will give you the biggest benefit if you solve it. The options with the lowest scores will probably not even be worth bothering with. Solving these problems may cost you more than the solutions are worth.

Example 2.6

A manager has taken over a failing service centre. He commissions research to find out why customers think that service is poor. He gets the following comments back from the customers:

1. Phones are answered only after many rings.
2. Staff seem distracted and under pressure.
3. Engineers do not appear to be well organised. They need second visits to bring extra parts. This means that customers have to take more time off work to be there a second time.
4. Customers do not know what time the engineers will arrive. This means that customers may have to be in all day for an engineer to visit.
5. Staff members do not always seem to know what they are doing.
6. Sometimes when the engineer arrives, the customer finds that the problem could have been solved over the phone.

The manager groups these problems together. He or she then scores each group by the number of complaints, and orders the list:

1. *Lack of staff training:* items 5 and 6: 51 complaints
2. *Too few staff:* items 1, 2 and 4: 21 complaints

>>

3. *Poor organisation and preparation:* item 3: 2 complaints.

By doing the Pareto Analysis above, the manager can better see that the vast majority of problems (69%) can be solved by improving staff skills. Once this is done, it may be worth looking at increasing the number of staff members. Alternatively, as staff members become more able to solve problems over the phone, the need for new staff members may decline.

The comments on poor organisation and preparation are few, and could be caused by problems beyond the manager's control. By carrying out a Pareto Analysis, the manager is able to focus on training as an issue, rather than spreading effort over training, taking on new staff members and possibly installing a new computer system.

Key points:

Pareto Analysis is a simple technique that helps you identify the most important problem to solve. To use it:

- List the problems you face, or the options you have available.
- Group options that are facets of the same, larger problem.
- Apply an appropriate score to each group.
- Work on the group with the highest score.

Pareto Analysis not only shows you the most important problem to solve, it also gives you a score showing how severe the problem is.

Paired Comparison Analysis

Paired Comparison Analysis helps you work out the importance of a number of options relative to each other. It is particularly useful when you do not have objective data on which to base your results. This technique makes it easy to choose the most important problem to solve, or select the solution that will give you the greatest advantage. It helps you set priorities where there are *conflicting demands on your resources.*

Paired Comparison Analysis is also an ideal tool for comparing completely different options, such as whether to invest in marketing, a new IT system or a new piece of machinery. These decisions are usually much harder than comparing three possible new IT systems, for example.

For each comparison, you decide which of the two options is most important and then assign a score to show how much more important it is. Follow these steps to use the technique:

1. List the options you will compare. Assign a letter to each option.

2. Mark the options as row and column headings on the worksheet.

3. Block out the cells on the table where you will be comparing an option with itself – there will never be a difference in these cells!

4. Now block out the cells on the table where you will be duplicating a comparison.

5. Within the remaining cells compare the option in the row with the one in the column. For each cell, decide which of the two options is more important. Write down the letter of the more important option in the cell, and score the difference in importance from 0 (no difference) to 3 (major difference).

6. Finally, consolidate the results by adding up the total of all the values for each of the options. You may want to convert these values into a percentage of the total score.

Example 2.7

As a simple example, a manager is looking at ways in which he or she can expand the business. He or she has limited resources, but also has the options listed below:

A. Expand into overseas markets
B. Expand in domestic markets
C. Improve customer service
D. Improve quality

Firstly, the manager draws up a Paired Comparison Analysis table:

fig 2.4 :: paired comparison analysis table

	Overseas market (A)	Home market (B)	Customer service (C)	Quality (D)
Overseas market	Blocked out			
(A)	(Step 3)			
Home	Blocked out	Blocked out		

>>

	Overseas market (A)	Home market (B)	Customer service (C)	Quality (D)
(B)	(Step 4)	(Step 3)		
Customer service	Blocked out	Blocked out	Blocked out	
(C)	(Step 4)	(Step 4)	(Step 3)	
Quality	Blocked out	Blocked out	Blocked out	Blocked out
(D)	(Step 4)	(Step 4)	(Step 4)	(Step 3)

Then the manager compares options, writes down the letter of the most important option, and scores the differences in importance. An example of how he or she might do this is shown in figure 2.5:

fig 2.5 :: paired comparison analysis table (filled in)

	Overseas market (A)	Home market (B)	Customer service (C)	Quality (D)

Finally, the manager adds up the A, B, C and D values, and converts each into a percentage of the total. This gives these totals:

• A = 3 (37.5%)
• B = 1 (12.5%)
• C = 4 (50%)
• D = 0.

The result shows that it is most important to improve customer service (C) and then to tackle export markets (A). Quality is not a high priority – perhaps it is good already.

Key points

Paired Comparison Analysis is a good way of weighing up the relative importance of different courses of action. It is useful where priorities are not clear, or are competing in importance. The tool provides a framework for comparing each course of action against all others, and helps to show the difference in importance between factors.

Decision Tree Analysis

Decision trees (also known as diagnostic trees) are excellent tools for helping you choose between several courses of action. They provide a highly effective structure within which you can lay out options and investigate the possible outcomes of choosing those options. They also help you form a balanced picture of the risks and rewards associated with each possible course of action. (See p. 116)

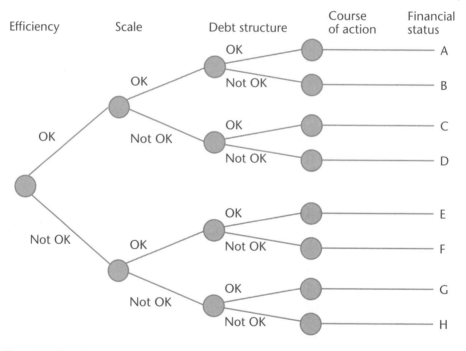

fig: 2.1 the decision tree

You start a decision tree with a decision that you need to make. Draw a small square to represent this towards the left of a large piece of paper. From this box draw out lines towards the right for each possible solution, and write that solution along the line. Keep the lines as far apart as possible so that you can expand your thoughts.

At the end of each line, consider the results. If the result of taking that decision is uncertain, draw a small circle. If the result is another decision that you need to make, draw another square. Squares represent decisions. Circles represent uncertain outcomes.

Write the decision or factor above the square or circle. If you have completed the solution at the end of the line, just leave it blank. Starting from the new decision squares on your diagram, draw lines representing the options you could select. From the circles draw lines representing possible outcomes. Again, make a brief note on the line saying what it means. Keep on doing this until you have drawn as many of the possible outcomes and decisions as you can see leading out from the original decisions.

Once you have done this, review your diagram. Challenge each square and circle to see if there are any solutions or outcomes you have not considered. If there are, draw them in. If necessary, redraft your tree if parts of it are too congested or untidy. You should now have a good understanding of the range of possible outcomes of your decisions.

Evaluating your decision tree

Evaluation is where you can work out which option has the greatest worth. Start by assigning a cash value or score to each possible outcome. Estimate how much you think it would be worth if that outcome came about. Next, look at each circle (representing an uncertainty) and estimate the probability of each outcome. If you use percentages, the total must come to 100% at each circle. If you use fractions, these must add up to 1. If you have data on past events you may be able to make rigorous estimates of the probabilities. Otherwise write down your best guess.

Calculating tree values

Once you have worked out the value of the outcomes, and have assessed the probability of the outcomes of uncertainty, start calculating the values that will help you make your decision. Start on the right side of the decision tree and work back towards the left. As you complete a set of calculations on a node (decision square or uncertainty circle), record the result. You can ignore all the calculations that lead to that result from then on.

Calculating the value of uncertain outcome nodes

To calculate the value of uncertain outcomes (circles on the diagram, see p.116), multiply the value of the outcomes by their probability. The total for that node of the tree is the total of these values.

Example 2.8

Calculating the value for 'new product, thorough development'

0.4 (probability good outcome) × R500,000 (value) =	R200,000
0.4 (probability moderate outcome) × R25,000 (value) =	R10,000
0.2 (probability poor outcome) × R1,000 (value) =	R200
Total	**R210,200**

In this example, the benefit we previously calculated for 'new product, thorough development' was R210,200. We estimate the future cost of this approach as R75,000. This gives a net benefit of R135,200. The net benefit of 'new product, rapid development' was R15,700. On this branch we therefore choose the most valuable option, 'new product, thorough development', and allocate this value to the decision node.

By applying this technique we can see that the best option is to develop a new product. It is worth much more to us to take our time and get the product right, than to rush the product to market. It is better just to improve our existing products than to botch a new product, even though it costs us less.

Key points

Decision trees provide an effective method of decision-making because they:

- Clearly lay out the problem, so that all options can be challenged.
- Allow us to analyse fully the possible consequences of a decision.
- Provide a framework to quantify the values of outcomes and the probabilities of achieving them.
- Help us to make the best decisions on the basis of existing information and best guesses.

As with all decision-making methods, Decision Tree Analysis should be used in conjunction with common sense – decision trees are just one important part of your decision-making tool kit.

Force Field Analysis

Force Field Analysis is a useful technique for looking at all the forces for and against a decision. In effect, it is a specialised method of weighing pros and cons. By carrying out the analysis you can plan to strengthen the forces supporting a decision, and reduce the impact of opposition to it. To carry out a Force Field Analysis, first download the free worksheet from www.magliolo.com (see fig 2.6). Then describe your plan or proposal for change in the middle. List all forces for change in one column, and all forces against change in another column. Assign a score to each force, from 1 (weak) to 5 (strong).

For example, imagine that you are a manager deciding whether to install new manufacturing equipment in your factory. Once you have carried out an analysis, you can decide whether your project is viable. In the example above, you might initially question whether it is worth going ahead with the plan. If you have already decided to carry out a project, Force Field Analysis can help you work out how to improve its probability of success. Here you have two choices: to reduce the strength of the forces opposing a project, or to increase the forces pushing a project.

Often the most elegant solution is the first choice: just trying to force change through may cause its own problems. People can be uncooperative if change is forced on them. If you had to implement the project in the example above, the analysis might suggest a number of changes to the initial plan:

- By training staff (increase cost by 1) you could eliminate fear of technology (reduce fear by 2).

- It would be useful to show staff that change is necessary for business survival (new force in favour, +2).

- Staff could be shown that new machines would introduce variety and interest to their jobs (new force, +1).

- You could raise wages to reflect new productivity (cost +1, loss of overtime -2).

- Slightly different machines with filters to eliminate pollution could be installed (environmental impact, -1).

These changes would swing the balance from 11:10 (against the plan), to 8:13 (in favour of the plan).

Forces for change   **Forces against change**

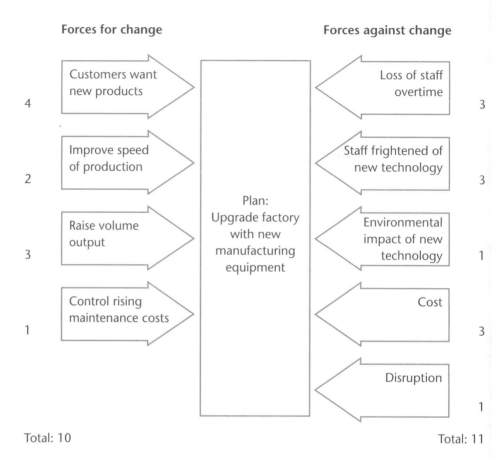

Total: 10   Total: 11

<u>**fig 2.6**: force field analysis</u>

Key points

Force Field Analysis is a useful technique for looking at all the forces for and against a plan. It helps you weigh the importance of these factors and decide whether a plan is worth implementing. Where you have decided to carry out a plan, Force Field Analysis helps you identify changes that you could make to improve it.

Six Thinking Hats

Six Thinking Hats is an important and powerful technique created by Edward de Bono in his book of the same name. It is used to look at decisions from a number of important perspectives. The method forces you to move outside your habitual thinking style and helps you get a more rounded view of a situation. Many successful people think from a very rational, positive viewpoint. This is part of the reason that they are successful. Often, though, they may fail to look at a problem from an emotional, intuitive, creative or negative viewpoint. This can mean that they underestimate resistance to plans, fail to make creative leaps and do not make essential contingency plans.

Similarly, pessimists may be excessively defensive and more emotional people may fail to look at decisions calmly and rationally. If you look at a problem with the Six Thinking Hats technique, then you will solve it using all approaches. Your decisions and plans will mix ambition, skill in execution, public sensitivity, creativity and good contingency planning.

You can use Six Thinking Hats in meetings or on your own. In meetings it has the benefit of blocking the confrontations that happen when people with different thinking styles discuss the same problem. Each Thinking Hat is a different style of thinking.

• **White Hat:** Focuses on the data available. Look at information you have and see what you can learn from it. Look for gaps in your knowledge and either try to fill them or take account of them. With this hat you **analyse past trends** and try to extrapolate from historical data.

• **Red Hat:** Looks at problems using **intuition and emotion**. Try to think how other people will react emotionally. Try to understand the responses of people who do not fully know your reasoning.

• **Black Hat:** Looks at all the **bad points of a decision**. Look at it cautiously and defensively. Try to see why it might not work. This is important because it highlights the weak points in a plan. It allows you to eliminate them or prepare contingency plans to counter them. This hat does toughen a plan. It can also help you spot fatal flaws and risks before you embark on a course of action. One of the benefits of Black Hat thinking is that it helps you see problems in advance. Many successful people get so used to thinking positively that they are underprepared for difficulties.

• **Yellow Hat:** Helps you **think positively**. It is the optimistic viewpoint that helps you to see all the benefits of the decision and the value in it. Yellow Hat thinking helps you to keep going when everything looks gloomy and difficult.

• **Green Hat:** Stands for **creativity**. This is where you can develop creative solutions to a problem. It is a freewheeling way of thinking, in which there is little criticism of ideas. A wide range of creativity tools can help you here.

• **Blue Hat:** Stands for **process control**. This is the hat worn by people chairing meetings. When running into difficulties because ideas are running dry, they may direct activity into Green Hat thinking. When contingency plans are needed, they will ask for Black Hat thinking, etc. A variant of this technique is to look at problems from the point of view of different professionals (eg doctors, architects, sales directors, etc) or different customers.

Example 2.9

Six Hat Thinking

The directors of a property company are looking at whether they should construct a new office building. The economy is doing well, and the amount of vacant office space is reducing sharply. They decide to use the Six Thinking Hats technique during a planning meeting to help them arrive at a decision. Looking at the problem with the White Hat, they analyse the data they have. They examine the trend in vacant office space, which shows a sharp reduction. They anticipate that by the time the office block would be completed, that there will be a severe shortage of office space. Current government projections show steady economic growth for at least the construction period.

With Red Hat thinking, some of the directors feel the proposed building looks quite ugly. While it would be highly cost-effective, they worry that people would not like to work in it. When they think with the Black Hat, they worry that government projections may be wrong – the economy may be about to enter a 'cyclical downturn', in which case the office building may be empty for a long time. If the building is not attractive, then companies will choose to work in another, better-looking building at the same rent.

With the Yellow Hat, however, some directors think that if the economy holds up and their projections are correct, the company stands to make a great deal of money. If they are lucky, maybe they could sell the building before the next downturn, or rent to tenants on long-term leases that will last through any recession.

With Green Hat thinking they consider whether they should change the design to make the building more pleasant. Perhaps they could build prestige offices that people would want to rent in any economic climate. Alternatively, maybe they should invest the money in the short term to buy up property at a low cost when a recession comes.

The Blue Hat is used by the meeting's Chair to move between the different thinking styles. He or she may need to keep other members of the team from switching styles, or from criticising other peoples' points. It is well worth reading Edward de Bono's book *Six Thinking Hats* for more information on this technique.

Key points

Six Thinking Hats is a good technique for looking at the effects of a decision from a number of different points of view. It allows necessary emotion and scepticism to be brought into what would otherwise be purely rational decisions. It opens up the opportunity for creativity within decision-making. The technique also helps, for example, persistently pessimistic people to be positive and creative. Plans developed using the Six Thinking Hats technique will be sounder and more resilient than would otherwise be the case. It may also help you to avoid public relations mistakes and spot good reasons not to follow a course of action before you have committed to it.

Cost-benefit Analysis

Strategists will find that even after intense analysis to generate solutions to a problem, the solutions may still not be worth implementing. Cost-benefit Analysis is a relatively easy and widely used technique for deciding whether to make a change. As its name suggests, to use the technique you simply add up the value of the benefits of a course of action and subtract the costs associated with it.

Costs are either once-off or may be ongoing. Benefits are most often received over time. Analysts build this effect of time into their analysis by calculating a payback period. This is the time it takes for the benefits of a change to repay its costs. Many companies generally look for payback over three years. In its simple form, Cost-benefit Analysis is carried out using only *financial costs and financial benefits*. For example, a simple Cost-benefit Analysis of a road scheme would measure the cost of building the road and subtract this from the economic benefit of improving transport links. It would not measure either the cost of environmental damage or the benefit of quicker and easier travel to work.

A more sophisticated approach to cost-benefit measurement models is to try to put a financial value on intangible costs and benefits. This can be highly subjective and needs to be well documented and researched, ie the stronger the assumptions obtained from the research, the stronger the argument for the results obtained from Cost-benefit Analysis and the less subjective the results will be perceived.

Where large sums of money are involved (for example, in financial market transactions), project evaluation can become an extremely complex and sophisticated art and require different analytical methods.

Example 2.10

A sales director is deciding whether to implement a new computer-based contact management and sales processing system. His department has only a few computers and his salespeople are not computer literate. He is aware that computerised sales forces are able to contact more customers and give a higher quality of reliability and service to those customers. They are more able to meet commitments and can work more efficiently with fulfilment and delivery staff. His financial cost-benefit analysis is shown below:

fig 2.7 ::

LIST OF COSTS			Cost per	
Item		Quantity	unit	Total
Computer equipment	• Network-ready PCs with supporting software	10	12,250.00	122,500.00
	• Server	1	17,500.00	17,500.00
	• Printer	3	6,000.00	18,000.00
	• Cabling and installation	1	23,000.00	23,000.00
	• Sales support software	1	75,000.00	75,000.00
Training costs	• Computer introduction (people)	8	2,000.00	16,000.00
	• Keyboard skills (people)	8	2,000.00	16,000.00
	• Sales support system (people)	12	3,500.00	42,000.00
Other costs	• Lost time: person days	40	1,000.00	40,000.00
	• Lost sales through disruption	1	100,000.00	100,000.00
	• Lost sales through inefficiency during first months	1	100,000.00	100,000.00
TOTAL				570,000.00

LIST OF BENEFITS: ESTIMATES

- Tripling of mail shot capacity: estimate R200,000/year

- Ability to sustain telesales campaigns: estimate R100,000/year

- Improved efficiency and reliability of follow-up: estimate R250,000/year

- Improved accuracy of customer information: estimate R50,000/year

- More ability to manage sales effort: R150,000/year

Total Benefit: R750,000/year

Payback time: R570,000 ÷ R750,000 = 0.76 of a year or 7.2 months

The payback time is often known as the break-even point. Sometimes this is more important than the overall benefit a project can deliver.

Cost-benefit Analysis can be carried out using only financial costs and financial benefits. You may, however, decide to include intangible items within the analysis. As you must estimate a value for these, this inevitably brings an element of subjectivity into the process.

The Break-Even Chart

Few managers go to the trouble of including a break-even chart with financial statements or when drafting a business plan. The reason for this is probably that assumptions have to be drawn up and a number of variables have to be calculated, ie a company's fixed and variable costs and unit price.

There are several ways to draw up break-even charts, such as using standard fixed costs or operating expenses, which is a better indicator for new businesses as the business owner is better off knowing what the break-even points are on real operations, rather than on what he or she perceives could be fixed costs.

Consider the factors and formulae outlined on the next page.

fig 2.8 :: elements of a break-even chart

Factor	Calculation	Formula
Average unit sale	Sales ÷ total units sold	Fixed Cost ÷ [1 - (Unit Variables Cost ÷ Unit Price)]
Average unit cost	Cost of sales ÷ total units sold	Fixed Cost ÷ [Unit Price - Unit Variables Costs]

THE ABOVE WAS CALCULATED USING:

Fixed costs = [Production costs + Sales & Marketing salaries + Administration expense + other operating expenses] ÷ 12

Unit variable cost = Cost of selling a unit ÷ units sold

It is difficult to draw assumptions as there are no obvious figures which can be easily read from a financial statement. You have to take annual estimates of the first year (sales or operating profit - whatever you are trying to calculate) and divide these figures by 12 to assess monthly fixed expenses. Even this figure is not the accurate fixed cost figure, but it can be used to determine a break-even point. Once this has been done, break-even points can be determined for any month or year.

The following example is a break-even analysis of a new company's first 12 months of operation. Note, no sales were made in the first month.

Example 2.11

The following has been calculated from assumptions and financial data:

Fixed costs	=	R 15,000
Variable unit costs	=	R 100
Unit price	=	R 1,000
Profits	=	Sales income - (units sold × unit variable cost)
		- Fixed costs

Operations	Months											
	1	2	3	4	5	6	7	8	9	10	11	12
Units sold	0	2	4	6	8	10	12	14	16	18	20	22
Sales income	0	2000	4000	6000	8000	10000	12000	14000	16000	18000	20000	22000
Profit	-15,000	-13,200	-11,400	-9,600	-7,800	-6,000	-4,200	-2,400	-600	1,200	3,000	4,800

Break-even calculation:

Break-even (monthly)				Calculation
Units break-even	=	Fixed cost	÷	[Unit price - Unit variable cost]
	=	R15,000	÷	[R1,000 - 100]
	=	R15,000	÷	900
	=	**16,67**		
Sales break-even	=	Fixed cost	÷	[1 - (Unit variable cost * Unit price)]
	=	R15,000	÷	[1 - (R100 *R1,000)
	=	R15,000	÷	[1 - R0,10]
	=	R15,000	÷	0.9
	=	**R16,667**		

It takes + 9 months to break even, ie 16,67 items are sold. Sales income = R16,667

The above calculations are graphically displayed in the following two charts:

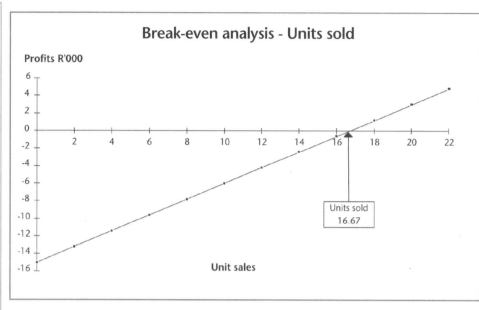

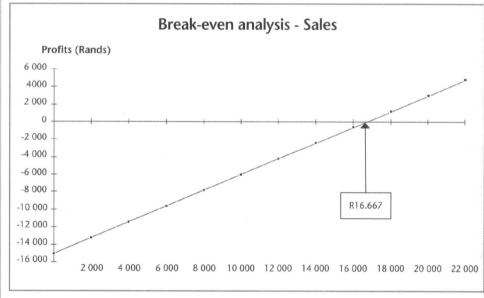

The lines on the above charts show:

- Profits increase and break even when 16.67 units are sold.
- Profits increase and break even when sales reach the R16,667 mark.

Impact Analysis

When things change in your organisation, do you ever wish that someone would think things through a little better to avoid the confusion and disruption that often follows? Or have you ever been involved in a project where, with hindsight, a great deal of pain could have been avoided with a little more up-front preparation and planning?

Impact Analysis is a useful and severely underused brainstorming technique that helps you think through the full impacts of a proposed change. As such, it is an essential part of the evaluation process for major decisions.

More than this, it gives you the ability to spot problems before they arise, so that you can develop contingency plans to handle issues smoothly. This can make the difference between well-controlled and seemingly effortless project management and an implementation that can negatively impact on the company.

Impact Analysis is designed to unearth the 'unexpected' negative effects of a change on an organisation. It provides a structured approach for looking at a proposed change, so that you can identify as many of the negative impacts or consequences of the change as possible.

Firstly, this makes it an important tool for evaluating whether you want to run a project. Secondly, and once the decision to go ahead has been made, it helps you prepare for and manage any serious issues that are may arise. All too often organisations do not undertake Impact Analysis. This is one reason that so many projects end in failure, as unforeseen consequences wreak havoc.

The challenge of Impact Analysis

The challenge in conducting an Impact Analysis is firstly to capture and structure all the likely consequences of a decision, and then, importantly, to ensure that these are managed appropriately. For smaller decisions, it can be conducted as a desk exercise. For larger or more risky decisions, it is best conducted with an experienced team, ideally with people from different functions within the organisation. With a team like this, you're much more likely to spot all the consequences of a decision than if you conduct the analysis on your own.

To conduct an effective Impact Analysis, use the following steps:

1. **Prepare for Impact Analysis:** Gather a good team, with access to the right information sources. Make sure that the project or solution proposed is clearly

defined and that everyone involved in the assessment is clearly briefed as to what is proposed and the problems that it is intended to address.

2. **Brainstorm major areas affected**: Brainstorm major areas affected by the decision or project, and think about whom or what it might affect. Different organisations will have different areas. This is why it's worth spending a little time getting this top-level brainstorming correct.

Major areas affected

The following three approaches provide analysts with different frameworks that can be used as a starting point for Impact Analysis brainstorming. Pick the framework that's most relevant for you, mix and match the approaches appropriately and include other areas where they're more relevant. Remember, involve people most likely to be affected by the decision as they'll most likely have more insight into the consequences of the decision than you have.

Approach 1: Organisational approach Impacts on different departments, business processes, customer groups and/or groups of people.

Approach 2: McKinsey 7-S's approach Uses the popular McKinsey 7-S's approach to thinking about the things that are important to an organisation: Strategy, Structure, Systems, Shared Values, Skills, Styles and Staff.

Approach 3: Tools-based approach There's a lot of overlap between Impact Analysis and some of the other tools already explained. The tools-based approach refers to using specific strategic methods or using a combination of tools. It involves the following:

*   **Identify all areas**: For each of the major areas identified, brainstorm all the different elements that could be affected. For example, if you're looking at departments, list all the departments in the organisation. If you're looking at processes, map out the business processes, starting with customer experiences, then moving on to the business processes that support this. The extent to which the strategist is able to undertake the assessment depends on the scale of the decision and the time available.

*   **Evaluate impacts**: Having listed all the groups of people and everything that will be affected in an appropriate level of detail, work through these lists identifying and listing the possible negative and positive impacts of the decision. Estimate the size of the impact and the consequences of the decision.

*   **Manage the consequences**: Turn information into action. If you're using Impact Analysis as part of the decision-making process, you need to weigh

whether you want to go ahead with the project or decision proposed. You'll need to ask yourself whether it's worth going ahead with the project given the negative consequences it will cause and given the cost of managing those negative consequences. If you're managing a project that has already been given the go-ahead, you'll need to think about things like:

- The actions you'll need to take to manage or mitigate these consequences.

- How you'll prepare the people affected so that they'll understand and (ideally) support change rather than fighting against it.

- The contingency strategy needed to manage the situation should the negative consequences arise.

Remember that few changes happen in isolation.

SWOT Analysis

One of the best techniques for analysing an organisation is SWOT Analysis, which can apply across diverse management functions and activities, but is particularly appropriate to the early stages of formulating company strategy.

Performing a SWOT Analysis means gaining a clear picture of the Strengths, Weaknesses, Opportunities and Threats that made the organisation what it is. Although this analysis should have an organisational focus, it should incorporate assessments of individual tasks, activities, people, functions and processes.

SWOT Analysis takes the following form:

- Internal resources and capabilities: strengths and weaknesses.
- Factors external to the organisation: opportunities and threats.

It is advisable to limit the exercise to the four or five most important factors that affect the organisation, focus on whether these are really threats or opportunities and avoid marginal strengths or weaknesses.

I have repeatedly been asked to give presentations and conferences in the past on the importance of strategy. I have argued that strategy is not just important, it is critical to creating sustainable competitive advantage in a global environment. This chapter has covered some tools that, at the very least, highlight how much you need to strategise before launching into a new venture. Strategy, however, is a vague concept to many managers. How can one determine whether a company is pursuing the right strategy?

Strategy is essentially about choices. You can't be all things to all people, but strategy must start with a different value proposition. A strategist delineates a territory in which a company seeks to be unique, and uses that to become efficient, effective and profitable. If all you are trying to do is the same thing as your competitors, or (worse) trying just to survive, then it's unlikely that you'll be very successful.

PART II:

THE STRATEGIC
ANALYST DIVISION

CHAPTER 3

THE THEORY BEHIND
THE STRATEGY TEAM

The strength of management lies in its ability to continually assess current organisational structures, ongoing events and potential risk, while keeping short- to long-term goals in mind. Strategies have to be continuously assessed and reassessed.

To facilitate this continuous assessment, I suggest that there needs to be a team in place.

One day, a company owner who is certainly well known in Johannesburg told me that he didn't have the time to continually strategise and certainly did not intend to deal with the media and analysts if he were to take his company through to a JSE or AltX listing. He asked if I could help him.

I developed a system for him that took into account the phases of research, due diligence, implementation and monitoring. This system gave him the freedom to concentrate on his company, while knowing that the media, investment community and clients were continually informed about changes to his company. In addition, strategic sessions were held every quarter to highlight programmes that had been achieved and tasks that had not been completed.

The 'system' was in fact a team. There are two ways in which this structure can be implemented: as a 'hired' or outsourced division or team, which in fact I propose calling 'insourced'; and as a complete division within the company, as part of the organisational structure and cost base, which I call The Chairman's Office, detailed in Chapter 4. In the 'insourced' version of the structure, the company introduces the strategist/corporate advisor as part of the in-house staff. He or she is employed by the company as its watchdog and fulfils the role of PR, analyst and development advisor.

STARTING WITH THE 'WHAT IF' MODEL

A number of techniques have been developed to aid the setting up a strategic/troubleshooting planning division and have been used successfully by a number of major stockbrokers and corporations. I have created a number of strategic systems that can be used by both investors and company owners, especially to account for the onslaught of global capitalism.

Depending on the company, what it does and how the operations are handled within the broader environment, strategic systems tend to be based on similar principles. The systems I have developed are essential 'what-if' scenarios. They are also called simulation models.

A simulation model is a system of mathematical equations, logic and data that describes the relationships among financial and operating variables. The main type of simulation model that business owners need tend to be financial models.

Simulation models have a number of common traits, or factors, usually where:

- One or more financial variables appear (expenses, revenues, investment, cash flow, taxes, earnings, etc.)
- The model user can manipulate (set and alter) the value of one or more financial variables
- The purpose of the model is to influence strategic decisions by revealing to the decision-maker the implications of alternative values of these financial variables.

In addition, what-if models attempt to simulate the effects of alternative management policies and assumptions about the firm's external environment. They are a tool for management, which can be deterministic or probabilistic.

Deterministic models do not include any random or probabilistic variables, whereas probabilistic models incorporate random numbers and/or one or more probability distributions for variables such as sales and costs. Financial models can be solved and manipulated to derive current and projected future implications and consequences. As a result of technological advances in computers (such as spreadsheets, financial modelling languages, graphics, database management systems and networking), more and more companies are using modelling.

How the model works

Generally speaking, the model consists of three important ingredients:

- Variables
- Input parameter values
- Definitional and/or functional relationships.

The development of financial models essentially involves two steps:

- Definition of variables and input parameters
- Model specification.

Definition of variables and input parameters

Fundamental to the specification of a financial model is the definition of the variables to be included in the model. There are basically three types of variables: policy variables (Z), external variables (X) and performance variables (Y). These are shown in the figure below.

Policy variables are the variables over which management can exert some degree of control. Policy variables are often called control variables. In finance, for example, such variables are cash-management policy, working-capital policy, debt-management policy, depreciation policy, tax policy, merger-acquisition decisions, the rate and direction of the firm's capital investment programmes, the extent of its equity and external debt financing and the financial leverage represented thereby, and the size of its cash balances and liquid assets position.

External variables are environmental variables that are external to the company but that influence the firm's decisions. For example, the firm is embedded in an industry environment which is influenced by overall general business conditions. General business conditions exert influences on particular industries in several ways, such as having an impact on such variables as total volume of demand, product prices, labour costs, material costs, money rates and general expectations.

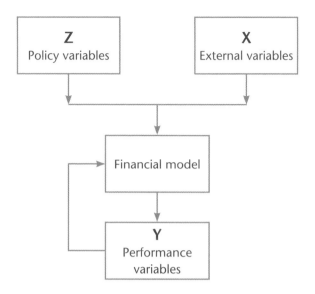

fig: 3.1 the three types of financial variables

My experience has shown that the quality and effectiveness of strategic planning depends strongly on an understanding at all levels of management of its purpose, use and benefit in managing the firm. This necessitates that a framework for setting strategy at the corporate level should be consistent with strategy set at the individual business and the served market level.

Once a business is defined at various levels a number of strategic management techniques can be used to address the issues of competitive position and market attractiveness. The result should be an integrated strategic plan that leads to objectives and a framework that culminates in the setting of action plans and responsibilities. It is important that from the start investors and corporate owners should expect that a planning process will continuously change and improve.

> Strategic management depends on the selection of significant market opportunities to achieve the long-term objectives of the firm. It is also important to manage future strategic changes so that the firm can capitalise on all opportunities.

THE PURPOSE OF THE TEAM

Setting up a separate strategic division is as much about survival as it is about success. Effectively, the main purpose of setting up a strategy team is knowledge-generation. This is achieved by studying a sample of the relevant market. This sample is determined by the method applied to assess resource constraints, accessibility of elements, etc. In recent studies, there has been a growing trend towards large sample sizes. This is due to the availability of tremendous computing power that modern information technology provides. High-quality secondary data sources also provide readily accessible data that can be analysed in batches of several thousands, if desired.

The strategic team acts as a corporate filter designed to determine if problems will occur and when, and what to do about these potential events. Its key functions are:

- **Research:** Global, regional and domestic research is crucial to identify main competitors, trends that could affect supply and demand, pricing, marketing, and financial and operational strategies. Many analysts know this market, but Africa provides unique challenges that must be continuously assessed. Numerous entrepreneurs have tried to enter this market before and have failed. A clear-cut industry analysis forms the foundation for a company's long-term success.

- **Due diligence:** Research enables a company to position itself to take care of future issues. A due diligence process of a company in relation to the research identifies whether a risk is pertinent to the company or not.

- **Review:** Issues assessed under research are discussed and reviewed with outside consultants to get an objective viewpoint and advice.

- **Implementation:** Changes that need to be made are implemented in the best possible manner, using the best methods, skills and investment returns possible.

- **Monitoring:** Once a strategy is implemented, regular checks are needed to determine whether the desired results are being achieved.

The researchers in a strategic team should be able to:

- Identify market opportunities
- Establish priorities for investment
- Pre-plan changes in products or services
- Formulate and implement strategic plans
- Optimally allocate resources to the strategic asset allocation
- Manage and control change
- Continually re-assess the company and its competitors

- Continually assess the shares/companies' sectors to ensure that these trends fit with those of its sectors.

Essentially, a strategic management team is the matching of:

- The organisation's resources
- Its distinctive competencies
- Its strengths and weaknesses

to:

- Environmental opportunities and threats in the face of local and global competitive action.
- The management of the changes necessary to sustain the competitive advantage.

OUTSIDE CONSULTANTS: THE ADVISORY COMMITTEE

The business development analyst

In drawing up a business plan, the first stop is with a business development analyst. He or she is the person who will provide the overall picture in terms of what information is needed, how it must be compiled and set out in a business plan. In The Chairman's Office, this task is part of the strategist's work.

The larger accounting houses all have development departments, which will assist you in drawing up a business plan. There are companies that charge a lot less than the accounting houses and often provide similar advice on tax and business structures. The Institute of Chartered Accountants of South Africa can provide details of their members and the areas in which they specialise.

Another source for advice, both technical and management, can be obtained from universities and technikons. Over the last decade, government funding of universities has decreased and this has forced some institutions to finance their work through consultancies for the private sector. However, it is important to remember that most consultants charge by the day (some by the hour), so it is imperative that you give them a clear brief outlining exactly what kind of advice or report you expect them to produce. You are paying for specific expertise, whether it be of a tax structure, where to locate your firm, marketing or of an engineering (technical) nature, so it is important to ensure that the advisor knows and understands what you intend to do in business.

Always try to negotiate a fee up front, rather than accept terms with unlimited time frames. Many consultants will be willing to negotiate a price rather than lose your business.

The financial advisor

The difference between business and financial advisors is marginal. While the business expert will outline issues like where to locate your business, which management structure to adopt and advice on sales, personnel, marketing and other such issues, the financial advisor will tell you how to spend your money efficiently. He or she will be able to advise you on taxation, pension or provident funds, customs and excise, the benefits and drawbacks of different forms of business enterprises, how to deal with staff, annual returns and audited accounts. In The Chairman's Office, this is also part of the strategist's task.

The best advice will come from someone who is thoroughly versed in accounting methods and financial management techniques. While you may believe you are qualified to handle your own affairs, there is no substitute for a good financial advisor. Establishing contact with a good advisor is an essential step to successful financial management. It is crucial to find someone who is adept at your particular type and size of business.

The bank manager

Once you have found business and financial advisors, the next step is to contact your bank manager. You have no choice; you will have to deal with him or her on a continuous basis, so it is advisable to outline your plans at an early stage. If you are unhappy with your personal bank manager, you could approach another bank. You will be surprised at how helpful the manager can be, providing you with practical and sound advice on who to contact for loans. He or she could make useful suggestions and arrange introductions to contacts who can help you, such as suitable accountants for your firm.

You may be able to judge from your bank manager's general demeanour and level of enthusiasm for your project – or lack of it – whether you want his or her bank to manage your business account. Just because he or she is a personal banker does not mean he or she has to handle your corporate work as well. Of course, much will depend on your existing relations, such as your track record regarding bank cheques and repayment of loans. Have you always kept the bank in the picture about your financial affairs – warning it, for instance about when you needed an overdraft? Much of the bank manager's judgement about your business will be based on your record of dealing with the bank.

Your decision will depend on financial constraints. However, accountants are usually well versed in drawing up business plans and introducing sources of finance, so it may be prudent to use your accountant's advice on the setting up of accounts, budgets and reporting structures, the appointment of key financial staff and the taxation implication of any given decision.

The legal advisor

Whatever type of business structure you use to run your business – from sole proprietorship to public company – there will be some form of legislation involved. Depending on the type of enterprise you choose, you will need to register the company. In addition, a time will come when you will need a lawyer to draw up sales/purchase agreements, register trademarks, copyright and patterns or you may have to sue debtors for unpaid accounts. You must therefore have a lawyer on your books as an advisor, but find out which lawyers deal with corporate issues, particularly those who practise and understand your area of specialisation.

For instance, if you are involved in producing or supplying goods or services to the public, you will need a lawyer with experience in consumer protection and product liability law. If you become involved in major takeover or merger deals, expertise in contracts is essential. When your company has expanded to require more staff, experience in employment law is desirable. If you will be dealing in property, conveyancing skills will be needed. Even within the structure of The Chairman's Office, this task has be performed by of an external consultant.

Other advisors

A business needs advisors in various arenas, and even in a firm using the system of The Chairman's Office, the following external advisors are essential.

fig 3.1 :: other outside consultants

Expert	Why you need them
Estate agent	Part of the business plan deals with the location of your business and you will, therefore, need an estate agent. It is important to choose an agent who specialises in the type of property you need – office, shop, industrial or agricultural. It is also better to choose an agent in the area where you intend operating from as this person will know the advantages and disadvantages of certain locations – traffic, access to highways and levels of crime. The estate agent can also give advice on a range of other pertinent issues, such as rentals and even negotiate these for you. He or she should be knowledgeable about planning regulations, rates and taxes and insurance valuations. In addition, ask the estate agent for the name of a reputable surveyor and architect, so that if you need to expand or change the layout of the premises to suit your needs, you will have an experienced advisor on your contact list.
Insurance broker	A wide range of insurance, against theft, fire, water damage etc. is essential. It is a commodity which is fairly easy to obtain, but it is crucial that you go to a reputable insurer. This reduces the risk of future problems in the eventuality of the insurer being declared insolvent. These agents will be able to give general advice on property, equipment, employer's liability and specialist advice on life assurance and pension/provident matters.
Advertising agency	An agency will provide advice on which media you should focus on to advertise your service or product. Should you use radio, television or the print media? They provide a full service and will prepare the advert for you.
Chamber of commerce representative	Local chambers of commerce can provide advice on markets, confidence indices and point you in the right direction.
Marketer	This person gathers and assesses data about the marketplace, customers and their needs, and approaches marketing companies. You or this person can assess your company through analysis of government survey statistics.
Human resources consultant	Personnel agencies provide advice on the availability of skilled, semi-skilled and unskilled labour, labour costs, methods of recruitment for different types of staff. They will undertake to find staff for you, do all the interviews and provide you with a shortlist of possible candidates.

>>

Expert	Why you need them
Stockbroker and merchant banker	You are unlikely to need these services in the near future, but is important to establish contact with a reputable stockbroker, who also has a research team. As a client, you would receive their research, which enables you to keep abreast of market and sector movements. For instance, if you want to set up a furniture shop, stockbrokers' reports on the furniture sector and on specific listed furniture companies (eg Ellerines, JD Group) will provide you with added insight into the industry.

Find advisors whom you trust and respect and who understand your particular business needs. While it will take time to build up a solid, trusting relationship with advisors, the benefits of having these contacts cannot be emphasised enough. It is, therefore, beneficial to appoint them at an early stage and – if finances permit – to pay them a retainer for their continued service. This helps to keep advisors fully informed on how your business is progressing, which will enable them to continually respond with the best advice.

TRUST

Often, one of the most serious challenges to ensuring positive relationships with customers, colleagues, government and employees is establishing trust. Trust is indeed the most fragile and vulnerable factor in a relationship between the strategist and his or her team, and the corporate owner.

Trust is defined generally as the absence of fear, the feeling of reliability, and the sense that adverse situations, pain or mistakes will have less impact or be pre-empted with the aid of the relationship.

It is often assumed that once a bond of trust is established, it is difficult to break. My experience demonstrates that trust is always fragile, and it takes many projects, late nights and continually proving yourself to each other to maintain it. Over time, trust builds between partners, but it is still possible to break that bond. There are many factors that can fracture such a bond, including the most commonly seen trust-busting behaviour listed below:

- **Acting unilaterally:** Taking action without consulting those directly or indirectly affected. Essentially, taking action without important input from key partners, particularly during the early stages of building trust.

- **Broken promises:** One of the crucial bases of trust is that each party can rely on the commitments of the other, both implied and explicit. When those commitments are broken without prior notification, understanding, explanation and warning, the first element of the relationship to suffer is trust.

- **Deception and fear:** Misleading intentionally through omission, commission, negligence or incompetence in a relationship creates a feeling of separation and distance.

- **Denial:** When mistakes are made, errors in judgement occur, a product underperforms, or there is a negative surprise, failing to promptly come forward and relate the circumstances candidly with empathy for those who are affected, changes a relationship of trust to one of suspicion and caution.

- **Disparaging the opposition:** Any time you hear the phrase, 'He's uninformed,' or 'They're just looking to raise money by their actions,' or 'It's politically motivated,' or 'They just don't understand,' you immediately suspect that the exact opposite is true.

- **Disrespect:** Even adversaries can trust each other to some extent, provided there is a sense of respect. When the reputation of an individual, product or organisation is minimised or humiliated, there is a sense of uneasiness that often leads to frustration and outwardly negative behaviour.

- **Holding back:** The essence of trust is having information and confidence so that no matter what happens, those in the relationship are able to count on the behaviour and attitudes of the others.

- **Ignoring the killer questions:** Too often, when preparing for adverse situations the very serious questions – those that can kill reputations and, therefore, destroy trust – are ignored so as to be nearly unrecognisable. The trustworthy organisation or individual prepares for the killer questions first and then determines other information that might be useful and helpful to explain or illustrate.

- **Lies:** What one individual or organisation sees as the truth can be seen as lies by a competitor or competing interest, simply based on the critic's or competitor's point of reference in relation to a given set of facts and information.

- **Danger signals:** The moment you hear the phrase, 'It's old news,' you instinctively understand that something new and adverse is about to happen, even if it is based on old circumstances.

- **Negative surprise:** Taking action out of character, out of sequence, out of selfish opportunity or simply without advance notice to those directly or indirectly affected can seriously damage the relationship of trust and will cause a loss of confidence in the relationship.

- **Not taking action:** A great source of frustration is when it's obvious that a situation could be resolved easily and quickly, but isn't.

- **Overrating your involvement in the relationship:** One of the most serious mistakes in a relationship is the assumption that everyone is prepared to manage adverse situations. Trust in relationships is often broken because when adverse situations occur, few step forward to resolve them. No matter how well the situation is dealt with, trust repair and maintenance must be key parts of any preparation and remediation process.

CHAPTER 4

THE CHAIRMAN'S OFFICE

The most successful entrepreneur is usually one with foresight. Telling yourself that you don't have all the expertise necessary to succeed, knowing it is easy to lose sight of the overall picture and understanding how easy it is to get embroiled in everyday operational problems takes sound business perception.

But there is a way of building the expertise you need around you, particularly if you run a medium- to large-sized company.

In the 1990s, I was hired as a business consultant by a Cape Town-based textile company to undertake an investigation into how to conduct a hostile takeover of a competitor. Part of the report dealt with the management of the target company. It had lost focus, the company's activities had become too diversified and the directors were so geographically divorced from the factories that the entire group had become ripe for a takeover.

In the report, I suggested a different form of management structure. Instead of having a full board of directors at head office, with each member sitting on a host of other boards of subsidiary companies, I recommended that a Chairman's Office be created. This would consist of the chairman, the managing director and the strategist or financial director.

These three people are the driving force behind any organisation. They see to the overall target objectives of the group, look to new markets, negotiate corporate finance deals and focus on expansion, profitability and general policy-making.

As the company expands, the next step is to create a full board of directors for each subsidiary and for each to run the company as if it were completely separate from the holding company. The chairman of each of these boards reports back to The Chairman's Office at the strategy meeting every quarter.

For the new business owner the situation is the same. He or she uses the principle of The Chairman's Office by finding two partners, each with specific skills. Preferably, one should be a strategist or financial accountant and the other an expert on economics, market trends or analysis or a corporate financier.

Once this team has been assembled, discuss each part of the business plan and decide who will draft which sections. The team members should be responsible for all aspects of their sections, including finding expert help to fulfil those functions that cannot be sorted out by The Chairman's Office.

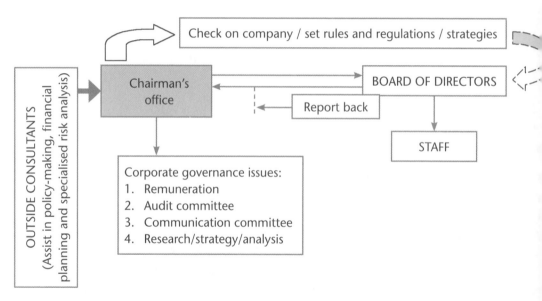

fig. 4.1: corporate structure including The Chairman's Office

This system enables the company to continuously assess what it is doing right and what it is doing wrong (or about to do wrong). Worst-case scenarios can be assessed and solutions drafted and the company will always be in a position to act quickly and decisively.

THE ROLES OF THE THREE DIRECTORS

The Chairman

According to the principles set out by Judge Melvyn King in his corporate governance report entitled King II, it is important to separate the function of chairman and managing director. Usually, the chairman is someone who is well versed in the industry, knowledgeable in the sector and in factors that could influence profitability. He or she is a suitable person to police the current and future policies of the business.

The managing director/owner

This person is closest to the business and thus knows and understands what works and what doesn't. However, while he or she doesn't have the time to undertake research and due diligence, experience shows that it is the managing director who effectively suggests what to analyse and what to assess for possible problems. This analysis and assessment is then undertaken by the strategist.

The corporate strategist/analyst

All new projects are handed to the strategist for research and due diligence before a final Yes or No is given for the acceptance or rejection of the project. For instance, if a company wanted to investigate the potential of expanding its X-TEC product into a new area, the strategist/analyst would be required to:

* Research the viability of selling the product into such an area.
* Perform due diligence on the effects (operational and financial) on the company of moving into such an area.
* Update the company's business plan to account for the target area.
* Update the corporate profile.
* Write a prospectus to raise funds for such a venture.
* Implement the targets set out in the research and due diligence.

The strategist performs detailed analysis, provides an assessment of key market trends, traveller patterns, possible competitive positioning of the major players in the future, consumer trends and new product development activity. Such people are chosen for their ability to ferret out current problems, present new problems and strategise for the future. Each new task is allocated and undertaken by a 'project manager'. This is set out later on in this chapter.

OUTSIDE CONSULTANTS

Where necessary, outside consultants are employed for additional information or to undertake specific skilled tasks. They may be engineers or geologists, lawyers, forensic auditors, etc. They can also fill the task of double-checking accounts or financial aspects of business, whether in a takeover, merger, opening new offices or expansion into new geographical areas or products.

REDUCING RISK

In an environment like South Africa, which has significantly differing levels of statistics (officially and unofficially), forecasts become difficult to reliably confirm. As such, the Chairman's Office would adopt the principle that the statistics and general information they use are only those that are confirmed by at least two other official documents, preferably from recognised global institutions, such as the United Nations, World Bank, IMF, etc.

BENEFITS OF THIS SYSTEM

The focus of The Chairman's Office is to maintain the independence of the strategist in order to avoid any conflict of interest. At the same time, the company can have a corporate advisor who has gone through the grindingly difficult task of getting to know the company in great and intimate detail.

The process is difficult enough without having to find skilled analysts every time a project is undertaken. Experience shows that setting up a strategic division expedites the planning of projects, their implementation and their follow-through.

Despite the complexity of the process of strategy, this division is structured for simplicity. There are only three directors or decision-makers, three is a number that enables quick decision-making, there can never be a stalemate and it is easy to co-ordinate meetings for such a few people.

IMPLEMENTING THE BUSINESS PLAN

Once the strategic division has been assembled, discuss each part of the business plan and decide who will carry out which sections. The team members should be responsible for all aspects of their sections, including finding expert help to fulfil those functions that cannot be sorted out by the corporate advisor, such as legal advice.

At the first meeting of the members of the division, the following factors should be assessed:

- **Set up a management structure.** Decide on the functions of the chairman, MD and corporate strategist.

- **Establish the focus of the division,** when it will meet and parameters for the strategist, ie how many hours he or she must be present at the company, duties for PR and analysis, etc.

- **Prioritise the business plan/prospectus.** State main objectives and time frames.

- **Decide on a short-, medium- and long-term strategy,** ie road shows, press releases, analytical reports creating databases, to whom this will service be provided and how it will be undertaken.

- **Decide what information is needed** to draw up the implementation plan.

- **Draw up a working schedule** to assess progress, ie meetings should be weekly or at most fortnightly.

If some team members are new, they will need to get up to speed on the research, due diligence and business plan. This is in addition to gathering general data about the business environment, such as who the customers are, how many there are, the products and services already provided, whether there is room for an additional service, the level of availability of skilled labour and what the factor costs of production are. Of course, if your product is unique, a number of the above facts are not needed, but those on potential consumer demand for your product are. Always remember that walls have ears and that a secret today could become someone else's business tomorrow. The bottom line is not to waste time. Gather the information quickly, assess the data and move on.

As the implementation plan takes shape, it will often necessitate changes in initial market and customer perceptions. This is normal and means that drafting a plan has worked. It has given the team new insight into their intended target markets and a sense of realistic expectation will take hold of the team. It is useless for the strategist to do all the work and be under unrealistic pressure to complete a task.

WORKING WITH THE CHAIRMAN'S OFFICE

Once a company expands or lists on an exchange, for the MD to follow up every existing and new task could become a nightmare. The strategic analyst's division provides the MD with a means to control events through a specific team that reports to the board on tasks, progress and implementation. Once the tasks have been completed and accepted by the board, the team conducts the investor relations, which is conveyed to shareholders, staff and general public.

The strategic division, in turn, works with project managers. Based on the objectives of management (board of directors), which are conveyed to the strategic division, the project manager would plan a process to deliver a specific result. The procedure is divided into a number phases.

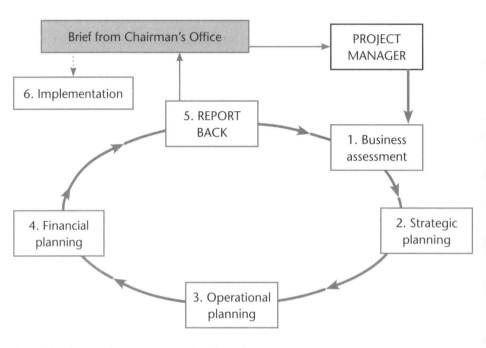

fig 4.2: the project manager's planning process

1. **Business assessment:** Gathering facts, undertaking analysis and forecasts in order to assess the company's current position, prospects, opportunities and threats in relation to a specific brief. This must include both a quantitative and qualitative assessment.

2. **Strategic planning:** Determining the grand design of the enterprise and the allocation of resources to opportunities, ie how does this project fit into the company as a whole and how will it affect its future profitability? The process of strategic planning is usually an agonising and lengthy process, but it leads to alternative ways of achieving goals. Examples include:

- Organic growth or acquisition
- Entry into new markets
- Increasing market share of those already served
- Buying assets or leasing them.

From this, strategy is determined, priorities established and decisions reached on the best reallocation of resources. It is also important to relay these strategies to analysts/media when drafting corporate strategies for communication purposes. While the process is under way, plans can be made and implementation action can begin to improve immediate profitability. These are based on the initial assessment of the company's performance, which invariably reveals opportunities for increasing profit or reducing cost.

3. **Operational planning**: Determining the form and content of major functions and activities and how they should be timed and interrelated. This usually involves making plans for each major activity of the business for the short to long term. The plans fall into a number of groups:

- Organisation
- Product and market development
- Marketing
- Resource development
- Manufacturing.

The planning in each of these areas should spell out what must be done annually in order to fulfil the objectives set out in the business plan, prospectus and project-related strategies. There must be a careful integration of all plans, which is facilitated by converting them into monetary terms and preparing projected financial statements for each year of the planning period. This helps to reveal whether:

- Plans are realistic
- Desired results are obtainable
- Financial resources are adequate.

Many adjustments are usually required to get a proper fit. A long-range planning document should then be prepared to incorporate the component parts of the strategic and operational plans.

4. **Financial planning**: Determine the potential financial impact of the project on the company as a whole. Can the company afford to take on a project if it

will cause financial stress, ie push gearing to heights considered unacceptable to shareholders? Or, if financed via a share issue, will the additional shares dilute EPS to an extent that it, too, will result in investor dissatisfaction?

Financial planning should cover the action to be taken and the results to be achieved within the next fiscal year and should be broken down to identify:

- Influence on cash flow, income statement and balance sheet
- Contribution of each manager to such tasks.

The annual company budgets have to be altered to take into account the cash requirements for the tasks being planned. Thus, the planned tasks are reflected in the plans for the year's activities, based on price and input costs. The budget should also reflect the results of action to be taken to increase immediate profitability, identified during the course of the business assessment.

5. **Report back:** To the corporate strategist, who in turn outlines the plans to the board of directors, the public and shareholders. Tied in with all the above must be a system of feedback reporting that permits periodic comparison of actual results with budget, performance standards or managers' priority plans. Out of feedback comes corrective action, desirably based on management by exception.

6. **Implementation:** Action undertaken by managers who are assigned the responsibility for specific activities to carry out the task. At this junction, short-term plans can be made. The project manager has reported back to the corporate strategist who has relayed the strategy, conclusions and recommendations to the board of directors. If the project viability is confirmed, the division can move ahead with implementation.

THE CONTINUOUS CIRCLE OF PLANNING AND IMPLEMENTATION

The planning process is continuous. The strategic and operational plans must be updated annually, modified where required to meet new circumstances and projected changes to the market, based on environmental factors. There must be a clear link between the grand design for the enterprise for the years ahead and realistic implementation action programmes for the short-term that have meaning for the individual project manager. Thus, there can be no separation of long- and short-term planning although each has its special role and characteristics.

The continuous inter-relationship of research, planning and implementation can be illustrated as follows:

- **Implementation should primarily be directed to effectiveness,** ie doing the right things by seeking out suitable opportunities and allocating resources to exploit them.

- **Operational and annual planning should concentrate on efficiency,** ie performing selected activities properly.

To be effective, business implementation must get down to and include the planning of results to be achieved by individual directors, managers and staff.

A perceptive company's forward plan may be rich with potential profit growth, but remains useless until managers at all levels implement such a plan. Their competence, judgement and enthusiasm will determine whether or not the company objectives are met. Thus, the annual planning and implementation of desired targets include working out with each manager an understanding of his or her key tasks and priorities that will enable him or her to concentrate on the really important profit-influencing tasks that measurably contribute to the achievement of the unit's objectives and hence the company goals.

PART III:

THE WORK OF
A STRATEGIST

CHAPTER 5

RESEARCH

The starting point for any strategic planning process must be research. Before you start, understand that research plans depend on the information you need and the available resources. Often an organisation will want to know everything about its products, services, programmes, etc. Your research plans depend on what information you need to collect in order to make major decisions about those products, services or programmes. Usually, you will be faced with a major decision that can be answered only once thorough research is undertaken.

The more focused you are on what you want to gain from the research, the more effective and efficient you can be, the shorter the time it will take and ultimately the less it will cost (whether in your own time, the time of your employees and/or the time of a consultant). There are trade-offs, too, in the breadth and depth of information you get. The more breadth you want, usually the less depth you'll get (unless you have a great deal of resources to carry out the research).

Alternatively, if you want to examine a certain aspect of a product or service in great detail, you will likely not get as much information about other aspects as well. Business owners who are just starting out may not have unlimited resources. The following various methods will give them a good mix of breadth and depth of information, and an understanding about specific areas, without going bankrupt.

It is important to stress that many managers find the process of conducting research far too ominous and 'scientific'. It's not. Usually, the first 20% of effort will generate the first 80% of the plan, and this is far better than nothing.

Remember that there is no perfect research design. It's far more important to do something than to wait until every last detail has been tested. In addition, it is important to keep research, because it forms a good foundation for the next time similar analysis has to be conducted.

DESIGNING A RESEARCH APPROACH

Consider the following key questions when designing a research plan:

- Why is the research being undertaken? What do you want to be able to decide as a result of the research?

- For whom is the information being prepared? Is it for capital funders, bankers, management, employees or customers?

- Specify the type of information you need to make a decision. Do you need information to really understand a process, customers, strengths and weaknesses of a product or service?

- Which sources will you use for information? Will you use employees, customers, groups of employees or customers or certain documentation?

- How can the information be collected and can it be done in a reasonable fashion? Will you use questionnaires, interviews or documentation, or observe staff and/or clients in the programme, or conduct focus groups among staff and/or clients?

- When is the information needed?

- What resources are available to collect the information?

- What information is needed to make current decisions about a product or service?

- Of this information, how much can be collected and analysed in a low-cost and practical manner?

- How accurate will the information be?

- Will the methods get all the needed information?

- What additional methods should and could be used if additional information is needed?

- Who can administer the methods now or is training required?

- How can the information be analysed?

Note that, ideally, the researcher uses a combination of methods, such as a questionnaire to quickly collect a great deal of information from a lot of people and then interviews to get more in-depth information from certain respondents to the questionnaires. Perhaps case studies could then be used for more in-depth analysis of unique and notable cases, eg those who benefited or those who did not benefit from the programme and those who quit the programme.

FOUR LEVELS OF RESEARCH RESULTS

There are four levels of information that can be gathered from customers or clients, including getting their:

- Reactions and feelings (feelings are often poor indicators of your service's lasting impact)
- Learning (enhanced attitudes, perceptions or knowledge)
- Changes in skills (applied the learning to enhance behaviour)
- Effectiveness (improved performance because of enhanced behaviour).

Usually, the further your research results get down the list, the more useful the information becomes. Unfortunately, it is quite difficult to get reliable information about effectiveness. Still, information about learning and skills is quite useful.

ANALYSING INFORMATION

Analysing quantitative and qualitative data is often the topic of advanced research and evaluation methods courses. However, there are certain basic rules that can help to make sense of reams of data.

- *Always start with a research goal:* When analysing data (whether from questionnaires, interviews, focus groups or whatever), always start from a review of your research goals, ie the reason you undertook the research in the first place. This will help you organise your data and focus your analysis. For example, if you wanted to buy a competitor by identifying its strengths and weaknesses, you can organise data into strengths, weaknesses and suggestions on how you would improve the weaknesses.
- **Basic analysis of 'quantitative' information:** Make copies of all data and store the master copy away. Use the copy for making edits and tabulate the information. For ratings and rankings, consider computing a mean, or average, for each question.

- **Basic analysis of 'qualitative' information:** Organise comments into similar categories, eg concerns, suggestions, strengths, weaknesses, similar experiences, recommendations, outputs and outcome indicators. Label the categories or themes, eg concerns, suggestions, etc. Attempt to identify patterns or associations and causal relationships in the themes. Keep all commentary for several years after completion in case you need it for future reference.

Effective analysis is about asking the right questions. It is important to keep in mind that the inferences drawn from information related to the past and present are not automatically valid for the future. Too often, analysts superimpose the past onto the future, assuming that things will be the same, or at least similar.

INTERPRETING INFORMATION

- Attempt to put the information in perspective, by comparing results to the following:
  - What you expected
  - Promised results
  - Management or staff expectations or beliefs
  - Any common standards for your products or services
  - Original goals, especially if you're conducting a programme evaluation
  - Indications or measures of outcomes or results (especially if you're conducting an outcomes or performance evaluation).
- Record conclusions and recommendations in a report, and associate interpretations to justify your conclusions or recommendations.

REPORTING RESULTS

The level and scope of the content depends on for whom the report is intended, eg funders / bankers, employees, clients, customers, the public, etc.

Be sure employees have a chance to carefully review and discuss the report. Translate recommendations to action plans, including who is going to do what about the research results and by when.

Bankers will likely require a full business plan that includes an executive summary, conclusions and recommendations, table of contents, description of the organisation, product, service, evaluation, explanation of the research goals, methods and analysis procedures.

From my experience it has become clear that in South Africa a business plan should include a research section from which assumptions are drawn. These are then used to draft financial forecasts and a valuation of the business.

Be sure to record the research plans and activities in a research plan that can be referred to when a similar research effort is needed in the future.

WHO SHOULD CARRY OUT THE RESEARCH?

Ideally, the organisation's management decides what the research goals should be. Then a research expert or corporate strategist helps the organisation determine what the research methods should be and how the resulting data will be analysed and reported back to the organisation.

If an organisation can afford any outside help at all, it should be for identifying the appropriate research and data collection methods. The organisation might find a less expensive way to apply the methods itself, eg conduct interviews, send out questionnaires and analyse the results returned, etc.

If no outside help can be obtained, the organisation can still learn a great deal by applying the methods and analysing results itself. However, there is a strong chance that data about the strengths and weaknesses of a product, service or competitor will not be interpreted fairly if it is analysed by the people responsible for ensuring that the results are positive. These people will be policing themselves. This caution is not to fault these people, but rather to recognise the strong biases inherent in objectively trying to look at and publicly report their work. Therefore, if at all possible, have someone other than those responsible for the product or service look at and determine research results.

The best kind of researcher is someone with good consumer/customer knowledge. A deep understanding of the consumer is essential, but it needs to be taken a step further. There is a tendency to focus all research on existing consumers. This is sufficient for studying daily functions. Emerging trends, however, take place at the fringes of consumer society. If the researcher wants to identify a new trend on its way up, the scope of the research net needs to be widened to include the fringes of society.

It takes special ability to be able to play with a large amount of information and come up with an absolutely new association of ideas. This comes from a special attitude and is true for both organisations and individuals. Attitude leads to a certain kind of organisational climate that can enable or destroy innovation. The organisational climate should be geared to absorb knowledge and connect that knowledge in new creative ways.

The following are a few more attributes of a good researcher:

- **Openness** – being able to absorb new influences and ideas, a willingness to step out of comfort zones and try out new ways of doing things. Openness works at two levels: at building knowledge capability and at encouraging experimentation.

- **Awareness** – the ability to spot breaks in continuity that others miss and the ability to abstract higher order concepts from them. There are again two strands here: awareness of what is going around you, in the vicinity and in the wider world, as well as the ability to stand back and see the wider perspective. This helps an organisation see concepts and insights in a new manner and then make connections.

- **Curiosity** – the need to know more is at the very base of knowledge acquisition. It is a child-like quality and adds to perspective, keeping awareness levels up. The second role it plays is in making unconventional associations between concepts, insights and facts.

- **Creative capability** – this is where it all comes together. Coming up with new ideas is all about linking insights, concepts and facts in a unique manner. There are two parts to this capability: an ability to bring two or more pieces of knowledge together in a novel way (there is a wide range of techniques that organisations can adopt) and putting in place the enablers that let this happen (putting processes in place).

  The big challenge in a large organisation is to facilitate the process of knowledge-sharing within and from outside. IT is a great enabler and a lot of companies use it to share information across functions. Organisations should encourage formal and informal channels of information-sharing. Informal networks can be great repositories of information as well as fountainheads of innovation.

  Innovation space is relevant both in the spatial-temporal sense as well as in the sense of providing people with enough sense of security to innovate. In the spatial-temporal sense it implies that, in the daily pursuit of efficiency and reliability, managers lose the focus on innovation, hence a special space needs to be created where innovation can happen. Organisations have experimented with lounges, special time zones, informal groups and project teams. The process that suits the organisation best needs to be picked up and implemented. Creative capability is all about making it possible for many kinds of knowledge to come together to create new ideas.

RESEARCH VERSUS DEVELOPMENT

Senior managers in most organisations do not possess scientific, analytical or engineering backgrounds. Even if they have formal qualifications in the scientific or engineering fields, the past decade's experience of handling finance, marketing or other broad business issues removes them from their original moorings. This makes senior managers feel intimidated by technologists who report to them since they have never handled technology, or stopped dealing with it eons ago.

It is well known that even the term 'R&D' can turn off even the most experienced of CEOs. This is due to an aversion to displaying ignorance in public. Analysts seldom overcome their habit of inserting jargon in their discourses or discussions even if they have been urged to maintain a high level of abstraction while communicating with other members of their organisation. Business reengineering processes, though applied uniformly all over the organisation, seem to act differently and produce different results in the R&D department when compared with other departments. The problem seems to rest with a gap in understanding of the real meaning of R&D.

For many years there has been a debate on the relative importance of research versus development. Arguments for indulging in more research rather than development, and vice versa, have been advanced. Most of these discussions, instead of enlightening management, usually lead to misleading conclusions. The reality is that R&D has to be managed.

Example 5.1

The Ford Ikon launch campaign

Ford gathered consumer knowledge to ensure that it got the right positioning of its new car, Ikon, in its launch campaign. The first step it took was to move beyond demographic positioning. A large-scale psychographic segmentation study was carried out, which threw up six psychographic segments of the target customer demographic.

This was coupled with another stream of knowledge that was consumer feedback on cars driven in car clinics organised by Ford. The Ikon came across as an attractive and peppy vehicle in this research.

>>

>>

These two pieces of information were put together.

The target segment chosen was 'full of life' and an 'affluent, young' segment of the population. These were the people who worked hard, played hard and enjoyed what they did. They needed a car to match this lifestyle. This target segment also turned out to be the trendsetter segment in the car market.

Ikon fitted these segments well and the campaign was just a logical extension of the research carried out by Ford. The campaign was very innovative and a great success because for the first time a car manufacturer was positioning a car not on features but on lifestyle and attitude. The Ikon also quickly became a market leader in its segment.

Expanding knowledge capacity is a sure-fire way of innovating.

RESEARCH – AN ACADEMIC DOMAIN?

During the last five years, despite research becoming more integrated into the business world, I have been repeatedly told that 'Research is for academics'. Academic research, carried out in universities and research institutes, aims at expanding levels of knowledge and technology. This type of research does not have any limits as it does not have any bounds in terms of tangible goals or outputs. Industrial organisations should not be concentrating on this kind of research through their R&D departments.

There are two types of industrial research: basic industrial research and applied research.

Basic industrial research is actually a disguised form of academic research. Because it seeks to push the frontiers of knowledge in that particular industry sector, the deliverables are fuzzy and this activity may not affect the bottom line of the business positively. It is thus best to contract out such work to universities or research institutes.

Applied research purports to have a goal or a set of outputs that apply to the sector or industry. But in most R&D departments the basic tract of research is pursued rather than the applied tract. The result is that nothing profitable comes out of this department. Remember that pre-existing knowledge determines the ability to absorb new knowledge. If your competitor launches a new product, you need to quickly launch a counter-product. Even if you do not want to invest in basic R&D, make sure there is something invested in applied R&D. You may not be the one to drive the bus, but make sure you don't miss it completely.

The answer is to incorporate a strategic division within a firm, so that the company can operate and grow with knowledge. Assuming that the department has several functions, it can remain independent and efficient, tackling tasks like broad-based economic empowerment, King II on corporate governance and valuations. This type of research is profitable to the firm, because it enables management to focus on the business while essential information is gathered and analysed.

> Managerial leadership in the modern business environment has increased in complexity, contextual unfamiliarity and knowledge. The need for solid, well-researched information is invaluable and must be part of any business.

CONDUCTING RESEARCH

Company owners must undertake extensive studies to determine the future level of competitiveness, complexity and rate of change of their target markets. This may involve not only extensive database work, but research considering external factors as well. Note that research in every phase includes an analysis of environmental factors.

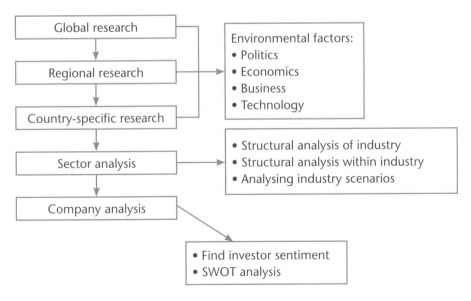

fig 5.1 :: information gained through research

Research is used to determine the viability of any future change in risk profile of the overall company or a specific project, today and for the future. As such, a due diligence report on the company or project would be carried out. Risk can be is assessed by:

- Structural analysis of the industry
- Structural analysis within the industry
- Analysing industry scenarios (present and future).

Environmental analysis

There are numerous books that set out environmental analysis as the strategic assessment of political, economic, social and technological circumstances and trends, ie PEST. During the past six years, I have changed that basic formula to merge social change with economic factors and have altered the label to 'Business'. The following are some issues that have influenced strategy in the past six years:

- **Politics:** war on terrorism, shift towards capitalism and democracy in Eastern Europe, strong movement towards bloc trading in Asia, Europe and Africa.
- **Economics:** opening up of new market potential in emerging economies, low interest and inflation rates in South Africa. Relaxation of exchange controls, streamlining of government, privatisation and deregulation.
- **Business:** merger and acquisition trends, globalisation, changing consumer demands and supply trends.
- **Technology:** the growth of the Internet and the advance of electronic communications, need for business management systems and changing consumer requirements in the SOHO arena.

Example 5.2

In 1990, South Africa saw the release of Nelson Mandela from prison. At the time many business owners were saying that this heralded a whole new way of business. Times ahead, they said, would be easier as sanctions would be lifted and business would become internationally accepted. These people were right – but it took almost a decade for stability to become a way of life, to be accepted as the norm. The first six years of the 1990s saw volatility and instability in business – even after 1994's historic elections.

Then, 1997/8 saw emerging market volatility and a stock market crash. Despite these volatile times, the All Share Index is today over 22000 – a climb of 130% from 1997's 9500 level. That level was, in turn, a climb of over 230% from 1990.

Yet many businesses failed during this period, many South Africans emigrated and the stock market has changed. The latest is the launch of AltX.

All these factors mean that the director who refuses to accept that change is inevitable faces financial suicide. To compound matters, the director who lists his or her company and who refuses to accept that the public needs to know about these changes, will face JSE disciplines of being suspended or delisted.

A company's future and, therefore, future profits cannot be left to chance. Profit opportunities must be aggressively pursued, evaluated and then organised to secure their full potential. Every action taken regarding markets, materials, staff, machinery and money has a bearing on profit. Making the right decisions at the right time, keeping resources in balance with opportunities means achieving optimum profit.

The essence of formulating a corporate competitive strategy is to relate that company's choices and commitments to its markets, business environment and the very nature of the company itself.

Business and strategic planning is the practice of seeking to do this continuously, methodically and with due care.

Structural analysis of the industry

This type of research is more general, looking at the company within its own environment. Although the relevant environment is broad, and encompasses factors such as socio-economic forces as well as political, business and technological factors, the key aspect of the firm's environment is the industry or industries in which it competes. Industry structure has a strong influence in determining the competitive rules as well as strategies potentially available to the firm.

Competition in an industry is rooted in its underlying economic structure and goes well beyond the behaviour of current competitors. The state of competition in an industry depends on a number of basic competitive forces, which determine the ultimate profit potential in the industry. Here profit potential is measured in terms of return on invested capital. It is the key structural features of industries that determine the strength of the competitive forces and hence profitability.

The underlying structure of an industry, reflected in the strength of the forces set out above, should be distinguished from the many short-run factors that can affect competition and profitability in a transient way. Fluctuations in economic conditions over the business cycle will influence the short-run profitability of nearly all firms in an industry, as can material shortages, strikes and major changes in supply and demand. Although such factors may have tactical significance, the focus of the strategist in the analysis of industry structure, or 'structural analysis', is on identifying the basic, underlying characteristics of an industry's roots in its economics and technology that shape the arena in which competitive strategy must be set.

Firms will each have unique strengths and weaknesses with regard to industry structure. In addition, industry structure can and does shift gradually over time. Yet, understanding industry structure must be the starting point of strategic analysis. A number of important economic and technical characteristics of an industry are critical to the strength of each competitive force.

- Threat of entry
- Intensity of rivalry among existing competitors
- Pressure from substitute products
- Bargaining power of buyers
- Bargaining power of suppliers
- Government as a force in industry competition.

Competitor analysis

Structural analysis applies to diagnosing industry competition in any country or in an international market, although some of the institutional circumstances may differ. The goal of competitive analysis for a company is to find a position in an industry where it can best defend itself against global forces or, alternatively, can influence or dominate them. Since the collective strength of global forces may well be painfully apparent to all competitors, the key for developing a strategy is to delve below the surface and analyse the sources of each.

Knowledge of these underlying sources of competitive pressure highlights:

- The critical strength and weaknesses of a company
- The areas where strategic changes may yield the greatest payoff
- The areas where industry trends promise to hold the greatest significance as either opportunities or threats.

While there is a debate among analysts as to what constitutes competitive factors, the research and experience I gained in stockbroking, specifically during the 1997 global market correction, suggests that the following forces are important:

- **Competitive rivalry** is particularly strong when there are a large number of organisations competing in the same market solely on price and quality, and where differentiation between products and services is minimal.
- **The power of buyers** is increased when their number is small relative to the number of organisations within an industry. This force is inextricably linked to the threat of substitutes.
- **The threat of substitutes** is high if a buyer can easily obtain a different product that meets the same need as an existing product, and an organisation is unable to raise prices too high.
- **The threat of potential entrants** is the ease with which another company can gain entry into a market and impacts on an existing organisation. In some industries, the cost of entry in terms of capital requirements is so high as to deter potential entrants. In others, economies of scale prevent small operations from obtaining a foothold. Effective strategies aim to swing these forces in favour of the organisation. (These forces are set out at great length in *Jungle Tactics*.)

The intensity of competition in an industry is neither a matter of coincidence nor bad luck. Rather, competition in an industry is rooted in its underlying economic structure and goes well beyond the behaviour of current competitors.

The state of competition in an industry depends on the six basic competitive forces mentioned above.

Predictions of turbulence

I have carried out well over 300 due diligence processes and other major research studies since 2001, and my work has shown that internal research (and especially the view of senior managers) about the future is usually flawed. Internal estimates of future turbulence are usually completely different to the actual level of turbulence that could occur. Such an error could be fatal for an organisation, since it could lead to all the firm's strategies consistently being developed for a much slower, less competitive and more predictable environment than is the reality.

This is the one area where external consultants can really provide a benefit for the firm. Not only do they bring their expertise to help the firm develop good tactical strategies, their external and independent view will generally also provide a fresh and possibly different approach and understanding of future potential chaos in an industry. My experience has shown that the predictions by outside consultants of future turbulence can be extremely accurate and thus should actually form part of the daily operations of the firm, as outlined in The Chairman's Office.

PRODUCT ANALYSIS

The firm's senior directors decide which products to invest in, which products to maintain and which ones to phase out. This area has traditionally been extremely weak for most firms, because many directors tend to keep the firm focused on historic areas of success and, secondly, the company's ability to assess future product demand tends to be much too simplistic as it does not account for changing demographics or global demand/supply trends. There are two starting points that a company can use.

1. The firm's management can either begin the product analysis with a narrow view that does not allow the firm to migrate to unrelated product areas, or they can proceed with no assumptions about what products the firm will pursue in the future.

2. Starting with a blank slat is more beneficial to the company. The strategists undertaking analysis will tend to consider the future growth and profitability of each product, in much the same way as a financial consultant would look for the highest profit fund or stock combination. By limiting the firm to historic areas of supposed competence, the firm will usually find itself in a low Return on Investment (ROI) situation.

    Ultimately, this means that the managers of the firm must learn to view all resources in terms of liquidity. If the firm's product has low future prospects, the firm's managers should systematically begin liquidating old, low-performing product families and replacing them with new, high-performing product items. This should be done regardless of whether or not the firm has any sort of 'competence' in the new product areas. Remember that in an environment of professional managers, capabilities can be bought.

Strategic diagnosis

This is normally accomplished with a carefully developed questionnaire. Usually, fewer than 20% of the questionnaires will be given to the senior managers of a firm. Generally, senior directors in emerging markets have an overoptimistic view of organisational values and leadership style. Accuracy is extremely important if the diagnosis is to lead to the development of an effective strategic plan. The incorrect use of technology or the lack of such systems to assess strength of leadership (analysis of questionnaires) can represent a critical gap. An external consultant could be extremely helpful in moving the firm's product technology strategy forward. If the gaps are not corrected, the outcome could be disastrous.

Gap analysis

Once the strategic profile has been developed, each specific gap is analysed. In order to make the analysis as clear as possible, it is very helpful to include three things in the analysis of each gap:

- The present level of the attribute under analysis
- The required future level the attribute needs to be at in the future
- The profit impact of the gap. This also helps managers set priorities for change by getting them to focus on the larger gaps first.

TURNING RESEARCH INTO A PLAN

At this level of planning, it is extremely important to gather input from all parties involved and all levels. The strategic plan should be as detailed as possible and each product and functional area should develop its own strategic plan, which will support the overall transformation and strategies of the firm.

It is important to plan exactly how each aspect of the change in products, assessments and functions will be carried out and for everyone to understand each step of the transformation that is to take place.

It is essential that you use a logical approach to implement any major change. This means that change initiatives must be carefully choreographed in such a way that the change involves a series of small changes instead of one giant leap.

The greater the change, the higher the likely resistance to such change. No matter how much change training is given, it is a simple fact that each person has an innate level of resistance to change. In order to facilitate the implementation process, high-resistance personalities must be kept out of early change initiatives. One good rule of thumb is to manage an initiative until it has penetrated around 25% of the organisation. From that point on, the initiative will normally diffuse through the organisation somewhat naturally.

In South Africa, resistance to change is linked, naturally, to the high rate of retrenchment, from manual labour through to managing directors. No wonder there is a resistance to change, because 'change' is often interpreted as a reason to retrench staff. Stated differently, the official term used is 'downsizing'.

Establishing and implementing excellent corporate strategy is complex and dynamic. When all the players come together in harmony, the result can be profitable. Unfortunately, that hardly ever happens.

Further academic reading on strategic segmentation can be found in H Igor Ansoff's *Workbook in Strategic Management* (1990).

:: CHAPTER 6 ::

TROUBLESHOOTING

There is a need to clarify a specific point about strategic troubleshooting. I have been told by business owners that once a company is running smoothly, there is no need to have a strategist conduct a troubleshooting analysis as there are no problems to be found, and that the exercise is expensive and a waste of time. This statement is shortsighted. The troubleshooter not only finds problems that exist but also sets up strategies to prevent problems from occurring. In addition, a troubleshooter can be used to determine whether a possible acquisition has inherent problems. It is better to know of problems before making an acquisition than afterwards.

Example 6.1

In 2002, I was requested to conduct a strategic due diligence process on a company based in Cape Town. The client wanted to buy the business and needed to know whether there were any current or possible problems within the firm to be acquired.

'If I buy this business, will I have problems of any kind in the future?' The instructions were clear.

After conducting initial in-depth analysis and research on the global markets, assessing company results and market potential, I determined that the firm looked solid and had sound financials and great prospects.

>>

>>

However, when I went to Cape Town to see the factory I spoke to the workers and quickly realised that they were highly dissatisfied with their working conditions, wages and work schedules. The related union is a militant one and this fact became a deal-breaker. The client heeded my warning not to buy the company and was proved correct some months later, when strike action practically crippled the company.

IT TROUBLESHOOTING

In today's world, a company's success is highly dependent on its IT network availability. As a result, companies are increasingly less tolerant of network failures. Therefore, IT network troubleshooting has become a crucial element to many organisations. Not only has the dependency on network grown, but the IT industry is also moving towards increasingly complex environments, involving multiple media types, multiple protocols and often interconnection to unknown networks. These unknown networks may be defined as a transit network belonging to a Internet service provider (ISP). The convergence of voice and video into data networks has also added to the complexity and the importance of network reliability.

More complex network environments mean that the potential for connectivity and performance problems in inter-networks is high, and the source of problems is often elusive.

The IT network troubleshooter is not the focus of *The Corporate Mechanic*. While there are similarities between the corporate and network troubleshooters' methodologies, ultimately the corporate strategist/troubleshooter will use IT experts to resolve problems with networks or computers. The same can be said of accounting forensics or legal diagnosis during a due diligence process.

WHAT IS STRATEGIC TROUBLESHOOTING?

Troubleshooting has been likened to detective work. Both gather information about a problem, which is then studied and analysed to find solutions. A troubleshooter tracks down the cause of a business problem by going out and getting the facts and then analysing them.

Detectives and troubleshooters proceed carefully and methodically, first looking for details, then questioning people, gathering all available facts and then analysing them to prove or disprove a theory. Like a good detective, a good troubleshooter also works systematically, getting information about a problem, coming up with ideas about what caused it and testing these ideas to see if they stand up against the facts.

Seldom is luck involved. A good troubleshooter depends on knowledge and on the way that knowledge is used, logically following a procedure that has proved itself. Many business owners probably use many of the analytical troubleshooting ideas already. In fact, this section of the book was developed by talking to strategists, analysts, entrepreneurs and business owners during the past decade, watching them on the job, asking them what worked for them and what simply didn't. This section takes what we learned from them and breaks it down into a series of steps. Each step is explained, and examples are given where possible, to show you how the ideas can be used in South African situations.

At this point, many readers will probably say that it is not their function to resolve corporate problems. When there is a problem, managers call in expert help. Don't be concerned. Everyone can benefit from these ideas. Besides helping you find the cause of problems, troubleshooting makes it easier to spot trouble as soon as it occurs. By following the steps set out below, you will find that the information passed along will be more accurate and useful to those who need to find its cause. And, if it's up to you to fix troubles, you will learn how to make more effective, longer-lasting solutions, without creating more problems in the process. Remember, when a problem occurs the intention is to get rid of it entirely.

Find the cause of the trouble quickly, efficiently, economically and with a minimum of wasted motion. A strategist can correct the cause of the trouble and not just the effect. In essence, the trouble is fixed for the life of the operation.

WHAT A TROUBLESHOOTER DOES

This may sound flippant, but troubleshooters exist because problems occur when people are involved. Human error is usually the main cause of a problem. A troubleshooter's basic job is to fix the problem, its cause and issues that may cause the problem to recur.

Every minute that a piece of equipment or a system isn't working, or a product isn't up to standard, the organisation is losing money and the client is not being satisfied. Few things are more important than getting back to normal. Everybody loses until the troubleshooter comes up with a solution and the trouble is fixed.

But it's not enough for a troubleshooter to get the equipment back in operation. He or she has to ensure that it doesn't create new problems in the process of curing the old ones. The troubleshooter thinks beyond the fix to prevent the same problem from occurring at a future date.

To find the cause of the trouble/problem quickly and efficiently, strategists have to have some kind of system to guide them as they work their way through the problem. If there is no system in place, time will be wasted because questions will have to be repeated, management and staff re-interviewed, things that could be ignored will be checked and actions that don't have anything to do with the real problem at hand will be taken.

To correct the cause of a trouble, strategists have to know for sure what the cause is. If they don't take time to identify the true cause, they are likely to end up taking an action which has no effect.

RECOGNISING AND DESCRIBING PROBLEMS

Every time a change is made – and that includes when something is fixed – the person who makes the change runs the risk of creating new troubles or problems. For example, a machinist who replaces a worn-out part with a new one, but from a different manufacturer, runs the risk that the item may not be the exact same size or material. Some small change that may seem insignificant may just be creating a much bigger problem.

In order to operate effectively, the manager and staff must know what their equipment, systems or products should be doing. Equipment is designed to work in a certain way and experience with it should enable you to know exactly how it should operate and what it should do. For example, an electric motor should make a certain sound and operate at a certain temperature. You know exactly what these should be from the specifications and your experience.

What makes good troubleshooting can be summed up in one phrase: 'Do it right the first time.' And doing it right means following a method.

Step One

The first step to any troubleshooting is to ask two questions:

- What is the item doing?
- What should it be doing?

If there is a difference between the Should and the Is, you have a deviation. Obviously, the more sharply you can define what should be happening, the more clearly you can recognise a deviation when it comes up. Some troubleshooters can spot deviations when others can't see anything wrong at all.

Essentially, troubleshooting starts with a clear notion of what should happen. 'Know your company's annual financial state of affairs' means 'Know every part of the financials, every minute detail and from every angle. Know what it should look like, how it should feel, what it should sound like.' Know the Should of an operation, backwards and forwards. Then you'll be able to spot trouble quickly.

Ask yourself, when you're in the middle of a tough problem, 'What should this thing be doing?' Follow the action through in your mind. Maybe the deviation will stand out a little clearer if you do. And when you are working with an unfamiliar piece of equipment, ask yourself: 'What did the engineers who designed this have in mind?' Establish the Should before you try to go any further.

If troubleshooters cannot initially resolve the cause of the problem, they follow the steps in Symptoms, Problems and Solutions (outlined later on in this chapter), including looking for differences and changes. Possible causes developed this way can be tested, verified and then fixed.

Remember that finding the problem (the difference between what the thing should be doing and what it is actually doing) is not the same as fixing the problem. For instance, finding the cause of lower productivity is not the same as finding a solution or implementing new strategies.

Step Two

Starting out with a clear, specific statement of the trouble gives you focus. It helps you communicate with other people and ensures that you get information that is relevant and useful. This statement is called the Trouble Statement.

The strategist may have an idea about what caused the problem, but isn't sure of it and needs to make sure before fixing it. Fixing the problem can only be done when all the facts have been gathered, including management performance, staff work ethics, target markets, the equipment, the location of the business, etc. The Trouble Statement should therefore identify the thing or group of things that are problematic, and what's wrong. For example, let's say your shop services a fleet of buses. 'The right, rear taillight on Bus No. 12 is broken' tells you what's wrong and the unit that's affected. This is a clear, concise Trouble Statement.

Sometimes you have to describe several related things, all with the same kind of trouble. 'The right, rear taillight is broken on 17 out of the 25 buses we service.' Again, this Trouble Statement tells you what you need to know in order to get started.

But don't try to include several different kinds of trouble in the same statement. That will only confuse matters. 'The right rear taillight on several of the buses is broken and they overheat and the brakes don't work on some of them' deals with several problems, each of which is separate and calls for a different kind of solution. Make at least three Trouble Statements out of this and things will be clearer.

Step Three

Having produced a Trouble Statement, you then need to create a Specification. This, as its name implies, is more specific.

Good analytical troubleshooting comes from having a precise, clear picture of the trouble. Poor troubleshooting comes from jumping to action on the basis of a loose, incomplete picture of the trouble.

The cause of a problem is a real thing. It has dimensions by which you can recognise and describe it. It leaves the tale of its dimensions in the effect it produces, the same way an animal leaves its story in its track in the sand. You can read the kind, shape, size, age and location of the cause by looking at the trouble. And unless you see the cause in operation you have no other way of ever finding out what it looks like, except by reading its signature in the trouble it produced.

THE DIMENSIONS OF A PROBLEM

There are four dimensions you can use to describe any kind of problem, no matter what the problem is:

* It has identity: you can name it, identify it, classify it by type or kind
* It has location: you can place it somewhere in space or in relation to other things
* It has timing: it occurs on a specific date, at a specific time
* It has an extent: it is of some size or affects so many things.

When you can describe the problem in these four dimensions, you can then use that description to trace your way back to its cause. In analytic troubleshooting, strategists get the description of a problem by asking management, staff and technicians/experts specific questions in each of the four dimensions. They don't just ask questions at random – that may lead to repetition or, worse, omission of important information. They ask questions in a systematic, orderly way, so the answers are as complete as possible.

Example 6.2

The identity of a problem

In an East London plant, a complex steel part was being formed, assembled and welded. Suddenly, quality control at the end of the press line spotted a hole punched in the side of the part. After management was called, a troubleshooter was commissioned to find the problem. Management stated that they needed the plant in full operation as quickly as possible, because it cost them over R1 million a day in lost revenue when the plant was closed.

After taking a look at the hole, the troubleshooter went into action, closing the plant for a day in order to move along, over, under and through the equipment. The next day the troubleshooter stopped it to examine a press or another piece of equipment. After 45 minutes, a loose welding electrode was found. Several times it had swung out of place, punched a few holes, then swung back into place. As a result, about 50 parts – worth R15 000 – had to be scrapped. The troubleshooter got the technicians to replace the electrode, lined it up carefully, tightened it and the job was done.

Sounds like a pretty good job of troubleshooting, doesn't it? The troubleshooter thought so, and so did the other employees who watched. But let's see how efficient this method really was. Here's what the troubleshooter did:

• Looked briefly at a damaged part at the quality control station
• Walked slowly along the press line, looking carefully at each press
• Examined the sheet steel coming into the press line at the head end
• Climbed up the catwalk above the presses, walked slowly along the press line looking at each press from above
• Stopped the press line, examined each press for unusual protrusions
• Stopped the press line, examined each press for loose fixtures and transfer equipment
• Stopped the press line, tested welding electrodes by hand for looseness
• Found the loose electrode, replaced it, lined it up and tightened it.

>>

Remember what was said earlier about getting facts and using them to solve problems? If the troubleshooter had just taken a few minutes to get the facts together before jumping into action, the trouble could have been solved in seven minutes, and at least R2 million of downtime costs would have been saved.

- By asking exactly *what was wrong with the parts*, the troubleshooter could have come up with a very precise description of the problem: the parts had a round, smooth hole, about 2 cm in diameter, punched into them.
- By asking *where the trouble was on the parts*, the troubleshooter could have located the source of the problem: each hole was in the lower right corner, about 5 cm in from the right side, 25 cm up from the bottom. That's all the troubleshooter needed to know.

By studying this skeleton Specification, it would have been apparent that whatever was causing the hole was 2 cm in diameter, had a rounded head and had changed its location in the press to a point 5 cm in and 25 cm up. Having thorough knowledge of the equipment, the troubleshooter could have thought a minute about what fit that description. He or she would probably have realised that on this press line an electrode is round, 2 cm in diameter and has a rounded head. It rides up and down with the press and could come loose. If it did, it could swing into a position where it could punch neat, 2 cm holes in the part.

Next step: stop the presses and look for a loose electrode located in the lower right corner. It would be clearly recognisable because it would be gouged and scarred and could be swung over to a point precisely 5 cm in and 25 cm up.

Uncanny? Not a bit. It's just plain, common sense. It's making the most out of the facts you've got in front of you. It's making sure you don't waste time checking out factors that are not part of the specific problem.

Identity

The troubleshooter in the above example would have had only to ask two questions about the problem. The answers to those questions would have given enough information to suggest a possible cause. But sometimes you need a more complete picture of the trouble in order to come up with possible causes or to test them sufficiently. So, there are additional questions you can ask to get information about a problem. After a while you will develop a sixth sense about which questions to ask. Until then, it's a good idea to ask them all, so you don't miss any valuable information. The two other questions you could ask are:

- What thing or group of things are you having trouble with?
- What is wrong with it or them?

You already have the answers to both these questions – in your Trouble Statement. So why do we ask you to repeat them in your Specification? Very simply, your Specification has to be more specific. For example, a Trouble Statement such as 'Parts have a hole punched in them' is perfectly good. It tells you what group of related things you are having trouble with (parts) and what's wrong with them (they have a hole punched in them). This is enough for a Trouble Statement, although it may not tell you all there is to know about the identity of either the parts or the holes punched in them.

So, in your Specification you would ask again, 'What thing or group of things are you having trouble with?' Answer: parts. Then you would ask, 'Which parts?' Answer: steel parts. 'Which steel parts?' Answer: we make only one kind of steel parts. You keep asking until you identify the problematic parts as specifically as possible. This technique of questioning until you get all the available information is called 'questioning to the void', and you should do it for each of the specifying questions.

When you asked 'What is wrong with the parts?', you would get the answer: 'They have a hole punched in them.' Questioning to the void you might ask, 'What kind of hole is it?' Answer: 'It's a round hole.' 'What kind of round hole?' 'One that's 2 cm in diameter.'

Questioning to the void will ensure that you get down any information about the defect that you might have overlooked. Do you know anything else about its colour, size, shape, taste, smell, texture, sound, etc? Use your five senses and get others to use theirs, to gather additional facts. For example, if water is seeping from a boiler, feel it. Is it hot or cold water? Is it boiler water or feed water? Knowing that one fact may really narrow your search for the source. If a motor is making odd sounds, exactly what are they? Listen for a minute. Is the noise high pitched or low, a whine or a scraping sound? Does it vary or is it steady?

If material has to be rejected because it is discoloured, exactly what colour is the defective portion? If the material contains foreign matter, what is its colour or texture? Can you identify it? It will help you if you know. The clue to a problem's cause often lies in one special characteristic of the defect, which may go unnoticed without thorough questioning.

Location

Locate the problem. Ask 'Where?'. This question asks for physical or geographical location. In what places or areas does the trouble show up? In the example of the punctured steel parts, the answer to the question 'Where is the problem?' was easy: 5 cm in from the right side and 25 cm up from the bottom. In many cases, however, it is very difficult to get a meaningful answer to this question. There is no physical, tangible flaw or defect you can see in front of you, therefore, there is no specific area you can limit it to. If a vehicle slows down going uphill, where on the vehicle is the trouble? Or, if a mixture is defective, where in the mixture is the trouble? In such cases, this question just does not apply.

If the steel parts discussed earlier were made on two lines, and it was only on line one that the holes were appearing, the answer to this question would be 'line one'. Then, questioning to the void, you'd ask 'Where on line one?' Answer: 'At quality control'. 'Where at quality control?' If there were more than one quality-control station you would try to determine at which station the bad parts were seen. If not, you would have reached the void.

Trouble is often noticed at more than one location and every place it shows up should be recorded. If, besides the quality-control reports, several customers had called to say parts with holes were delivered to their plants, the answer to this question would have been 'at quality control and at customers' plants (specific locations)'.

Timing

Time the problem. Ask when the trouble was first noticed. Here, as with all your answers, you want the most precise information you can get. Don't put down 'This morning', if you can find out precisely what time this morning. Don't settle for 'Between nine and 10' without asking if anyone knows when between nine and 10.

After you have pinpointed the first occurrence of the trouble, you want to find out if there have been any other occurrences. Again, you are trying to get each date and time the trouble showed up, as completely and precisely as possible. From these facts, a definite pattern may emerge and, if there is another variable that has the same pattern, you may be able to match the two: effect and cause.

If you don't get precise dates or times, put down the best available information. 'It's happened two or three times since last January.' 'It comes and goes.' Sure, it's not much, but if it's all you've got don't let it get lost. Write it down: just remember that it's 'soft' data and keep looking for better information.

One word of caution: troubleshooters are often tempted to answer the first two 'When?' questions with events instead of times. There is a universal human tendency to jump to a cause, then try to make the facts fit that cause. 'When were the holes first noticed?' 'Oh, right after they got a new supplier for the steel.' Or, 'When, since it started in January, have you noticed a higher reject rate?' 'Every time Van Tonder is on the machine!' If these events are related to the cause, they will come out later in your problem analysis, take my word for it. But they don't belong in your Specification.

Every thing has a life cycle. This is simply the total time from its conception – as an idea or a design – until its disintegration or destruction. The life cycle consists of a series of steps or stages it goes through: design, parts manufacture, assembly, inspection, testing, shipment, sale, use by buyer, etc. Trouble may show up at any point in the life cycle and knowing at what step it was first noticed can be very helpful. Knowing that holes first show up in a part during its quality-control inspection allows the troubleshooter to limit the search for cause to the steps before quality control.

The extent

How much of the thing is affected? This question obviously applies only if you are dealing with a group of related things. If you produced 240 steel parts on the first shift, how many of them had a hole? Or, if there are three compressors in your cooling system, how many of the three are malfunctioning? In the case of a damaged part, where you can examine the surface, you can see if one third or one half or 95% of the part is defective. But it makes no sense to ask how much of a car has trouble when it is slowing down going uphill.

TESTING POSSIBLE CAUSES

You've asked every question to the void, noted which ones you may need more data on and which ones didn't apply. You have a pretty good description of what the trouble is, where it is, when it is and to what extent it is. You know all there is to know about the trouble. Or do you? You know all about what the trouble is, but do you know what it is not?

Why is it important to determine what constitutes a negative stance, ie what the trouble is not? Take the case of a business, say a vehicle panel-beating and spray-painting company, which has two compressors that are exactly alike.

Assume one blows up under high pressure, whereas the other is all right. This is information that is important. Something must be different about the bad compressor. You compare them carefully and notice that the bad compressor has a different type of high-pressure hose, it is clean and looks new. You follow this up and someone tells you they put a new kind of hose on that one compressor yesterday. No matter how good the supplier says the new hose is, it becomes your prime suspect once you've spotted it. And you spotted it by being aware of *what was not giving you trouble.*

The more you can limit the trouble you're trying to explain, the easier the job of explanation becomes. You have to check into fewer possible causes. If you realise the trouble is occurring on one unit, but not on six others, you don't bother looking at anything that is common to all seven. You've got a focus. If you find a limited effect, you look for a limited cause. If you find a round, 2-cm hole and not any other shape or size of hole, you look for a round, 2-cm cause. Asking yourself what the trouble is not, for instance, might help point to the shape of the trouble and underline some of its peculiarities.

You get the IS NOT information for your Specification the same way you get the IS: by asking questions in the *what, where, when* and *extent* dimensions. For every IS question there is a corresponding IS NOT question. I recommend asking first the IS question, then its companion IS NOT question, to gather specification information efficiently.

---

fig 6.1 :: trouble specification

What the problem IS	What the problem IS NOT
• What thing or group of things are you having trouble with?	• What thing or group of things could you be having trouble with, but are not?
• What is wrong with it or them?	• What could be wrong with it or them, but is not?
• Where is the thing when the trouble is noticed?	• Where could the thing be when the trouble is noticed, but isn't?
• Where is the trouble located on the thing?	• Where could the trouble be located on the thing, but isn't?
• When was the trouble first noticed? (date, time)	• When could the trouble have first been noticed, but wasn't? (date, time)

▷▷

What the problem IS	What the problem IS NOT
• When has the trouble been noticed since then? (date, time)	• When could the trouble have been noticed since then, but hasn't? (date, time)
• When in the history or life cycle of the thing was the trouble first noticed?	• When in the history or life cycle of the thing could the trouble have first been noticed, but wasn't?
• How many units of the thing have the trouble?	• How many units of the thing could have the trouble, but don't?
• How much of any one unit has the trouble?	• How much of any one unit could have the trouble, but doesn't?
• How many flaws or defects are on any one unit?	• How many flaws or defects could there be on any one unit, but aren't?

What a good troubleshooter wants in the IS NOT section are the things, defects, places, times, etc that are most closely related to the IS questions. That is, the things, defects, places, times, etc that are going to give the least number of differences when compared to the IS section. The less differences, the better the chances of finding that one difference that holds the key to the problem!

After you've worked with the same equipment for a while, you have a pretty good idea of what can go wrong with it. And, for most of these troubles, you also have an idea of some of the things that could cause them.

A good way to identify the most useful IS NOTs is to think in terms of what you could reasonably expect. If what's wrong with your car is a loss of power, you shouldn't be thinking about defects like air-conditioning not working or worn brake linings. What you want to ask yourself is 'If this car's engine is losing power, what other kinds of problems could I reasonably expect there to be with the way the engine is running?'

One last word about IS NOTs. They are of great value in testing possible causes. Every so often, however, you will come across a case where there is no IS NOT, which makes sense: your organisation makes or repairs only one, very specialised part – there is no other thing you could be having trouble with. You install a piece of equipment in one place and it is never used anywhere else – there is no other place it could be used.

There is no doubt that it will take a while to get used to specifying a problem. As with any new skill, practice makes perfect, and it will eventually become second nature to you to ask these questions as soon as you discover trouble. After some time you won't have to refer to the list of questions and you'll probably write down the answers only if you're dealing with a particularly difficult or complex problem. Otherwise, you'll take a few notes or specify mentally. It will take just a few minutes, but the payoff from stopping to specify, before leaping into action, will be tremendous.

SYMPTOMS, PROBLEMS AND SOLUTIONS

Failures in companies are characterised by certain symptoms, which might be general (such as staff being incapable of completing designated tasks) or more specific (problems caused on purpose or through negligence). The strategist should always apply the specific context in which he or she is troubleshooting to determine how to detect symptoms and diagnose problems for their specific environment.

Each symptom can be traced to one or more problems or causes by using specific troubleshooting tools and techniques. After being identified, each problem can be remedied by implementing a solution consisting of a series of actions.

General problem-solving model

When you're troubleshooting in a complex business environment, a systematic approach works best. An unsystematic approach to troubleshooting can result in wasting valuable time and resources, and can sometimes make symptoms even worse. Define the specific symptoms, identify all potential problems that could be causing the symptoms and then systematically eliminate each potential problem (from most likely to least likely) until the symptoms disappear.

Step 1: Make a clear problem statement

Define the problem in terms of a set of symptoms and potential causes. To properly analyse the problem, identify the general symptoms and then ascertain what kinds of problems (causes) could result in these symptoms.

Step 2: Gather the facts

Gather the facts you need to help isolate possible causes. Ask questions of affected management, staff and other key people. Collect information from these sources set out in the following table, which provides an overview of the basic methods to collect data.

<u>fig 6.2 :: methods of collecting facts</u>

Method	Overall purpose	Advantages	Challenges
Questionnaires, surveys, checklists	• To quickly and/or easily get lots of information from people in a non-threatening way	• Anonymous • Inexpensive to administer • Easy to compare and assess • Administer to many people • Can get lots of data • Sample questionnaires already exist	• Might not get careful feedback • Wording can bias client's responses • Are impersonal • Don't get full story
Interviews	• To fully understand someone's impressions or experiences, or learn more about their answers to questionnaires	• Get full range and depth of information • Develop relation-ship with client • Can be flexible with client	• Can take time • Can be hard to analyse and compare • Can be costly • Interviewer can bias client's responses
Documentation review	• To get an impression of how operations are functioning without interrup-ting them; review finances, memos, minutes, etc.	• Get comprehensive and historical information • Doesn't interrupt • Information already exists • Few biases about information	• Often takes much time • Info may be incomplete • Need to be quite clear about what looking for • Not a flexible means to get data; data restricted to what already exists

>>

Method	Overall purpose	Advantages	Challenges
Observation	• To gather accurate information about how an operation actually works. • Look at procedures	• View operations as they are actually occurring • Can adapt to events as they occur	• Can be difficult to interpret seen behaviour • Can be complex to categorise observations • Can influence behaviour of participants • Can be expensive
Focus groups	• Explore a topic in-depth through group discussion	• Quickly and reliably get common impressions • Can be an efficient way to get great range and depth of information in a short time • Can convey key information about operations	• Can be hard to analyse responses • Need a good facilitator for safety and closure • Difficult to schedule 6-8 people together
Case studies	• To fully understand or depict a client's experiences and conduct comprehensive examination through a cross-comparison of cases	• Fully depict a client's experience in the company • Powerful means to portray operations to outsiders	• Usually time-consuming to collect, organise and describe • Represent depth of information, rather than breadth

The above should, of course, be undertaken alongside the research methods set out in Chapter 5.

Step 3: Consider possible problems

Consider possible problems based on the facts that you have gathered. Using the facts, you can eliminate some of the potential problems from your list. Depending on the data, for example, you might be able to eliminate financial mismanagement as a problem, so that you can focus on operational issues. At every opportunity, try to narrow the number of potential problems so that you can create an efficient plan of action.

Step 4: Create an action plan

Create an action plan based on the remaining potential problems. Begin with the most likely problem and devise a plan in which only one variable is manipulated. Changing only one variable at a time enables you to reproduce a given solution to a specific problem. If you alter more than one variable simultaneously, you might solve the problem, but identifying the specific change that eliminated the symptom becomes far more difficult and will not help you solve the same problem if it occurs in the future.

Step 5: Implement the action plan

Perform each step carefully while testing to see whether the symptom disappears.

Step 6: Whenever you change a variable, be sure to gather results

Generally, you should use the same method of gathering facts that you used in Step 2 (that is, working with the key people affected, in conjunction with utilising diagnostic tools).

Step 7: Analyse results

Determine whether the problem has been resolved. If it has, then the process is complete.

Step 8: What if?

If the problem has not been resolved, you must create an action plan based on the next most likely problem in your list. Return to Step 4, change one variable at a time, and repeat the process until the problem is solved.

> If you exhaust all the common causes and actions and still can't solve the problem, either those outlined in this book or ones that you have identified for your environment, contact me at bci@magliolo.com.

PREPARING FOR SUCCESS OR FAILURE

It is always easier for a company to recover from a failure if it is prepared ahead of time. Possibly, the most important requirement in any environment is to have current and accurate information about that company, its networks, systems, operations, etc. Only with complete information can intelligent decisions be made about future changes to systems or operational functions, and only with complete information can troubleshooting be done as quickly and as easily as possible.

During the process of troubleshooting, the company is expected to exhibit abnormal behaviour as staff become wary of strangers among them or systems (factories, even) have to be shut down. Therefore, it is always a good practice to set up a time frame for troubleshooting to minimise any business impact. This can be done effectively when troubleshooting becomes part of the firm's corporate structure. Always document any changes being made, so that it is easier to back out if troubleshooting has failed to identify the problem within the maintenance window.

To determine whether the company is prepared for a corporate failure, answer the following questions:

- Do you have an accurate physical and logical map framework of all its operations, including computer networks?

- Does the organisation or department have an up-to-date outline of physical location of all devices on the network and how they are connected, as well as a logical map of network addresses, network numbers and subnet works?

- For each business and corporate set of rules and codes of behaviour, do you have a full list of staff numbers and contacts associated with them?

- Do you know all the points of contact to external staff and all clients, including any connections to the Internet?

- Has the organisation documented normal behaviour and performance at different times of the day so that you can compare the current problems with a baseline?

If you can answer yes to all questions, you will be able to help it recover from a failure more quickly and more easily than if it is not prepared. Lastly, for every problem solved, be sure to document the problems with solutions provided. This way, you will create a problem/answer database that others in the organisation can refer to should similar problems occur later. This will invariably reduce the time to troubleshoot the company and, consequently, minimise any negative impact on business.

START-UPS

A strategist may be called in to help in the formation of a new business, or a new business owner himself or herself may be the strategist. The following list sets out some factors that owners face when starting up a business.

New business owners must:

- Save money
- Stay in a field they understand
- Know their business before they start: research, research and research some more
- Use winners in their business field as mentors
- Specialise, even to a single product
- Find a product or service that is:
  - Needed or desired
  - Thought by customers to have no close substitute
  - Not subject to price regulation.
- Set a cap on their liability
- Learn computer skills
- Learn communication skills
- Have a strategic structure in place, including a lawyer and accountant, before they start
- Prepare a business plan
- Prepare the site criteria model for their particular business
- Do 'for and against' lists for major decisions
- Be contrarian: buy when everyone is selling (and vice versa)
- Deal with those they like, trust and admire
- Learn accounting skills
- Create their own internal control plan
- Give back to the community.

New business owners should not do the following:

- Sign a lease without a lawyer's review
- Rush: there is no such thing as the last good deal
- Set up a 'commodity' business (one without pricing power)

- Work to the detriment of family and health
- Compete in markets dominated by few players, unless they have a special niche
- Avoid a long-term financial plan.

AN EXPANDING COMPANY

Before expanding a business, the CEO should always consult a lawyer and an accountant must be part of the team. They can help to develop benefits for future employees as well as for the management. The goal is to provide benefits sufficient to recruit and maintain outstanding managers. Provisions can be considered for retirement plans, health insurance and holiday benefits. These costs should then be included in a budget.

When a business starts to grow, the management must:

- Identify and acknowledge problems with brutal honesty .
- Immediately reduce losses by unemotionally cutting costs to maintain a positive cash flow and profitability. This is the first and most important action to take.
- Stay with the business they know unless its future is fatally defective.
- Take the initiative to explain to their creditors what the problems are and why slow or smaller payments will be necessary. Never write post-dated cheques or send late payments without an explanation.
- Not cut value or quality of the products or services. Make them even better.
- Improve every aspect they can of performance and image.
- Look for opportunity in adversity. Sometimes there will be bargain opportunities during business slumps.
- Remember that businesses have cycles. They should hang in there and ride out the adverse periods.

Some of the common mistakes made when businesses begin to expand can be deadly; they include the following:

- **Uncontrolled cash flow:** Businesses fail because they run out of money, so their cash flow projections for current operation or any expansion should be prepared very conservatively
- **Forecast income** (sales) very low or forecast expenses very high
- **Unanticipated contingencies not provided for**

- **A drop in sales or insufficient sales**: If this happens, income and cash flow will be impacted. Immediately take the necessary remedial steps by ruthlessly cutting costs.

- **Higher costs**: Can you increase volume of sales? Can you offset with higher prices?

- **New competition**: The reality of corporate life! Can you learn from them? Can you neutralise their opening impact?

- **Business recessions**: You will need to promptly cut costs to maintain earnings and cash flow.

- **Incompetent managers or employees**: Act swiftly to get rid of them.

- **Dishonesty, theft**: Study the ways the most successful competitor controls all forms of dishonesty that your business is exposed to, including shrinkage (shoplifting) and employee dishonesty. Each business will be different.

- A combination of any or all of the above.

FINANCIAL TROUBLESHOOTING

Occasionally, a business problem will involve financial difficulties. The first step in financial troubleshooting is to identify the type of financial problem that the business is experiencing. Is the problem one of profitability, liquidity or solvency or a combination of the above? Still worse, is it more than one of the above? Income statements, cash flows and balance sheets can be used together to characterise financial performance. Several years of data summarised in a trend sheet provide an ideal measure to start the analysis. Failing that, financial statements calculated for a typical year can help sort out the long-term problems from situations arising from a specific year.

A business that is experiencing financial difficulties is, in most cases, in that predicament for several reasons. It is extremely rare to find a situation where a single management problem or decision is the sole cause of poor financial performance. The consequences of financial difficulties will be low profitability, liquidity or solvency. The underlying cause generally will be associated with one or more diagnostic or causative factors of efficiency, scale and debt structure.

Efficiency

As used in this book, 'efficiency' refers to the relationship between inputs and outputs in a business. Efficiency can be measured in physical terms, such as crop yields, computers sold, vehicles manufactured, etc. Efficiency can also be examined using economic measures, such as variable costs per acre or returns per rand. There are no perfect measures of efficiency. Normally you will have to examine several aspects of the business before a clear picture begins to emerge. Efficiency, to a large extent, is determined by the management's managerial and technical skills. In larger operations, efficiency will reflect the performance of the owner as well as hired managers and workers.

Companies with low efficiency generally will show below-average profitability. Efficiency and profitability are two sides of the same coin. Low returns and high costs also can affect liquidity. In the long run, poor profitability translates into losses in earned equity and reduced solvency, although some businesses may have sufficient equity to withstand low efficiency for many years.

Improving efficiency, in most cases, requires improving basic management and technical skills. This is not easy. Detailed production records can help identify problem areas. Outside technical or managerial consultants or experienced specialists also can be helpful. Ultimately, improving efficiency means improving resource allocation, enterprise choice and the motivation and coordination of employees.

Scale

This refers to the size of the business. Companies can be too large or too small. In large or complex operations, managerial control or input can be spread too broadly. The efficiency of the business suffers as a consequence. Scale problems occur more frequently with businesses that are too small. In particular, scale problems occur when the labour supply is large relative to the capacity of the company to fully employ and support it. Even large, complex businesses can have scale problems of this sort, such as when several families attempt to work together. Small firms also may have higher production costs per unit, because fixed investment costs are spread over relatively low output levels.

Scale can be assessed by determining the labour requirements for the firm and comparing that to the existing labour supply after making allowances for off-premises work. Other labour-based measures of scale include sales per worker or workers per specified area. A similar set of measures can be developed for the capital stock, considering investment per acre, per product produced or per worker.

Full employment is, in most cases, necessary to ensure an acceptable standard of living. If labour is in excess, the funds withdrawn for wages or family living expenses can adversely affect the profitability and liquidity of the business. If the scale of a business is inadequate, for example a farm is too small relative to its labour supply, a number of options can be considered. The labour supply can be reduced through casual employment or by eliminating hired or family employees. Or labour utilisation can be increased through expansion, by purchasing or leasing additional assets, shifting to more labour-intensive enterprises, or attempting to improve productivity through more intensive management.

Debt structure

This refers to the amount of outstanding debt, its term and cost. A firm can have too little debt, limiting its size, efficiency, growth and earning capacity. For the most part, however, debt structure problems arise when the debt load is excessive, too costly or must be paid off over too short a term. Debt structure influences profitability through interest costs, liquidity through debt-servicing requirements and solvency through the value of the assets available to secure the firm's liabilities. Some debt-structure problems are relatively easy to resolve – for example, by lengthening loan terms to improve cash flow. Most, however, involve adjusting the asset or liability structure of the business. The owner might sell assets and reduce liabilities. Or he or she may simply attempt to eliminate assets that have debt-service requirements in excess of their cash-generating potential. Lenders in certain situations may be willing to consider debt write-off or sale-lease back options. Adjusting debt structure usually requires a negotiated settlement between borrower and lender.

TROUBLESHOOTING WITH A DECISION TREE

A decision tree (also called a diagnostic tree) is a procedure that involves examining the efficiency, scale and debt structure of a business.

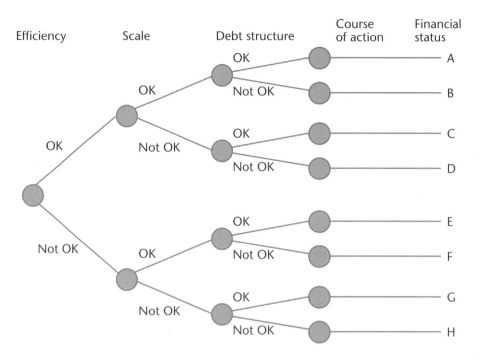

fig: 6.3 the decision tree

In the interest of simplicity, the strategist decides whether or not the factor is OK or Not OK at each node (oval) in the decision tree. This oversimplifies the process, but it demonstrates the interrelationship of efficiency, scale and debt structure, and the courses of action that might be appropriate to remedy each problem.

The decision tree also implies that a range of specific management options or adjustments exists for a firm on each branch. A firm with acceptable efficiency but unacceptable scale and debt load faces choices that are quite different from a firm with poor efficiency, acceptable scale and unacceptable debt load. Further, there is always a question of order or priority in attempting to resolve financial problems. Which problem should be fixed first?

The following tables presents several management courses of action for each branch on the decision tree.

fig 6.4 :: financial troubleshooting diagnostic factors and courses of action

Diagnostic factors	Courses of action
Financial status A	
• E: OK • S: OK • D: OK	• Review financial performance annually • Keep current on new technology • Examine potential for expansion • Consider off-firm investments.
Financial status B	
• E: OK • S: OK • D: Not OK	• Restructure debt: lengthen term or reduce interest rate to improve cashflow • Sell assets to reduce debt • Reduce debt through 'shelving' or write-off • Consider bankruptcy.
Financial status C	
• E: OK • S: Not OK • D: OK	• Address scale problem or else cashflow problems will develop • Expand by adding an enterprise or expanding existing enterprises. Use records to make expansion decisions • Investigate company and its products. • Use resources fully: machinery, labour. • Examine whether management ability and emotional stability are sufficient to handle the additional stress of expansion. • Increase temporary or casual employment, but assess its effect on efficiency. • Consider retiring, if appropriate.
Financial status D	
• E: OK • S: Not OK • D: Not OK	• Identify several low-cost ways to expand, such as renting additional space. • Increase off-firm income, but assess its effect on efficiency • Scale back the business to allow a significant increase in casual employment. • Declare bankruptcy and start again.

Key:
• E = Efficiency   • S = Scale   • D = Debt structure

The lists are by no means exhaustive. They simply illustrate ways in which profitability, liquidity or solvency problems might be resolved, given a firm's efficiency, scale and debt structure.

FINANCIAL TROUBLESHOOTING FOR A FARM

The following text illustrates the financial consequences of inadequate efficiency, scale and debt structure on a farm business using Decision Tree Analysis. Although the financial measures are shown to be significantly affected by changes in the three factors, the specific relationships among the financial measures may not apply to other farm conditions or situations.

The farm produces corn and soybeans on 1,000 hectares. It also has a 250-sow furrow-to-finish enterprise, marketing approximately 4,000 hogs per year. About 70% of the corn crop is fed to hogs. The farm is managed by a single family. One spouse works part-time off the farm. They employ one full-time worker plus seasonal labour. About 7,000 hours of labour are used on the farm. The farm's financial statements are summarised in the following tables.

The farm is assumed to have generally acceptable (OK) levels of efficiency, scale and debt structure.

fig 6.5 :: diagnostic factors of a farm's financial troubles

Diagnostic factors	Courses of action
Financial status E	
• E: Not OK • S: OK • D: OK	• Improve enterprise record-keeping and analysis • Re-orient priorities: spend more time on management • Deal with facts. Management is a personal thing and affects self-worth • Work to improve and sustain management • Use advisory services • Improve marketing skill and performance • Examine family living expenditures and operating costs • Evaluate whether the operation is too large to manage efficiently • Discuss whether to quit farming while equity is still good • Establish a point where additional credit should not be extended • Decide if an off-farm job would be better than self-employment.
Financial status F	
• E: Not OK • S: OK • D: Not OK	• Determine if debt problems are due to poor efficiency or outside circumstances. Will debt problems develop again if solved now? • Evaluate long-term. Is there a future in farming?
Financial status G	
• E: Not OK • S: Not OK • D: OK	• Determine if farming is a 'hobby' rather than a business • Consider leaving before equity is gone • Determine if resources can be employed better elsewhere • Obtain off-farm employment.
Financial status H	
• E: Not OK • S: Not OK • D: Not OK	• Decide if resolving this difficult situation is worth the hassle • Consider the effects on marriage, family, health and so on • Consider selling out or declaring bankruptcy.

Key:
- E = Efficiency
- S = Scale
- D = Debt structure

The following sets out the balance sheet, income statement and cash flow for the farm.

fig 6.6 :: balance sheet

	Assets (R)	Liabilities (R)
Current	596,300	158,400
Intermediate	547,900	155,700
Long-term	1,401,800	140,300
Non-farm	172,900	88,000
Total	2,718,900	542,400
Net worth		**R2,176,500**

fig 6.7 :: income statement

Revenue	Rands
Crops	175,800
Livestock	442,600
Total	618,400
Cash expenses	
Operating	328,900
Interest	34,000
Hired labour	25,000
Total	387,900
Net cash income	230,500
Depreciation	95,800
Net farm income	134,700

fig 6.8 :: cash flow

Net cash farm income	R230,500
Non-farm income	15,000
Total outflow	R245,500
Family living	R 30,000
Taxes, social security	54,400
Debt service	85,800
Total	R170,200
Net cash flow	**R 75,300**

The following changes are made to the farm example to illustrate the impact of altered levels of efficiency, scale and debt structure on common financial performance measures.

Efficiency of the farm is reduced by increasing the crop production expenses by 10% and reducing hog marketing rates by approximately 17%, from 8.4 to 7.0 pigs marketed per litter. These changes reduce gross farm income by 9.5% and increase cash expenses by 1.9%.

Scale is reduced by increasing hired labour by 3,500 hours. This represents the addition of a second family to the farm business – an increase in yearly labour costs of approximately R30,000 per year. Total full-time equivalent increases from 2.5 to 4.0 as a consequence.

Debt structure. In the base analysis, the farm business has a total debt-to-asset ratio of 20%. To illustrate an unsatisfactory debt structure, the debt-to-asset ratio is increased to 70%. Long-term liabilities increase six-fold. Intermediate and current liabilities also are increased.

Analysis of the example. Two critical steps in financial troubleshooting involve determining whether or not a financial problem exists and, if so, determining its most likely cause. Debt-structure problems, in this example, are most clearly indicated by high debt-to-asset ratio, negative or low cash flows and other liquidity measures, and low returns-to-equity. The assumed change in debt structure is rather large.

Consequently, the observed change in financial measures is dramatic. Scale problems, represented by increased labour, reduce profitability and expense measures. Net farm income falls by the increase in labour expense. However, liquidity is not as adversely affected because the increase in expenses results in reduced tax liability. The output of the farm measured by the turnover ratio is not affected by this change, since this ratio measures only efficiency of capital use and not efficiency of labour use. Finally, a reduction in efficiency alone results in fairly pervasive changes. Net farm income and all the associated profitability measures decrease. Further net cashflow is reduced by nearly 50%.

fig 6.9 :: financial troubleshooting combinations

	A	B	C	D	E	F	G	H
Net farm income (R1,000)	134.7	28.7	105.0	-1.4	68.8	-31.5	38.7	-61.7
Return on assets (%)	4.9	4.9	3.8	3.8	2.4	2.7	1.3	1.5
Profit margin (%)	24.4	24.4	18.6	18.6	13.4	14.6	7.0	8.2
Turnover ratio (%)	20.2	20.2	20.2	20.2	18.2	18.2	18.2	18.2
Return on equity (%)	4.4	-1.8	2.9	-5.7	1.3	-9.2	-0.1	-13.0
Operating expense ratio (%)	57.0	57.2	62.1	62.1	64.5	63.5	69.8	68.8
Net cash flow (R1,000)	75.3	-134.5	-58.3	-159.0	-38.5	-189.5	-24.1	-219.7
Current ratio (%)	3.8	1.4	3.8	1.4	3.8	1.5	3.7	1.4
Term debt coverage ratio (%)	164.0	64.1	150.0	57.5	133.0	49.4	120.7	41.3
Net worth (R1,000)	2176.0	873.0	2176.0	873.0	2176.0	873.0	2176.0	873.0
Debt-to-asset ratio (%)	20.0	68.0	20.0	69.0	19.7	69.0	17.8	69.0
Cost of debt (%)	6.4	7.6	6.4	8.4	6.4	7.6	6.4	7.8

The specific combinations of A to H follow the decision tree diagram in Figure 6.3. A is the base analysis, B is a debt structure problem only, C is a scale problem only, and E is an efficiency problem only. The remaining branches are combinations of the three problems.

The procedure outlined helps the analyst go from symptoms to cause to cure. The difficulty, however, is that poor financial performance can be caused by several interacting factors. And the resolution of the problems will, in most cases, reflect the unique situation of a given farm business.

This suggests that effective troubleshooting involves more than simple rules or financial guidelines. Appropriate financial analysis can come only from careful attention to the resources and needs of the individual farm family.

Troubleshooting a farm business requires an orderly approach, good data and occasional intuitive leaps of faith.

FINAL WORD ON TROUBLESHOOTING.

A troubleshooter should continually review case histories of the businesses in his or her field – and not only the successes, but also the failures. Determine the reasons they failed and ask whether it was due to inadequate testing, planning and experience? Did they have a solution to the problem? And did the solution resolve the issue? Forewarned is better than fire fighting.

CHAPTER 7

CORPORATE
DEALS

At a recent conference, I was asked an unusual question: What would I consider to be the 10 Commandments of the strategist planning for an acquisition? I had to consider a number of issues before I could answer the question.

Fundamental to a purchase is determining the most basic of factors: is this a good business? The list of 10 rules thus consists of those that cannot be bent, avoided or broken. Any business that is sound and has a profitable future must subscribe to all 10. There are, in my opinion, more than 10. For example: according to the second Commandment, you would not buy a cheap business. It would be like acquiring a bad used car. You would spend all your time trying to patch over problems and there would be little or no time left for building the business. Buy a good business, a solid one that through your talents can grow and flourish. Start off with a strong foundation and build from there. As stated, this is only one of 10 commandments, yet there are a host of other factors that would flow from this single item.

To keep the answer succinct, here is the list:

- **Commandment 1: The past is only an indicator of the future.** The past financials will help determine the purchase price, but they do not guarantee what the business will look like in the future. You must evaluate the business for what it can expect to provide you with after you buy it.

- **Commandment 2: Identify the strong features of a business and find the weaknesses.** All good businesses possess certain common features.

Determine whether the one you're considering already has these in place. Find and eliminate problems.

- **Commandment 3: The whole is sometimes worth less than the parts.** There have been times when analysis of a potential takeover shows that the value of the two companies combined will be less than the two apart. Strategy can help with resolving valuation problems or identifying solutions to amalgamate at lower prices.

- **Commandment 4: Always determine bottom-line profit.** This traps so many buyers when they look at a product and not the profit. Judgement can be clouded by the popularity of an item. You must remain objective!

- **Commandment 5: Concentrate on core skills.** Make certain that you already possess what the business really needs.

- **Commandment 6: Apply technology.** In order to grow any business, you must take advantage of technology. Can this business improve its systems and run on its own so you can focus your attention on driving the profits? Where can you access the technology and what are the costs?

- **Commandment 7: Exploit.** Nearly all businesses possess certain components that have not been exploited. Identify these 'hidden' values.

- **Commandment 8: All businesses must have three personal things:**
  - You MUST be able to explain strategy in simple terms to others.
  - You MUST be able to explain strategy with great enthusiasm.
  - It MUST be a business that makes you very proud.

- **Commandment 9: Evaluate and identify problem areas.** No business is perfect and every business needs attention. Sometimes the smallest improvements yield the greatest results. Pinpoint all of them.

- **Commandment 10: Valuate and revaluate.** Only you can truly evaluate the benefits of any venture. You'll understand how to take a realistic approach to this crucial exercise only once you have conducted research and used valuation techniques and undertaken an analysis of how much a new venture will improve your business.

A SUCCESSFUL BUSINESS ACQUISITION

Merger and acquisition activity is continually on the rise, particularly in a global market. Having survived recession, war and a rapidly changing global business environment, many companies are now focusing on growth. Specifically, companies that downsized during the last few years have saved some cash and are now poised to spend money and grow through acquisition.

Though it can seem exciting, growth by acquisition is filled with corporate traps and possible financial problems, particularly for the inexperienced. Simply having the money to buy a company does not, in itself, ensure success. Neither does securing capital for an acquisition from a bank or through investors ensure success. Obtaining the enthusiastic support of your management team also does not ensure success.

The three factors that have the greatest impact on the success or failure of a business acquisition are:

1. Having a thorough understanding of the acquisition target prior to closing the transaction, so there are no surprises after the acquisition has been completed.

2. Developing a post-closing plan that offers maximum potential to effectively integrate, operate and grow the acquired company in a post-transaction environment

3. Executing that post-closing plan, which can be difficult and is highly dependent on how the employees of the acquired company not only accept, but proactively participate, in the plan.

If The Chairman's Office has a dedicated 'insourced' strategist at its quarterly meetings, the process of any future corporate deal will tend to run more smoothly. Alternatively, should a company be pursuing a corporate deal and not have the necessary professional experience resident within the organisation, it is critical for management to use dedicated outside advisors who understand their business as well as the business environment, and can adequately represent management through this tedious and difficult process.

Whether it's a merger of equals or one company acquiring another, operational effectiveness and financial success can hinge on the ability of the post-transaction management team to understand both corporate cultures, and to integrate the employees of each company into an emerging culture that fits the objectives underlying the transaction. This is the task of the corporate strategist, which will lighten the duties of the managing director.

Of course, a smart strategist doesn't try to force-fit one culture into another. In this regard, large company transactions can be particularly difficult due to the sheer size and complexity of the merging organisations. But small company transactions can be challenging as well. For example, there may exist within the acquired business a deeply rooted, 'family-oriented' culture that has been nurtured over the course of numerous generations of ownership.Having been acquired by a larger and more formal company, the smaller informal business may now be required to adhere to more structured policies, procedures and demands. Additional reporting requirements to the new owners introduce another layer of 'work', the value of which employees of the acquired company may not see. The transition can be time-consuming and, at times, frustrating.

But skilled strategists understand how to manage these environments-in transition.

The same dynamics are at work in the aftermath of a corporate acquisition. Whose system do you use? Where do you locate a particular resource? What vendors should you retain? The best answers emerge when each party listens to the other and contributes to a decision that's in the best interests of the whole.

WORKSHEETS FOR A DEAL-MAKING STRATEGIST

The following worksheets form a starting point for the strategist in the process of any corporate deal. Some of the questions posed in the following tables will be put to colleagues and members of the company to be acquired. However, most are formulated and brainstormed internally (in The Chairman's Office) before they are directed at individuals.

fig 7.1 :: trouble specification

Steps in the process	Questions to consider
First-level proposal review	• Does the project or corporate deal fit within the company? • How will the project benefit the company? • Is there a need for the services/outcomes? • Is the approach solid? • Are there better approaches for achieving the outcomes? • Does the project fit with your organisation's theory of change? • Does it build on other grants?
Second-level proposal review	• Does the project fit with the organisation's mission and theory of change? Does it shift the organisation away from its mission? • Does the project design make sense? Do the proposed activities fit with the overall project goals? • Do the costs make sense? • Is the programme likely to succeed in achieving its desired results? What are the major challenges to success? How will these challenges be addressed? • Is this the right organisation to do the job? Are there others doing anything like this, and if so, might they do it better? • Does the organisation have a successful history of running a similar project? If the proposed scope of work is new for the organisation, does it have the capacity to meet the goals?
Discussion with colleagues	• How are the organisation and its key staff leadership perceived within their peer group and by other funders or competitors? • Does the organisation have a positive history of working and networking with other organisations in the community?

Steps in the process	Questions to consider
First level of financial consideration	• Become familiar with the project budget. • Review the description of the project's staffing: Does the proposed project staff design seem adequate? • Consider how the project supports or doesn't support the work of the organisation: Do the two fit together?
Financial document review	• Does the organisation have working capital that is equal to the current liabilities plus three months of operating budget? • Does the organisation have positive net assets? • Does the organisation have an operating deficit (expenses exceeds revenues)?

NOTE:

• Working capital is equal to current assets minus current liabilities.

• Net assets is also called net worth or profitability in the business world. This is equal to revenues minus expenses.

fig 7.2 :: organisational history and track record

Area of review	Question	Notes
History	• Set out the history of the organisation. • What were the key milestones in its development? • What were the most significant accomplishments of the past three to five years? • What were the most significant challenges?	Red flags?
Recent accomplishments	• What were the most important accomplishments in the past three years?	

fig 7.3 :: governance and executive leadership

Area of review	Question	Notes
Role of the board	• Describe the board and the role it plays in the organisation. • How do the board and strategist work together? How are decisions made? • What is the board's role in strategic planning? In fundraising? In financial oversight?	
Structure of the board	• How does the board make decisions? Do appropriate committees exist? How often does the board meet? • If applicable, what is the role of any advisory board(s)? Who serves on it?	
Composition of the board	• Who is on the board? What do they bring to the organisation? • How are board members recruited and selected? Who is involved in this process? • Describe the commitment of the CEO and other managers to diversity of staff and board members.	**Red flags?**
Relationship between strategy and chairman	• Describe the partnership between the MD and the board chair. • How do they work together?	
Executive leadership	• What are the managing director's background and qualifications? How long has he or she been with the organisation? • How does he or she work with the staff? How does he or she work with the board of directors? • Describe the leadership the managing director brings to the organisation.	

fig 7.4 :: organisational vision and strategy

Area of review	Question	Notes
Vision	• What is the organisation's mission? • What is the vision for the organisation?	
Strategy formation	• How do you set the overall direction for the organisation? • Does the company have a current strategic plan? If not, how does the MD develop strategy? • Who else is involved in the strategic planning and thinking? • How does he or she incorporate current strategies into your work?	Red flags?
External environment	• How does the organisation keep abreast of the latest thinking in its business? • What are the top three challenges facing the organisation over the next five years?	

fig 7.5 :: proposed project: planning, outcomes and evaluation

Area of review	Question	Notes

Project planning	• Describe the basis for the project manager's approach to this project. What research is he or she relying upon for his or her proposed approach?
	• Describe the resources needed to accomplish the goals, and the project manager plans to obtain them.
	• If relevant, discuss the following:
	  - Scalability of model
	  - Potential for broad impact
	  - An innovative approach	

>>

>>

| Outcomes | • What are the goals and outcomes identified for the project?
• What was the process for developing the outcomes? How will the project manager use lessons learned from previous years/ projects?
• Describe the organisation's greatest strengths in terms of the capacity of the company and its directors to achieve the intended outcomes.
• What significant challenges exist in the manager's capacity to achieve his or her intended outcomes? | Red flags? |
| Evaluation | • How does he or she evaluate programmes? What tools does he or she have in place?
• How does the manager incorporate what he or she learns into ongoing and future work?
• What is the plan for evaluation for this project? What resources are allocated for evaluation in the project budget? | |

fig 7.6 :: human resources

Area of review	Question	Notes
General staff and HR concerns	• Describe the organisational structure and staff roles/reporting relationships. • How are staff recruited and hired by the firm? • How are staff oriented and trained for their jobs? • How does the organisation handle staff performance reviews? • How does the organisation invest in professional development for staff?	Red flags?
Project staff	• Who are the staff members responsible for the proposed project? What are their backgrounds and qualifications?	

fig 7.7 :: external communications and relationships

Area of review	Question	Notes
Communications	• Who are the key audiences? How do management and the board of directors communicate with those audiences? • How do management and the board of directors disseminate information about their work and/or share what they learn with others in the corporation?	Red flags?
External relationships	• What partnerships or collaborations are management and the board of directors involved in? What role do they play? • How do management and the board of directors approach and develop partnerships or collaborative relationships with others? • Who is the company's main competition? How does the company work with them?	

Listen to the views and concerns of all employees regarding work in the 'new' environment.

The ability of an organisation's top management to keep listening to what their employees are saying, either directly through standard communication channels or implied by certain behaviour, is perhaps the single most difficult task to undertake on a consistent basis. Why? Because the pace of corporate life and the myriad responsibilities of senior executives and mid-level managers make it all too easy to shuffle to the middle of the 'to do' list what might initially appear to be small or trivial issues that have the potential, over time, to mushroom into much larger concerns.

Implicit in listening is management's commitment to a relationship with their employees based on mutual respect – management respect for employees' opinions and employee respect for management's ability to make thoughtful decisions.

:: CHAPTER 8 ::

DUE
DILIGENCE

> An idea is an opportunity when it is timely, attractive, achievable, durable, fills a need and provides value to the buyer. An idea is an opportunity only if there is reason to believe the market will validate the idea and the management team has the ability to execute the idea. Only proper, strategic due diligence can determine such factors with pinpoint accuracy.

In business, there is a perception that there will never be two transactions that are exactly the same, which would mean that there cannot be a definitive methodology to due diligence. However, while all projects will differ to various degrees, there will always be a similarity between company objectives, management and shareholder structures, products sold or services provided and so on. These factors, together with an analysis of a transaction's financial strength and the strategic methods to determine it, are the starting point for all due diligence processes. The main difference is in the interpretation of results and conclusions drawn from the analysis.

Ultimately, due diligence is the best method strategists use to consider the potential impact of risk on changes to a company, present and future.

START WITH THE BASICS

- Get advice: Few mid-market companies have the in-house skills needed for a complex transaction. Therefore, the earlier they involve internal and external advisors to begin any corporate process, the more likely it is that their expertise will favourably influence the approach and final outcome of the deal, whether to solve problems, conduct an acquisition or prepare for the future.

- **Find crucial information:** Since deals generally have a steadily accelerating pace, particularly when there are many parties involved, starting early can give you, the strategist, more time to investigate important issues and options.

- **Improve the deal:** A well-planned and -executed due diligence process can also put the company strategist in control of the process. It can provide a strong knowledge base from which to improve the ultimate outcome.

- **Take and keep control:** Once negotiations are underway, it quickly becomes difficult to slow the pace to make major changes of approach without potentially losing the deal. Even less can be changed once the deal is signed.

- **Conduct 'what if' scenarios:** Without adequate knowledge, the company may lose legal or business opportunities –- making the deal less beneficial. There is also the potential of losing the entire deal if 'deal-breakers' are not adequately investigated and resolved. There is the potential of a threat to a company's growth (or even survival) if a deal is fraught with problems not seen as a result of poor research.

WHY IS DUE DILIGENCE CONDUCTED?

The strategist needs to confirm that the business is what it appears to be. He or she therefore needs to:

- Identify actual or potential defects that could affect the future profitability of the business
- Research and assess factors that will be useful for valuing assets
- Negotiate the ultimate price, when conducting an acquisition
- Verify that the transaction complies with investment or acquisition criteria.

The aim of due diligence is to identify problems within a business, particularly any issues that may give rise to unexpected liabilities in the future. When due diligence is carried out as part of the steps leading to an initial public offering (IPO), the exercise takes on added meaning and encompasses a wider scope. These issues are comprehensively set out in *A Guide to AltX: Listing on South Africa's Alternative Exchange.*

During my investigation of a complex mining deal that transcended emerging markets and included the potential to be listed on the London Stock Exchange in 2006, it became clear that the reason so many deals fall short of their promise is inadequate due diligence. This is a key factor in the failure of deals to live up to expectations. In too many cases, the people behind these deals do not effectively size up their risks before proceeding. Typically, acquisitions fail because the buyer has little experience with the complexities of the acquisition process.

The process of due diligence, in the case of an acquisition, includes a number of serious risk variables. Too many analysts avoid assessing these factors when conducting due diligence on not only an acquisition but also during most due diligences. There is *always* a need to include the following:

- Strategic fit (product, service or new company)
- Correct valuation of all aspects of a business
- Warranties and indemnifications
- Unrecorded liabilities
- Payment and other financing structures
- Environmental liabilities and impact studies (particularly when the company involves environmental and geological impact studies)
- Information systems compatibility
- Analysis of assets (must include redundant assets)
- Inventory and receivables valuations
- Management, directors, staff, workforce and shareholders
- Pension, provident funds and severance payouts
- Operational integration.

Any one of these risks can prevent a deal from being concluded. Worse, if not properly recognised and addressed in advance, they can destroy value in the overall business. Getting a corporate finance deal off to the right start is key to identifying and managing these risks.

WHO SHOULD CONDUCT DUE DILIGENCE?

For the due diligence exercise to be carried out in an unbiased manner and to achieve its purpose of accurately presenting the state of affairs of the company, it is important that it is carried out by an independent professional.

The process in itself calls for professional input from both financial and legal advisors, in addition to other technical advisors, such as engineers or IT professionals.

This will depend on the genre of the business being studied. However, as mentioned previously, the success of the due diligence exercise is largely dependant on management's co-operation – physically, in the time spent with advisors, and mentally, in their positive attitude towards the whole process.

HOW IS DUE DILIGENCE CONDUCTED?

Conducting due diligence generally starts with the creation of a checklist of necessary information. Management prepares in particular financial statements that need to be reviewed to incorporate realistic forecasts. In addition, interviews and site visits must be set up and conducted. Finally, thorough research is conducted into customers, suppliers, industry experts and trade organisations.

HOW MUCH DUE DILIGENCE NEEDS TO BE CONDUCTED?

There is no correct answer to this question. The amount of due diligence conducted is based on the size of the business, prior experiences, the size of the transaction, the likelihood of closing a transaction, time constraints, cost factors and resource availability. It is impossible to learn everything about a business in the time available, so it is important to learn enough to enable the buyer to lower risks to an appropriate level and make good, informed business decisions.

In practical terms, the due diligence process aspires to achieve the following:

- Assess the reasonableness of historical and projected earnings and cash flow
- Identify key vulnerabilities, risks and opportunities
- Gain an in-depth understanding of the company and the market in which the company operates such that the company's management can anticipate and manage change
- Set in motion the planning for the post-IPO operations.

Since due diligence is such a crucial part of any corporate finance strategy, serious attention must be given to these issues before embarking on any strategic alliance. Remember, though, that it may not be necessary to investigate every possible avenue of consideration. Too much due diligence can kill a small transaction.

Ultimately, what is listed in *The Corporate Mechanic* is meant as a menu of items to choose from. Use this menu to select what to investigate and what to overlook. Make conscious and informed – not random – decisions of the possible lines of investigation. A way to do this is to develop a due diligence strategy considering the following factors:

- What's important to the company and what isn't?
- Which problems will be costly? Which ones will be minor?
- Where are the problems likely to be?
- How complex is the corporate deal, problem or issue? What will the investigation cost in time and in money?
- What is the risk if the unexpected causes the transaction to go bad?

THE FIVE AREAS OF INVESTIGATION

There are five essential areas in which to conduct due diligence:

1. corporate image
2. social responsibility
3. environmental accountability
4. financial soundness
5. industry attractiveness.

These are the absolute minimum requirements for responsible due diligence.

Corporate image

- What is the company's public image? Have there been any tensions between the community and the company?
- Has negative media publicity been dealt with?
- Are there any pending lawsuits against the company?
- Is the company looking solely for investor relations opportunities by aligning itself with a potential partner?
- Is the company willing to engage with a partner in a transparent and open manner without expecting an exclusive relationship (ie barring competitors)?
- In the case of a merger, which corporate image will be dominant?

Social responsibility

- Is the company primarily involved in the manufacture or sale of firearms or narcotics, ie does involvement in these activities constitute a significant share of the company's total portfolio?

- Does the company have a good reputation, especially in areas of corporate social responsibility? In the case of new companies, are they committed to instituting/improving sound policies?

- Does the company have policies barring harmful child labour or forced labour?

- Does the company have a non-discrimination policy governing the hiring and promotion of minorities and women? Does it comply to black or economic empowerment policies of the country where the deal is to be struck?

- Does the company accept unions or attempts to organise a union?

- Does the company have a health and safety action plan for workers, including the handling of hazardous materials and the prevention of environmental accidents?

- Does the company have a policy for codes of conduct and labour standards?

Environmental accountability

- Does the company collect and evaluate adequate and timely information regarding the environmental, health and safety impacts of its activities?

- Does the company set targets for improved environmental performance and regularly monitor progress towards environmental, health and safety targets?

- Does the company assess and address, in decision-making, the foreseeable environmental, health and safety-related impacts associated with the processes, goods and services of the enterprise over its full life cycle? And provide the public and employees with adequate and timely information on the potential environment, health and safety impacts of the activities of the enterprise?

- Does the company maintain contingency plans for preventing, mitigating and controlling serious environmental and health damage from its operations, including accidents and emergencies, and mechanisms for immediate reporting to the relevant authorities?

- Does the company continually seek to improve corporate environmental performance, by encouraging, where appropriate, the adoption of technologies and operating procedures in all parts of the enterprise that reflect environmental best practices? Are its products or services designed to have no undue environmental impacts, be safe in their intended use, and be efficient in their consumption of energy and natural resources?

- Is the company ISO or SABS (where needed) certified?
- Is the company free from regulatory lawsuits?

Financial health

- Is the company a publicly traded company?
- Does the company publish annual reports?
- Does the company have audited financial statements?
- Has the company been in business for several years?

Industry attractiveness

- Is the industry an attractive opportunity (enough to warrant a due diligence)?
- Is there a system to place a score on various aspects of the industry?
- Are there barriers to entry?
- What are the price factors involved in entering the market?
- Do institutions control the market?
- Are the shareholders broad-based?
- What are the skills available in the market? Assess engineering, technical, managerial and strategic skills.
- Determine pricing, demand and supply factors.

A MORE COMPREHENSIVE APPROACH

The due diligence process should ferret out problems such as a company's tax, corporate or shareholding structures. It should assist the directors in taking hard decisions, such as selling non-core, non-profitable assets, activities or entire divisions. It will also result in a critical analysis of the control, accounting and reporting systems of the company and concomitantly a critical appraisal of key personnel. It will identify the value drivers of the company, thus enabling the directors to understand where the value is and to focus their efforts on increasing that value in the future.

Proper due diligence goes way past looking at the financials, both historical and prospective. Several guides have been written to assist in conducting due diligence, but reduced to its basic terms the due diligence exercise involves a close examination of a number of different areas of the business. The following is a list of the key areas that would come under scrutiny and a brief description of what the due diligence exercise should focus on in each area:

fig 8.1 :: key areas of due diligence

General field of investigation	Reason
Financial statements	Ensure accuracy
Assets	Confirm value, condition and legal title
Employees	Identification and evaluation of key directors
Sales strategy	Analyse policies and current procedures
Marketing	Key value drivers and such efficacy
Industry in which the company operates	Understand trends and new technologies
Competition	Identify threats
Systems	Efficacy of current systems. Do they need to be upgraded?
Legal, corporate and tax issues	Do any tax issues need to be resolved?
Company contracts and leases	Identify risks and obligations
Suppliers	Are they expected to remain around?

A comprehensive list of documents to be acquired for in-depth due diligence is set out in the Appendix.

The aim of due diligence is to identify problems within the business, particularly any issues that may give rise to unexpected liabilities in the future. This may be evident when the process is instigated by a prospective purchaser, who is interested in knowing as much as possible about the company that is to be acquired. When due diligence is carried out as part of the steps leading to an IPO, the exercise takes on added meaning and encompasses a wider scope. The above table illustrates the general fields of investigation and reasons for conducting such research.

As stated at the beginning of this chapter, every strategist will perform a due diligence review differently. Some will get advisors (usually from large accounting firms) to perform the task, whereas others will handle it themselves.

SOURCES OF INFORMATION

The information the strategist wants is usually drawn from two sources: interviews and documents. Interviews may be conducted with management, bankers, lawyers, accountants, major clients or suppliers.

Do some groundwork in advance and ensure that the following documents are readily available when needed. Assign responsibility for ensuring good copies are prepared, and keep track of where they are located in case a key person is out of the office when the information is requested. For the operations and technical review, consider what is specifically appropriate to the business. From experience, there are two crucial issues to always remember: insist on getting the documents you need (don't be put off with excuses) and ensure that the documents are the originals.

Due diligence will require documents for the following reviews:

- **Legal review**: legal documents, contracts and other legal issues
- **Financial review**: company's financial status
- **Management review**: team's capabilities
- **Marketing review**: marketing plan and activities
- **Operations and technical review**: equipment, plant and processes.

Legal review

Documents

- Corporate minute books and documents (eg articles of incorporation, by-laws). Get a summary (and copies) of the main contracts in place (eg shareholders' agreements, employment contracts, leases, patents, insurance policies, mortgage documents and sales or supply contracts).
- A summary of all outstanding or pending litigation with an accompanying opinion letter from lawyers explaining the expected outcome of each lawsuit.

Legal review should start early. The request for information and a confidentiality agreement prior to the exchange of initial information is probably the first legal document that will be required. A lawyer will also help you structure the letter of intent. As negotiating draws near, it is important to increase the legal review of the proceedings to determine what is legally advisable and feasible.

Typically, in an acquisition scenario, the seller will want to have as few representations and warranties in that agreement as possible. Representations and warranties are legal commitments from the seller to the buyer regarding the assumptions on which the purchase is proceeding. Buyers are entitled to legal and financial recourse in the event that these commitments are not upheld. Such items may include:

- The capacity of the seller to sell
- The absence of legal impediments to the sale
- The accuracy of the financial statements
- The absence of unrecorded liabilities
- The absence of significant changes since the financial statements were produced
- Other more specific requests regarding contracts and mortgages.

There are far more legal issues than can be discussed in *The Corporate Mechanic*. For example, a commitment by the seller that, subsequent to signing (but prior to closing), he or she will preserve the assets and continue to run the business so that business and goodwill will not diminish. Or, has the company disclosed all details relating to bank financing, or a list of actions that must be taken prior to closing? Another area that needs to be carefully assessed is the issue of restraints of trade. These specify a period of time during which a seller or departing key employee cannot compete directly with the acquisition target.

Latent liability is a major area of legal concern. This risk can appear in a variety of forms, from product failures to health and safety concerns, to environmental liability and, of course, outright financial fraud. The strategist needs to be aware that current or future owners could be held accountable for civil and/ or criminal liabilities committed by past owners. Insurance and indemnity from civil prosecution is obtainable to limit the effect on the company's financials.

Financial review

Documents

- Published financial statements for the last three to five years.
- Company-prepared interim financial reports and analyses.
- Recent business income tax returns and payment schedules.
- Auditors' working papers and all pertinent correspondence with the auditors.
- Recent appraisals of tangible assets.

A due diligence review will *always* include a detailed look at the financial status of the company. The strategist will want to verify the information contained in the investment proposal against the financial records of the company. When the strategist is confident that financial records are accurate, the credibility of forecast data is enhanced. If this review hasn't taken place, then wait until it is completed before moving on to the next review. It's essential that all weak areas in financial material are assessed, so that you are properly prepared to explain them to the client.

A strong balance sheet makes an investment more attractive. A certain amount of debt is expected, but if the company's debt load is excessive, the strategist will be concerned about the investor's real intent for the funds generated from the investment. Is the intent really to expand, or will existing debt be offset with new capital?

The strategist wants to ensure that a capital structure will sustain the business through its growth period. A company with an unbalanced financial structure (too much debt or equity) is likely to encounter difficulties ranging from a lack of liquidity to poor rates of return. These types of problems often ruin a business.

Management review

Documents

- A strategic plan that focuses on the big picture for the next five to 10 years and that incorporates the directors' and owners' vision of the company.
- Historical and future forecasts, along with actual figures, to assess management's ability to produce accurate forecasts and to determine

future expectations. These are usually found in budgets compared to actual sales, expenses and profit statements.

- In the case of due diligence that involves another company, get all key management biographies and résumés.
- An organisation chart and copies of any employment, consulting and confidentiality agreements with key employees.
- A list of primary and back-up suppliers (especially if you buy a speciality product or service).

The purchaser is buying not only a business, but also the management team of the company being acquired. Evaluating a management team's capabilities will be an integral part of a due diligence review. Always be open and honest about management shortcomings or past failures. Most new owners look for people who have learned from their mistakes (and can avoid them in the future) rather than people who claim to be perfect. Besides, experienced directors, through their own skills or their extensive network of contacts, can probably fill the gaps in management – but first they have to be aware that those gaps exist.

The following list provides an example of issues that need to be addressed during this important part of the due diligence review.

- Review the background and employment history of key employees carefully, so if there are any unexplained gaps or blemishes, be prepared to explain them.
- Ask for business and personal references for each key member of management.
- Are the management and staff encouraged to improve their skills and knowledge?
- Are external consultants used to ensure that products or marketing strategies are at the cutting edge? Is management up to date on research, industry and market trends, locally and internationally?
- Is the chemistry within the management team positive? Look for a good cross section of skills, complementary personalities and a cohesive approach to problem-solving. Also look for a team with demonstrated strengths that compensate for any identified weaknesses.
- Is there a natural leader and will this be apparent beyond the share structure? Meet the management team to find out.

Marketing review

Documents

- Press releases, speeches by management and marketing materials released in the past year.
- A list of key customers with historical and projected sales data and order backlog, if available.
- Market strategies.

All aspects of a marketing plan that were included in an investment proposal will be thoroughly examined at this stage. The analytical review will include an assessment of market dominance and market share compared to present and future competitors. Strategists tend to be wary of anyone who either claims there is no competition or completely discounts the competitors' ability to challenge them in the marketplace. The strategist will review the underlying market research data that the company summarised in its investment proposal.

The information required will vary depending on the type of market. In any case, the owners of the company to be acquired must be prepared to disclose market research data, questionnaires, responses and analyses. The strategist may be required to undertake market demographic studies. If a new market is to be created after due diligence, a detailed analysis has to be conducted of the potential for the market, future demographics and how the company will develop its share in that market. Reports prepared by outside consultants (particularly those recognised as experts in their field) will add significant credibility to your estimates of the market size and how your product will serve the target market.

Operations and technical review

Documents

- If the company is a manufacturer, you will need returns and warranty data to assess the quality of the product and to assess any contingent liability related to the products.

Many strategists develop a gut feel for the type of people that are worth investing in, what the truth is and whether the company engineers actually know what they are doing. You should ensure that everyone on the staff, including people in the factory and office, is aware that a strategist will be touring the facility, so they can put their best foot forward.

The strategist may have unique industry knowledge in the operations area and may be able to critique the manufacturing layout. This could be a positive development. Some strategists prefer to make surprise visits during the financing process to ensure that the employees are not just 'acting' while visitors are present.

Here are some thoughts to keep in mind when conducting a plant tour.

- Ensure that premises are neat and tidy but also look like an ongoing operation
- Ensure that there is appropriate safety equipment available
- Talk to employees to get a flavour of the culture and the communication within the company
- Make sure that if you stop and talk to employees that they take appropriate safety precautions, such as shutting down equipment that requires constant monitoring
- Have members of the management team, who are specifically involved in each process, accompany you to provide an overview during the visit. For example, a production manager should accompany you on a tour of the production line.
- Make on-the-spot requests, such as to see the order book.

If the business depends on specialised technology, the strategist will want to exercise extensive due diligence in this field, on his or her own and with a specialist in the area.

THE FIVE-STAGE MODEL FOR DUE DILIGENCE

The following five-stage approach has been designed to help manage a corporate finance process effectively and timeously. These processes can be viewed as a cycle of due diligence, containing critical points at which to decide whether or not to move forward. If each stage is 'favourable' move to the next stage. If not, either shelve the project or reject it outright. For example, if a company plans to buy out a competitor, only to find out that there is a legal action pending, it could shelve the project until after the legal action, or it could determine that the action and the publicity would be negative to it and abandon the purchase.

By following the five-stage model, the strategist and buyer can be reasonably sure that their efforts remain focused, relevant and controlled.

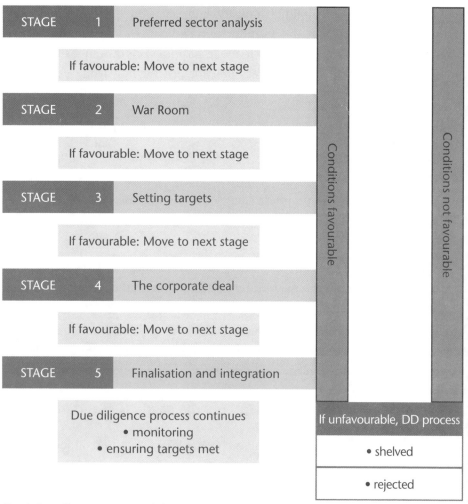

fig 8.2 :: five-stage model

STAGE 1: Preferred sector analysis

Is the project viable at the macro level? Conduct preliminary research, before undertaking due diligence.

Before setting up the corporate team and allocating responsibilities, the strategist needs to conduct the necessary macro-research to determine whether a project will be profitable and within sectors that are appropriate to the company's designated long-term plans.

For instance, take the example of a strategist who has been commissioned to undertake due diligence on the potential of expanding a business into a new field. He or she should undertake research to assess whether the new product or service of the new partner will be of benefit to the client or not. If the research shows that there would be no benefit, why waste time and funds (expensive at that) setting up a team of specialists when the outcome is already forecast?

There are strategists who will carry out due diligence anyway, given that it is their livelihood to provide such a service. This can be avoided by setting up a Chairman's Office, as discussed in Chapter 4.

Macro-research includes company, external and change perception.

An analysis of the business's competitive environment need not be complex, expensive or time-consuming. The strategist's aim, at this stage, is to understand the industry and its future potential within the company's current strategy. In particular, the strategist needs to understand the strengths and weaknesses of the business and the threats and opportunities that exist for the business in the future.

The assessment can result in the strategist identifying problem areas that must be overcome or, alternatively, strengths that must be improved before the project can be carried out. An example would be finding out that the market is right for expansion and profitability will be enhanced, but that the company needs to improve its skills base before the project can be carried out.

When looking at the external situation, an intimate knowledge of the client's business and industry begin to pay off. The Chairman's Office structure would provide a far better insight into how markets and customers, supply chain and competitors are changing and how these factors will affect the company than outside consultants would. An external assessment may reveal competitive threats that call for a defensive strategy, or it may point to emerging opportunities that the company must be prepared to take.

It is crucial to know whether management will accept (and be willing to) change in the future. Does the company have a capacity to change? By assessing the company's current position in the market and where it aims to be according to long-term goals, the strategist will conclude what the gap is between company vision (and expectations) and reality. The macro-research could find that the gap could be reduced by the company improving its knowledge base, implementing new technology or raising production capacity.

At the extreme, a business in which no one makes money is of no interest, and is worthless. However, a business in which almost everyone makes high returns, regardless of competitive position, is near impossible. My own experience is that industry attractiveness is far less critical than a company's competitiveness when determining long-term profitability and viability. In fact, industry attractiveness is about 66% less important than competitive superiority in the market.

Analysing macro issues

The best empirical measure of industry attractiveness is the Return on Capital for the industry, weighted by sales. Not everyone has to earn a high return, but the players supplying the bulk of the market should have a high average, well above the cost of capital. Many theories about particular industries' attractiveness can be quickly disproved by looking at the weighted average returns on capital in them.

Barriers to entry is another macro-factor that must be analysed. This includes investment scale, branding, service, distribution channels or sources of raw material, property/location, corporate expertise or access to highly skilled people, patents, ability to produce at low cost, corporate aggression and secrecy.

The industrial demand/supply factors are also clearly important. Barriers to exit include costs of firing employees, investment write-offs, disengagement costs, costs shared with other parts of a business, customer requirements for goods and services and non-economic reasons, like the desire to keep a large empire.

Market growth shows how healthy demand currently is, and how well the industry is coping against competing products. The *threat from substitutes* can arise from competing technologies, or simply from products that consumers tend to prefer over time. The relative bargaining power of the industry vis-à-vis its suppliers and its customers is pivotal. Broadly speaking, if an industry has a more concentrated structure (fewer suppliers accounting for, say, 75% of total output) than its suppliers or customers, it will tend to have greater bargaining power.

Now is the time to develop 'what-if' scenarios, to further refine strategic options.

STAGE 2: The War Room

Once it has been established that the new project's targeted industry is reasonably likely to succeed, a project leader is elected and a team of specialists chosen, and a specific room for the due diligence process should be selected. This is the place where all research will be coordinated and documents stored.

When setting out on the path of due diligence, the first step is to make a strategic assessment of the company's own current operations and competitive situation. Ideally, the assessment team should be made up of internal advisors, with some outside expertise as required.

The team

It is crucial that the people assembled on the due diligence assessment team are as objective as possible during the process. There are three ways to reduce the subjectivity of the team: gather perceptions of the organisation from outside; use outside consultants; and analysis by the team itself during extended meetings.

Despite most corporations having the finances to set up internal organisational strategy structures, they still use outside consultants and analysts. Distinctive competence – the organisation's competitive edge – may best be determined by outside consultants querying customers. For example, one organisation that was convinced its competitive strength lay in the quality of its professional staff was surprised to learn that many of its customers viewed it as a cost-driven operation in which staff qualifications were of secondary importance.

However, the focus of *The Corporate Mechanic* is the establishment of an internal strategic team.

Once the team is clear about what research has to be completed, and, therefore, what factors and industry micro-patterns are most relevant, it can start a historical analysis that shows what actual steps the organisation has taken over time. If desired, this analysis can identify developmental stages that highlight particular tendencies. For instance, the focus might be on reconstructing the firm's technical skills base over the last five years. A study could reveal the extent to which skills were purchased from the outside, generated in-house or developed in collaboration with other organisations.

During the analytical process the team members learn to work with each other, understanding skills levels and weaknesses in each other. In addition, this process usually identifies leaders within the team. The lead strategist can then set up reporting structures.

One observation here. It is essential that the team works together in one room. My experience is that many companies tend to underestimate the isolating effects of distance. In one firm with which I am familiar, people in the same building but three floors apart interact with each other formally on the job about as much as they do with others in the same corporation who are based overseas.

Another benefit of the team working together is that a bonding takes place among team members, which is important before the corporate deal takes effect. The more a group of people jointly seek to make sense of the organisation they are strategising for, the more unified they will become. At the same time, this process of inquiry will generate creative tension towards improving the organisation. In all, considerable team-building is a natural by-product of organisational health.

Some areas of teamwork within the due diligence team that require systematic self-analysis are organisational style, organisational expectation, individual expectation and cultural bias. These areas can be explored by two respective techniques, namely decision analysis and norm specification.

Decision analysis

Who is involved in decision-making on the due diligence team, when and in what ways? These are the questions that decision analysis addresses. There are three ways to make a decision, which correspond to the three types of decision system: to delegate (decentralised system), to mandate (centralised) and to collaborate (shared). When a manager delegates, he or she transfers decision-making authority to a subordinate. When he or she mandates a decision, a manager decides unilaterally. When a manager collaborates, he or she enters into a joint decision-making process with others.

Collaboration typically takes one of two forms. Under the first form, consultation, a manager solicits input from subordinates before making a decision, but retains go/no-go authority. Under the second form, consensus, manager and subordinates jointly shape the decision or solution or course of action.

Consensus is thus a more complex process than consultation. It means that everyone on the team has had input prior to the decision point, and everyone is willing to go along with the team's decision, even though this decision may not be everyone's first choice.

The three basic decision-making modes are summarised in the following table.

fig 8.3 :: modes of decision-making

Definition	Decision-maker	Strengths	Weaknesses
Delegate			
	Subordinates decide (within boundaries set by manager)	Authority moves closer to action; the subordinates 'own' the decision; the delegator's time is freed up	Can be risky – assumes the subordinates are competent; may ignore inter-dependencies among subordinates
Mandate			
	Manager decides unilaterally	Global perspective; can reach a decision quickly	Possible insensitivity to local conditions; implementation may be difficult because the implementers do not own the decision
Collaborate			
Consultation	**Manager** decides after consultation with subordinates	Multiple resources brought to bear; implementers have some decision ownership	Somewhat time-consuming decision process
Consensus	**Manager** and subordinates jointly decide	Multiple resources brought to bear; implementers own the decision	Time-consuming, even frustrating decision process

By mapping the patterns of delegating, mandating and collaborating, the team can clarify the kind of decision system by which it will operate. A key consideration should be simplicity. And the reality for most, if not all, organisations is that the strength of consulting input for any given decision area will vary with the particular situation and the needs at that time, hence, some manoeuvring room is essential.

The next step is to generate a set of the major decisions and decision areas with which the organisation is concerned. These decision areas then need to be 'exploded' into a larger number of narrower decisions. The analytical task is to review each decision to clarify who is involved, at what point, and how.

After completing decision analysis, the team can review dominant patterns in order to characterise the organisation's decision system in terms of decentralisation/ centralisation/ sharing.

Norm specification

A norm is a tacit rule of behaviour, a usually unwritten understanding of what is right and what is wrong. Every social system – from the family to the nation – has a distinctive set of norms, or behavioural ground rules. By making explicit the norms by which the organisation operates, the team can gain considerable insight into stylistic patterns.

As an organising framework to stimulate thinking about norms, I have often used a mnemonic based on the letter 't': taboos, traditions, trappings, turf, tempo, technology, trust and teamwork. The strategist could draw up a chart with these headings and rate the norms accordingly.

The business plan

At this point in the assessment of the business, the strategist and his or her team will be able to identify important issues and considerations for survival and growth, and develop various 'what-if' scenarios and forecast various potential financial consequences for the business. At this stage, the team can determine whether or not the project is the right fit. If it is, a plan must then be prepared to delegate responsibilities to the team members, with timeframes. Remember, this is still early in the due diligence process, and – at this stage – you must concentrate on business planning.

Once it appears that a corporate deal is in the making, it is time to gather information to assess and change the company's business plan. From my experience, the strategist will find that many companies in South Africa operate without a business plan. If there is a business plan, move on to drafting the due diligence. Unfortunately, if a business plan does not exist, one will have to be drafted.

An alternative is to draft a plan that is specific in identifying key criteria that will make the corporate deal a success and part of the existing business. Examples of these criteria are industry, size, location, products and services, personnel, profitability, growth rate and resources required to complete the deal.

All documentation formulation must be completed at this stage. The aim of Stage 1 and 2 is to set up the information so that there is an in-depth understanding of the business and its strategic priorities.

STAGE 3: Setting targets

The objective of this stage is to set targets for the team.

A Letter of Intent and Confidentiality Agreement must be drafted and signed by the parties before due diligence can proceed. This letter prepares the way for the next stage of a detailed due diligence. This signifies genuine interest by the parties in reaching a final agreement.

Therefore, this stage concentrates on finalising the team and planning an initial exchange of information between the team and the client. It is critical that the client employs a team of highly skilled advisors, both internal and external, with the right blend of skills and perspectives to make the best, most well-informed set of decisions possible. Understand that, even with a confidentiality agreement, the strategist may not be able to obtain all the information he or she requests in the initial exchange.

Some of the team's tasks include:

- Quantifying the costs and benefits associated with a particular corporate deal, including transaction and post-transaction costs. This includes determining whether there is a need to replace incompatible equipment and systems. Should redundant assets be liquidated? The team can also conduct audits and other potentially expensive activities.
- Assessing the suitability, capability and value of specific assets and resources
- Evaluating facilities, locally developed computer systems and management

- Uncovering important information about the business, such as unrecorded liabilities, inventories that cannot be sold or uncollectible receivables, potential non-renewal of contracts, among other issues

- Providing objective assessment of risks, ranging from financial, to product liability and environmental issues

- Developing tactics and strategies to identify risks

- Helping to arrange financing

- Helping to negotiate resolutions to potential 'deal-breaker' issues

- Structuring the terms and conditions of the deal.

The possible roles of the advisors on the team are many and varied. Many of these roles will carry on throughout the remaining stages of the corporate deal. Therefore, it makes sense for the strategist to involve the most important advisors early in the planning stage. In this way they will have the maximum opportunity to positively influence the way the due diligence assessment will unfold.

The strategist's first choices for the team should be people within the client's business, who possess specific knowledge, skills and experience needed. It is important, however, to ensure that not the entire management group is included on the team. A clear and separate focus on the ongoing business needs to be maintained so that it continues to do well. Again, The Chairman's Office provides solutions to all these issues.

Outside consultants should be included, because of the specialised expertise, objectivity and/or wider experience they bring, particularly in areas which cannot be addressed sufficiently by internal members of the team. In the early stages, high-level guidance from outside experts is all you require, so involving them need not be expensive. More time-intensive work will not be required until after the next stage has been passed, and detailed due diligence begun.

Depending on the nature of the corporate deal, external members of the team may include, among others:

- Accountants
- Actuaries
- Appraisers
- Bank representatives
- Business valuators

- Engineers
- Environmental consultants
- Lawyers

Professional advisors are exactly and only that – advisors. They should not take over and transact the deal. If advisors are to be effective, the strategist must trust their abilities, their integrity and their common sense. With the team in place, the strategist can now focus on the due diligence process.

It is thus important that the initial exchange is made at the correct time, ie after the team has been established. Initial exchanges are often good indicators of how the transaction will proceed. The strategist will begin watching for danger signals in the early stages of contact and remain observant throughout the transaction.

Such danger signals might include:

- An attempted imposition of an unrealistic timeframe for the completion of the corporate deal
- Withholding of key information to gain reasonable access to information and people
- The material provided is unclear and ambiguous
- Information provided turns out to be significantly misleading or false under closer examination
- Management places unreasonable restrictions on whom the strategist brings to review the proposed transaction.

These signals often signify real warnings of increased risk and can constitute fair reason to reject the project. The alternative is to intensify due diligence by investing more time, money and effort to determine a realistic assessment of the situation and evaluate its implications. The final step in this stage is to perform a high-level strategic and financial assessment of the information obtained in the initial exchanges.

The team should be able to review this material quickly, which may help to uncover previously unaddressed high-level issues. To properly complete the initial assessment, it is necessary to have several meetings with specific members of all the relevant parties. At this stage it is crucial to do some probing to confirm the general accuracy of the information provided.

Remembering that only an initial assessment has been completed, the strategist must be cautious about entering into any binding agreement or commitment on material issues before having obtained all the necessary information. It is vitally important that he or she obtain legal advice at this stage so that he or she understand precisely what commitments, if any, have been undertaken.

Before entering into the next, highly detailed stage of due diligence, the strategist should:

- Begin defining requirements from financial and strategic perspectives
- Expand contact with the opposing corporate finance team, to begin to understand their skills, temperament and motivation in preparation for negotiating and for working with them later
- Establish an informal means of dialogue with this team, to check out or clear up misunderstandings, and to handle those difficulties that arise that may be slow or difficult to resolve in more formal negotiations.

STAGE 4: The corporate deal

The next stage is the detailed action plan and budget. The budget should include all significant and foreseeable transaction costs and expenses related to corporate activities.

At this stage, it has to be determined whether the corporate deal should be carried out or not. If yes, negotiations have to start. This topic is, in itself, the subject of entire books. What can be said is that without detailed due diligence negotiations become guesswork. The following example amply highlights this issue.

Example 8.1

In 1992, I was commissioned to undertake analysis on a car rental company. The client wanted to buy a small Johannesburg-based company that had only 15 vehicles, but was important in that it provided a service to politicians. Initial analysis indicated that there were credibility problems. I found that the owners were not honest, financials were not up to date and revenue figures did not seem to meet actual budgets. My recommendation was not to go ahead with negotiations. In-depth analysis and due diligence were required before negotiations could start.

The client declined, believing in the directors, and urgently wanted to buy the firm. Negotiations went ahead, without the assistance of thorough knowledge. Three months after the company was acquired, the police arrived at the company's offices, stating that the company had, in fact, stolen two vehicles. The

> agency was bought without the purchaser knowing that he had actually bought
> 17 vehicles. Two had been sold by the directors of the original company, before
> the negotiations had been completed.

This stage is your most challenging in terms of managing costs and achieving the information objectives. In general, the internal strategic team and external consultants will have to do a thorough job, so as not to leave any important stones unturned. As leader of the team, your primary tasks are to:

- Monitor progress
- Ensure effective communication and execution is taking place
- Make decisions about where extra due diligence is likely to be of greater value than the expense to be incurred, given the time available.

This detailed stage will produce information that will help refine the client's negotiating position and strategy, influence the final terms and price of the corporate deal and help to begin operational planning for post-transactional integration. At this stage, there will be sufficient information to determine whether the deal should be finalised.

Several key areas of due diligence investigation include valuation, tax issues, impact studies, financing options and a detailed analysis of final issues.

Final issues analysis

The purpose of such analysis is to obtain enough information about the deal to minimise the risk of unpleasant surprises surfacing after a deal has been concluded. The most important thing to remember is that you can never achieve absolute certainty. Further, risk tolerance is different from that of another person facing similar decisions. Caution is important.

NOTE: No set of procedures exists to produce a final issues analysis. Instead, the strategic team must decide what detailed investigations need to take place and determine who on the due diligence team will perform these investigations. In addition, analyse the results of the due diligence assessment and consider the impact on future negotiations. Simple issues include a financial check on the directors of the parties involved in a corporate transaction, a check on the assets of the company and its debt levels (determine whether these are accurate), and compare these to the research undertaken in previous stages. The aim, therefore, is to assess whether everything said is actually the truth.

Now, the team must determine and arrange the appropriate type and amount of financing to close the corporate deal. The types of financing that the team must consider, alone or in combination, include:

- Assumption of the liabilities of the business; include payable amounts to suppliers, long-term debt or mortgages

- Consider financing options, terms, conditions and timing of payments

- How will the company raise funds to carry out the corporate deal? It may be necessary to use external sources, such as banks, venture capitalists or even listing on an exchange. These methods form the basis of the last chapters of *The Corporate Mechanic*.

- Tax considerations are key factors in determining the pricing and structure of any corporate deal. In the case of an acquisition, understand what requirements are motivating the seller. As such, it is necessary to have a tax expert as part of the corporate team. Typically, the seller's primary focus is on achieving the greatest after-tax proceeds possible. Often a seller will accept a lower price for the business if it is structured in a way that minimises the tax consequences. Unfortunately, some of the tax structures and strategies that help the seller minimise taxes on the transaction will ultimately result in higher taxes for the buyer. Tax considerations include:
  - Maximising tax values, in relation to future tax deductions
  - Ensuring that tax losses are used in future deductions
  - Creating the most efficient tax structure for the future of the business
  - Other taxes that may be involved, such as VAT, land transfer duties and payroll taxes.

At the end of this stage, information has to be coordinated to include the final issues analysis, tax and financing consideration. At this point, the strategist has to ask the team: Should the transaction be finalised? Is this corporate deal expected to offer the returns first forecast? Remember, far too many poor acquisitions have been made as a result of people not wanting to lose a deal, despite negative issues and problems raising their heads.

If the decision is to go ahead with the deal, move to the next and final stage.

STAGE 5: Finalisation and integration

The objective of this stage is to finish negotiations and to close the deal on reasonably reliable and satisfactory terms.

By now the strategic team should have a clear idea of the following issues:

- How and when the deal will add to profitability, ie forecast return on investment
- Major risks regarding the transaction
- Principal outstanding issues regarding the deal
- How the deal will be structured
- The amount, type and cost of the financing available to the company
- The price range within which the deal will be negotiated
- In the case of an acquisition, the seller's stated or likely opening negotiating position
- Some idea of where the seller will be flexible during negotiations. Research at such a stage will offer the team negotiating power.

By this time, the team must have worked out a plan for post-transaction. How will the acquisition, merger, etc be integrated into the company? Planning should thus be well advanced in all aspects of corporate finance. The next step is to approach the other party to start negotiations. If they agree to proceed, then the strategist can begin formal negotiations.

To complete any corporate finance deal, the following has to be undertaken:

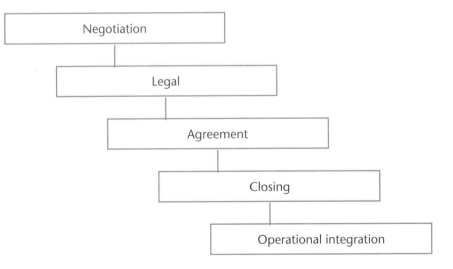

fig: 8.4 :: steps in completing a corporate finance deal

Negotiation

While every set of negotiations is as unique as the people involved in them, generally there are three negotiating stages. First, determine all parties' stated goals, apply the information gathered during research and, finally, reach an agreement, normally completed through trade-offs and compromises.

In a sense, then, negotiation has been carried through all stages. As negotiation commences, both sides of the corporate deal should start to find common ground and an increased commitment to make the deal succeed.

The following guidelines on negotiation are useful to remember.

- Honesty and integrity are key. Negotiations usually break down when trust is lacking. If even a few items of the information supplied are in doubt or disputed, the participants will soon tire of the negotiation.

- The fewer people involved in the negotiations the better, especially regarding the key issues of price and terms. Smaller numbers mean smoother communications and faster decision-making.

- Only deal with decision-makers.

- The better prepared the parties are, the better the negotiations will go. Ensure that priorities and strategy are clearly understood by all members of the team who will be involved in or are supporting the negotiations. Having to retract something committed to in error is very disruptive and it undermines the negotiating process as well as the credibility of the offending party.

- Keep lines of communication open at all costs, including informal lines for off-the-record discussions.

- Agree to a timetable early in the negotiations and keep to it as much as possible. As momentum builds, the strategist may have to give way on what he or she has left to the end. It is best not to get down to one negotiating point, creating a win/lose focus which some parties may not be able to accept.

- Get agreement from both sides on an acceptable price range early in the process. Then leave the final price negotiations to the end, when they can be traded off against some other concessions.

- To move things along, make strategic, large trade-offs, rather than bargaining over each and every aspect trying to make small gains.

In short, each side should want the other to feel confident about the information and shared common ground in order to proceed to a final agreement.

There are three key factors in any negotiations, namely information, time and power.

- **Information:** In addition to all facts gathered during due diligence, there is a need to have a solid understanding of the personalities and motivations of the key people involved. Remain aware of the dynamics of negotiations as they are occurring, especially as the pace begins to increase. Be aware that not all people are driven by logical and sound corporate finance sense. Ego can sometimes overwhelm pure financial logic. You may be willing to trade off going for the absolute lowest price in exchange for actions or information that will bring you peace of mind. Alternatively, the seller can be motivated to reduce the risk of not receiving full payment, and to avoid reducing the final price. Often, opposing objectives must be harmonised in order for the negotiations to be successful.

- **Time:** Both sides are usually under some kind of time pressure to close the deal. Most often, however, the side under the greatest time pressure is at the greatest disadvantage. Pareto analysis (see Chapter 2) states that 80% of concessions during negotiations are made in the last 20% of the time. For this reason, resolve as much as you can as you proceed.

- **Power:** No one should be forced to negotiate. Nevertheless, it sometimes feels that there is no option but to close a deal. The common mistake is to believe that, due to so much having been invested in the corporate process, it is better to go through with it in order to justify the time and money already spent. The correct way to think about time and money already invested is as past history. Pouring good money after bad will not change what has happened. When the strategist concludes that a deal is not a good one, there is a need to do what can be done to make the deal work. However, if it is determined that a deal will not work, move on.

Legal issues

It may take several sets of negotiation and revision to get to a final agreement of purchase and sale acceptable to both sides. Even after negotiations are concluded, much can be gained or lost depending on the structure and wording of the final agreement. The document must reflect exactly and precisely what was negotiated and agreed upon. This document should be reviewed by the legal and financial advisors of both sides before it is signed.

CLOSING

The exchange of title and effective date of all of the terms and conditions of the purchase and sale agreement may occur at the time of signing, but often take place a specified period of time after the agreement has been signed.

Post-transaction integration

During a corporate deal, it is important to keep considerable management energy focused on maintaining and strengthening the existing business base. Therefore, not all members of the management team should be appointed to a corporate finance team. However, as a project unfolds, key members of the company should be made aware of progress, and, as appropriate, included in the planning and execution of the integration of the acquired company into the ongoing business.

When the corporate deal involves the integration of a company that has been acquired, it becomes imperative to make the amalgamation of the new work force into the acquiring company a primary issue. Sometimes, people or positions are made redundant through acquisitions. If downsizing and elimination of some jobs are to take place, or if the knowledge, skills and attitudes of newly acquired staff truly do not measure up, it is best to make changes as quickly as possible. Failure to effectively plan and execute the post-transaction integration phase, which can last several years, can prevent anticipated productivity, synergy and profitability from ever being realised and lead to the ultimate failure of the acquisition.

:: CHAPTER 9 ::

VALUATION

Recently, a client approached me and asked about selling a portion of his business to potential buyers.

'How much do you want to sell and at what price?' I asked. These were standard questions, but the client's answer highlighted his lack of preparedness. He stated: 'I was hoping that you can tell me how much of my business I should sell and also value the company.'

Many such instances are being played out in South Africa today, where companies need to be valued or grow by acquiring competitors, yet they do not know the value of their company or whether they are paying too much for the acquisitions or not.

Placing a value on a company is a complex procedure. The methodology can vary depending on the type of business and the reason for the valuation. There is a wide range of factors that go into the process, from the company's book value to a host of tangible and intangible elements, and the strategist must consider all the relevant facts.

Business valuation should be considered a starting point for any corporate deal, whether to sell shares, the entire company or when conducting a merger or setting up a share incentive scheme. The more informed the parties in a transaction are, the better the likelihood of a good deal taking place. Of course, each party has different motivations, but fair market value is the price a seller will accept and a buyer will pay.

A major factor for conducting a valuation, one that is seldom stated, is simply to avoid surprises in the due diligence process, which can quickly kill a deal. Full financial disclosure at all times is extremely important. Bad news that is disclosed upfront might have an impact on price, but at least the deal is far more likely to survive.

With precise earnings information in hand, the strategist can employ several business valuation methodologies and weight the various results according to their pertinence to the business in question. For instance, a business with significant tangible assets would be different to a service-based company. Every business thus has a range of fair market values and the business valuation process is not totally scientific. The challenge of the business valuation process is to determine a business's true earnings, to assign fair value to its intangible assets and to uncover the hidden value drivers of the business that reside below the radar of superficial business valuation techniques.

These factors mean that the strategist has to determine the value of a company based not only on assets or managerial skills, but also relative to other comparable companies and relative to environmental influences. In fact, businesses that have completed a formal valuation do tend to sell quicker than those without one.

Although various techniques can be used to value businesses, over the past six years I have discovered that a combination of these methods produces a fairer and more realistic valuation when undertaking a strategic due diligence assessment.

GENERAL VALUATION TECHNIQUES

Let's reiterate: the purpose of company valuation is to measure the 'right or fair value' of a business. That can be a subjective issue, but finding a value is still crucial for many reasons. How can corporate owners sell a portion of their business if they don't know what to charge and how does the strategist determine whether an opportunity is really a profitable venture without a valuation?

It is thus important to remember that the true value of a business is what someone will pay for it. To arrive at this figure, strategists use various valuation methods.

Industry rules of thumb

In some industry sectors, buying, selling or listing a business is common. This leads to the development of industry-wide rules of thumb.

The rules of thumb are dependant on factors other than profit. Some industries have peculiarities, such as:

- Turnover for a computer maintenance business or a mail order business
- Number of customers for a mobile phone airtime provider
- Number of outlets for a food franchise.

Buyers will work out what the business is worth to them. Take the example of a computer maintenance business with 10,000 contracts but no profits. A larger competitor may pay R100 per contract to buy the business. This is because it could merge the two businesses and make large profits. The key source of value of a business may be something that cannot itself be measured. A strong relationship with key customers or suppliers may be critical and thus rules of thumb are used. For example: if a business holds the licence or distributorship rights of a potentially successful product, the business's value will increase accordingly.

Management stability may be crucial if the purchaser is not bringing in a strong new team. If the owner-manager or other key people are going to leave, the business may be worth far less. For example, the profitability of an advertising agency may collapse if the key creative person leaves or if key sales people leave, because they may take important customers with them.

There are some factors that affect rules of thumb. For example, restrictive covenants contained in employees' contracts could damage the value if a potential buyer intends to radically change the staffing arrangements. The more risks there are, from a purchaser's perspective, the lower the value will be. There are specific actions the buyer can take, with a view to building a more valuable business.

- Set up excellent management information systems, including management accounts. Good systems make nasty surprises unlikely.
- Spread sales across many different customers
- Tie in key customers and suppliers through contracts and mutual dependence
- Minimise exposure to exchange rate fluctuations and other external factors.

Point scoring

A method to determine a value is to work out a point-scoring system. This places some analytical value on a rule of thumb method. This scoring is subjective and its purpose is to create logical handles to use on the multiplier of the restructured cash flow. The items must be chosen based on experience and study of the business.

fig 9.1 :: point-scoring system of valuation

Valuation issues	Allocated points			
	One	Two	Three	Four
Length of time in business	1 year	3 years	5 years	7 years
Location	Poor	Fair	Good	Excellent
Time left on the lease	<5 years	5 years	10 years	>10 years
Turnover growth (%)	5%	10%	15%	25%
Depth of management	No depth	One key director	Three directors	>Three directors
Reputation of the business	Poor	Fair	Good	Excellent
Financing	Poor	Fair	Good	Excellent
Cash flow	5% cash flow	7.5% cash flow	20% cash flow	+20% cash flow

Next, divide the answer by 28 points, which is the maximum number of points that can be achieved. Complete this exercise for the various options. The company that has the highest value is the one to analyse. It must be stressed that it is not the company to invest in. This method is a filter and the above variables can be changed to suit the company, industry or geographical region.

Entry cost valuation

An entry cost valuation reflects what this process would cost to start a business from scratch. To make an entry cost valuation, calculate the cost to the business of:

- Purchasing its assets

- Developing its products

- Recruiting and training the employees

- Building up a customer base.

Once the cost has been calculated, make a comparative assessment of how the following two factors could affect a cost valuation: the use of better technology, and the effect of cheaper rental by locating in a less expensive area.

The entry cost valuation can then be based on cheaper alternatives, which is more realistic.

Asset valuation method

The most basic valuation method is based solely on the values recorded in the firm's financial statements. This method is based on the assumption that the value of the firm is merely the sum of its assets and ignores the capacity of the company to generate future values. These methods provide for a quick evaluation of a company, but have two major disadvantages:

- **Outdated information:** the information recorded in the financial statements reflects the state of the company at a given (specific) time. Thus, developments and operations made by a company from that moment on are not considered as part of any valuation. Remember, even when a listed company releases results it has a 'post balance sheet' item, outlining events that have occurred after the balance sheet has been completed, but before the annual statements have been published. In my opinion, this methodology is best used as a negative measure of valuation, ie it enables the strategist to reject companies that do not meet investment criteria. It is quick to assess, but this system does not consider the company as a going concern.

- **Inaccurate information:** this system does not account for non-monetary values, such as managerial skills or company innovation, as well as the firm's capacity to create value in the future, the required funds to maintain the company running, the market value of the assets and liabilities and the value of money in time.

Accounting-based valuation takes into account the accounting information obtained from the company's balance sheets. However, this is done without performing any kind of adjustments.

The value of the company is thus given as the difference between the total assets and total liabilities.

> Corporate value = Total assets - Total liabilities

Adjusted asset valuation

This method aims at adjusting the asset valuation, by moving the assets towards the realisation value, as follows:

- Deduct non-value assets, such as accrued charges and the cost of installation

- Include intangible assets that could be sold, such as patents or copyrights

- Revalue fixed assets (property and equipment) to reflect the market price of the assets.

Liquidation-based method

Some directors believe that the worst thing they could do, when their business cannot be saved from financial ruin, is to sell all the assets. They are wrong. There assets could be sold 'as is' in an auction after being attached by the courts. The liquidation valuation approach assumes:

- **The owner sells the assets:** Where a company can progressively sell its assets to termination point, assets are valued at liquidation value [AssetLV]. Using this method, assets are priced at a lower value than their liquidation value, and some liquidation cost is not considered (such as penalty cost of personnel dismissal), while the liabilities are kept at the book value.

- **Forced liquidation:** This method provides for the liquidation of assets at the book value, but the liabilities are adjusted to include liquidation-related obligations (such as personnel dismissal cost).

> Corporate value = [AssetLV] - (Liabilities)

Intrinsic value method

The most basic form of valuation is to calculate the cost of rebuilding a company. Therefore, if it costs R1 million to buy a company's assets and an additional R1 million to rebuild the company, then the valuation of the company (under this method) is R2 million. The condition here is to rebuild the company to its current state. Another way of seeing this is to assess the replacement value of the assets.

Economic value method

The value of the company is calculated by applying the following rules:

- Adjust assets to replacement value
- Include all leased assets
- Include all assets not required for operations
- Include required capital for working capital.

Under this method, a company's value is determined as the assets and funds required for operations.

Revenue-based valuation

Revenues are the sales generated by a company for providing goods or services. Whether a company has made profits in the last year, there are always revenues. Therefore, revenue-based valuations are achieved using the price:sales ratio, often simply abbreviated as PSR.

The PSR takes the current market capitalisation of a company and divides it by the last 12 months' trailing revenues. The market capitalisation is the current market value of a company, arrived at by multiplying the current share price times the shares in issue. This is the current price at which the market is valuing the company. For instance, if XYS has 10 million shares in issue, priced at R10 a share, the market capitalisation is R100 million.

Conservative investors add long-term debt to the total current market value of its stock to get the market capitalisation. The logic is that if you bought the company, you would also acquire its debt, effectively paying that much more. This avoids comparing PSRs between two companies where one has taken out enormous debt to boost sales.

The next step in calculating the PSR is to add up the revenues from the last four quarters and divide this number into the market capitalisation. If XYS had R200 million in sales over the last four quarters and currently has no long-term debt, the PSR would be:

$$\frac{10 \text{ million shares} \times R10/\text{share} + R0 \text{ debt}}{R200 \text{ million in revenue}} = 0.5$$

The PSR is a popular valuation technique when making an acquisition. As this is a perfectly legitimate way for a company to value an acquisition, many simply expropriate it for the stock market and use it to value a company as an ongoing concern.

The lower the PSR, the better. For instance, if XYS lost money in the past year, but has a PSR of 0.50 when many companies in the same industry have PSRs of 2.0 or higher, it can be assumed that, if it can turn itself around and start making money again, it will have a substantial upside.

For example, there are some years during recessions, when no auto company makes money. Does this mean they are all worthless and there is no way to compare them? Another common use of the PSR is to compare companies in the same line of business with each other. Finally, new companies in 'popular' industries are often priced based on multiples of revenues and not multiples of earnings.

Yield-based valuations

A dividend yield is the percentage of a company's share price that it pays out as dividends over the course of a year. For example, South African mines declare results every quarter, so if a mining company pays R1.00 in dividends per quarter and its share price is trading at R100, it has a dividend yield of 4%. Four quarters of R1 is R4 and this divided by R100 is 4%.

Member-based valuations

Sometimes a company can be valued based on its subscribers or its customer accounts. Subscriber-based valuations are most common in media and communication companies that generate regular, monthly income, ie cellular, satellite TV and online companies. Often, in a subscriber-based valuation, strategists will calculate the average revenues per subscriber over their lifetime and then figure the value for the entire company based on this approach.

For instance, if ABC Limited has six million members and each sticks around, on average, for 30 months, spending an average of R20 a month, the company is worth:

6 million $\times$ R20 $\times$ R30 = R3.6 billion

This sort of valuation is also used for satellite TV, Internet and cellular phone companies. Although member-based valuations seem rather confusing, their exact mechanics are unique to each industry. Studying the history of the last few major acquisitions can tell an inquisitive investor how the member model has worked in the past and can suggest how it might work in the future.

Earnings-based valuations

Price/earnings ratio (PE) is a more common yardstick of a company's value than Net Asset value.

By definition, PE is the current share price divided by the EPS for the past year. For example, a share trading at R20, with earnings of R2 per share, has a PE of 10 times. While there is no set rule as to what is a good PE, a low PE is generally considered cheaper than shares with a high PE. As with all these ratios, however, it's important to compare a company's ratio to the ratios of other companies in the same industry.

Therefore, for the strategist the most common way to value a company is to use its earnings. Earnings, also called net income or net profit, is the money that is left over after a company pays all its bills. To allow for apples-to-apples comparisons, most people who look at earnings measure them according to EPS. In South Africa, Headline Earnings Per Share (HEPS) was introduced in the 1990s and this figure excludes extraordinary items from the profit figure. It is a more accurate figure because it removes figures that are one-off, such as the sale of property.

However, EPS alone means absolutely nothing.

To look at a company's earnings relative to its price, most investors employ the PE ratio. There are lots of individuals who stop their entire analysis of a company after they figure out the PE ratio. A small unquoted business is usually valued at between two and five times its annual post-tax profit. For example, using a PE ratio of five times for a business with taxed profits of R100,000 gives a PE valuation of R500,000.

PE ratios are used to value businesses with an established, profitable history. Remember this, quoted companies have higher PE ratios than unlisted ones. This is an important issue when valuations are undertaken, as listed companies' shares are easier to sell than unlisted ones. Typically, the PE ratio of a small unquoted company is 50% lower than that of a comparable quoted company in the same sector. These issues have been used in developing the Indicative Strategic Valuation method, as set out below.

As intelligent strategists value companies based on future prospects and not past performance, stocks with low PEs sometimes have limited futures. This is not to say that investors cannot still find some great low PE stocks that for some reason the market has simply overlooked – you still can and it happens all the time. Rather, you need to confirm the value in these companies by applying some other valuation techniques. Again, this is another reason for the discount rates used in the Indicative Strategic Valuation method.

Free cash flow valuation

This is a measure of financial performance calculated as operating cash flow, minus capital expenditures. In other words, free cash flow (FCF) represents the cash that a company is able to generate after costs to maintain its asset base are paid. Free cash flow is important because it allows a company to pursue opportunities that enhance shareholder value. Without cash, it is not easy to develop new products, make acquisitions, pay dividends, reduce debt, etc.

Many strategists believe that stock exchange analysts concentrate far too much on earnings, while ignoring the real cash that a firm generates. Earnings can (and often are) clouded by accounting methods, but cash is tougher to manipulate.

It is important to note that negative free cash flow is not bad in itself. If free cash flow is negative, it could be a sign that a company is making large investments. If these investments earn a high return, the strategy has the potential to pay off in the long run.

Alternatively, it is quite possible for a company to report positive earnings while experiencing negative cash flows. Growing companies can experience this phenomenon, especially when they need to reinvest much of their earnings in the business in order to maintain and increase growth rates. Companies can and do engage in earnings 'smoothing' so as to make their earnings numbers look good for Wall Street.

When companies report their earnings, these earnings are reported on an 'accrual' basis according to generally accepted accounting principles (GAAP). These earnings usually are not based on cash receipts. For example, a company may make a sale in December and not receive payment until January. Similarly, a company may claim a depreciation expense for production equipment, but it didn't actually have to pay out any cash for this expense. It does, however, have to make new investments in order to remain competitive, but these investments are often not completely reflected in the reported earnings.

Free cash flow analysis puts all business activity back on a cash basis. Therefore, it attempts to answer the following questions:

- Where did the cash come from, and where did it go?
- How much of that cash is (or might be) available to investors (both equity holders and debt holders)?
- How much investment is required on an ongoing basis to maintain and grow these cash flows?

Multiplier or market valuation

The aim of this approach is to calculate a valuation by using an 'industry average' sales figure as a multiplier. This industry average number is based on the price at which comparable businesses have sold recently. As a result, an industry-specific formula is devised, usually based on a multiple of gross sales. From experience these formulae are not reliable, as they do not account for the differences that two businesses in the same industry may have.

Discounted cash flow valuation (DCF)

DCF is the most widely used technique to value a company. It takes into consideration cash flow and also the time value of money. What actually happens in this method is as follows:

- Cash flows are calculated for a particular period of time
- The time period is fixed taking into consideration various factors
- These cash flows are discounted to the present at the cost of capital of the company
- These discounted cash flows are then divided by the total number of outstanding shares to get the intrinsic worth per share.

> **Equation: The valuation is based on the sum of the dividends forecast for each of the next five years (at least) plus a residual value at the end of the period.**

This is also the most technical method of valuing a business. It depends heavily on assumptions about long-term business conditions. It is used for cash generating businesses that are stable and mature. For instance, a publishing house with a large catalogue of titles, or a water company with a local monopoly.

The value today of each future dividend is calculated using a 'discount interest rate' which takes account of the risk and the time value of money. For instance, in an inflationary environment (such as South Africa) R1 received by a business today is worth more than R1 received in the future.

If a business can inspire confidence in its long-term prospects, then this method underlines the business's solid credentials. The most common application of the discounted cash flow is to separate businesses that truly generate cash from ones that just consume it. The most straightforward way for an individual investor to use cash flow is to understand how cash-flow multiples work. In a private or public market acquisition, the price-to-cash-flow multiple is normally in the 6.0 to 7.0 range. When this multiple reaches the 8.0 to 9.0 range, the acquisition is normally considered to be expensive.

DCF is divided into two parts

In the first part, explicit projections of cash flow are made for each year. This is referred to as the explicit value period, since explicit forecasts of periodic cash flows are used in the valuation. After the explicit value period, instead of projecting cash flow forever, it is common to estimate a continuing value. However, it does not rely on explicit forecasts of the cash-flows that are to be received during the continuing value period. Instead, the forecast of cash flow is implicit in the assumptions that are used to estimate continuing value.

Projecting cash flow

Cash flow problems often catch small business owners by surprise. An accurate cash flow projection can protect businesses against this situation. A cash flow projection charts the amounts of money your business expects to receive and pay out each month in a rolling six- or 12-month period. This forecast takes into account the lag time between billing your clients and getting paid; incurring an expense and paying for it; and collecting taxes that aren't due to the government until a later date. A well-prepared cash flow projection will allow you to plot anticipated cash flow positions over time. It will help you anticipate shortfalls in time to do something about them, protecting you from a cash flow crisis. Also, a cash flow projection can help you spot sales trends, tell you if your customers are taking too long to pay, and help you plan for major asset purchases. In addition, should you decide to seek a loan, banks will ask to see one-year cash flow projections by month, and three- to five-year projections by quarter.

The following step-by-step process will guide you through preparation of a cash flow projection:

Step 1: Cash on hand: Count your cash at the beginning of the first month of your projection. This amount is your 'cash on hand'. In succeeding months, the ending cash balance from one month will be carried over as the beginning cash balance of the next month.

Step 2: Cash receipts: Record cash sales, credit card sales, collections from credit accounts and any interest income. The key to doing this successfully is recording receipts in the months you actually expect to get the money, not the month a sale is made.

Step 3: Accounts receivable: Record anticipated receivables in the months you expect them to be paid. If you have not kept records that show you how long it takes individual customers to pay their bills, calculate your 'average collection period' by dividing your total sales for the previous year by 365. That gives you your average daily sales volume. Then, divide the rand value of your current accounts receivable by the average daily sales volume. That number is the average number of days it takes you to collect on a bill. Using that number as a guide, record payments as they will come in over the next year.

Step 4: Miscellaneous cash: Account for anticipated miscellaneous cash infusions, including new loans from banks or family members, or stock offerings.

Step 5: Total cash available: For each month in your projection, add the amounts in steps one to four. This figure shows the total cash available to you in each month.

Step 6: Cash paid out: Now it's time to calculate how much cash you anticipate spending in each month of your rolling projection. First, assess operating expenses. Again, the secret is to note every expense in the month it will be paid, not the month it is incurred. Be sure to include the following items in your list of operating expenses:

• Gross wages, including anticipated overtime and bonuses

- Owners' remuneration

- Payroll taxes and benefits, including paid holidays, paid sick leave, health insurance and unemployment insurance

- Subcontracting and outside services, including the cost of labour and materials

- Purchases of materials for use in making the product or service, or for resale

- Supplies for use in the business

- Repairs and maintenance

- Packaging, shipping and delivery costs

- Travel, car and parking costs

- Advertising and promotion, including fliers, direct mail, print or TV ads, yellow pages listings, website maintenance and design

- Professional services, such fees paid to attorneys, bookkeepers, accountants, consultants, etc.

- Rent

- Telecommunications, such as phone, fax, Internet Service Provider

- Utilities, such as water, heat, electricity, gas

- Taxes

- Interest due on loans

- Other expenses focusing on costs specific to your business

- Miscellaneous (include a small cushion for miscellaneous expenditures).

When you're finished recording these, subtotal your operating expenses.

Step 7: Other costs: Calculate the other ongoing costs of doing business. Be sure to include the following items:

- Loan principal payments: vehicles, equipment purchases, etc.

- Capital expenditures: depreciable expenditures, such as equipment, vehicles, construction of new or improvements to existing buildings, and improvements to leased facilities and offices

- Start-up costs: expenses incurred prior to the first month of operation and paid for over the course of the following year(s)

- Reserve: money set aside monthly for taxes paid at the end of the year.

Step 8: Total cash paid out: Once you have listed all other costs of doing business, add them to your subtotal for operating expenses. This figure is your 'total cash paid out', and reflects your estimates for the total cash you will have to spend each month.

Step 9: Determine your monthly cash flow: subtract your total cash paid out (Step 8) from your total cash available (Step 5). The difference is your monthly cash position or cash flow. As you plot your projected cash flow, check to be sure your cash position at the end of each month is positive. If it is not, take steps early to cover these anticipated shortfalls.

Update your cash flow projection monthly, making adjustments whenever you encounter an unexpected expense or income. As actual sales and disbursements are made, list the actual amounts next to the estimates on your cash flow projection. Check for accuracy in your forecast, and make adjustments to future months as needed. As one month ends, add another month to the end of your rolling projection

The Indicative Strategic Valuation Method

Indicative Strategic Valuation combines factors that are pertinent in any valuation, including business skills, balance sheet strength, future potential and historical performance, analysing competitive positioning, inherent strengths/weaknesses and the opportunities/threats presented by the business environment. In addition, it is important to forecast operating performance, estimate cost of capital and continuing value, interpret results, analyse the impact of prevailing regulatory frame work, the global industry outlook, impact of technology and several other environmental factors. Single valuation techniques omit too many of these factors, which distorts true valuation.

This valuation method requires an examination of several aspects of a company's activities, which allows the strategist to standardise the valuation methodology for all corporate finance deals. The essence is that, without variation in the valuation methodology, the strategist can make comparisons between various projects.

This method has two parts, as detailed in the diagrams below: In the first part, a gross value is determined, which in Part 2 is discounted by a variety of factors.

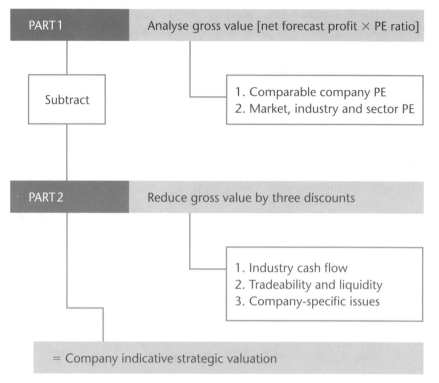

fig: 9.2 :: indicative strategic valuation method

The method is illustrated in the following case study.

Case study for De-ez Property Realtors Ltd

The company is strictly focused on selling residential property. De-ez is not involved in the sale of commercial or office property, nor does the company rent property.

Analysis of the company, environmental factors and competitors results in the following net taxed profit forecast:

	Actual	Forecast	
De-ez Property Realtors Ltd	2006	2007	2008
Net taxed profit	R1m	R5.2m	R6.1m

The industry has a multitude of competitors, both listed and unlisted.

The industry has a poor cash flow, highlighted by a 36% discount between share prices and cash flow. The level of skills and expertise in this industry is limited.

The company has depth of management. The company has a strong cash flow and shareholder support is sound.

PART 1: Determine gross value

The aim is to establish a fair and realistic value that is based on research as set out in the previous chapters. There is no point in conducting research if it is not used. The intention is to assess the company relative to comparable exchange-listed companies. This is only the start and this gross value needs to be discounted to include risk-free rates, liquidity, tradeability and director/owner (company-specific) issues.

The methodology is as follows, and uses the De-ez example above:

- Step 1: Assess all listed companies' price earnings. Find the one that is the most comparable to the company being valued. Price earnings is determined by comparing companies of similar size, track record, growth prospects and risk profile.
- Step 2: Assess the All Share, industrial and sector indices. These provide a solid indication of whether the relative company PE is too high, too low or fair.
- Step 3: Choose the minimum and maximum price earnings. This will calculate the gross value.

STEP 1: Determine De-ez's listed competitors. The following shows some of the price earnings ratios.

fig 9.3 ::

	JSE Real Estate listed companies	PE ratios	Type of company
1.	Acucap	11.59	Invest
2.	Octodec	12.5	Prop loan stock
3.	Orion	19.6	Commercial prop
4.	Paraprop	12.2	Prop loan stock
5.	Premium	13.8	Prop loan stock
6.	Putprop	12.1	Commercial/industrial
7.	Redefine	18.5	Prop loan stock
8.	Resilient	15.9	Prop loan stock
9.	SA retail	12.3	Prop loan stock
10.	Sable properties	8.5	Commercial, retail, residential and industrial
11.	Siyaprop	212	Prop loan stock
12.	Spearhead	12.4	Prop loan stock
13.	Vukile	9.9	Prop loan stock
AVERAGE		22.84	

The only comparable company to De-ez is Sable, which has a PE ratio of 8.5.

STEP 2: Assess market conditions and thus industry earnings ratios.

<u>fig 9.4 :: industry earnings ratio</u>

ALL SHARE INDEX

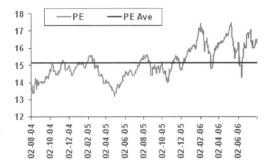

Comment:
- Ave: 15.11x
- Current: 16.3x
- All Share Index PE is above the average rate and thus can be considered 'expensive'.
- As such, BCI asserts that this level does not represent a fair and realistic current value.
- However, it is realistic to state that this level can represent the maximum forecast value for De-ez.

INDUSTRIAL INDEX

Comment:
- Ave: 12.4
- Current: 12.9
- The Industrial Index is 'bouncing' off the average PE of 12.4 and thus can be seeing as reasonable and fair for industrial companies listed on the JSE.
- This ratio can thus be seen as an average gross value for De-ez.

>>

REAL ESTATE INDEX

Comment:
- Ave: 23.5
- Current: 24.5
- The ratio is falling, as listed real estate companies' results fall from a high base.
- It has broken through the support average level of 23.5 times and is expected to fall to at least close to the Industrial Index price earnings ratio.
- These ratios are considered not to be fair and realistic.

Therefore, the minimum ratio to determine gross value is 8.5 times and the maximum 12.4 times.

fig 9.5 :: forecasting gross value

De-ez Property	ACTUAL		FORECAST			
Realtors Ltd	2006		2007		2008	
	min	max	min	max	min	max
Pre-tax profit (rands)	R1,0m		R5,2m		R6.16m	
Price earnings ratio (times)	8.5x	12.4x	8.5x	12.4x	8.5x	12.4x
GROSS VALUE: (PE x Profit)	R8.5m	R12.4m	R44.2m	R64.5m	R52.4m	R76.4m

The gross value of De-ez is a minimum of R8.5m and a maximum of R12.4m for 2006. This valuation is expected to rise to R52m (min) to R76.4m (max) by 2008.

PART 2: Discount 1: Industry Cash Flow

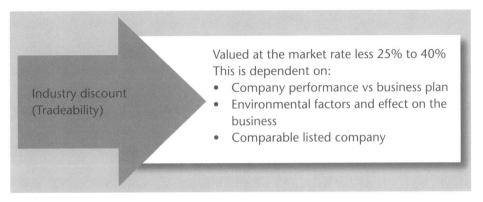

Industry discount
(Tradeability)

Valued at the market rate less 25% to 40%
This is dependent on:
- Company performance vs business plan
- Environmental factors and effect on the business
- Comparable listed company

fig: 9.6 :: Discount 1

In many instances, small-to-medium-sized companies do not have steady cash flows, not enough or, at least, not established. Without such statistics, it is not realistic to use Discounted Cash Flow methods as an indicator for conducting valuation.

However, if an indicative gross value is used, this can be discounted by an Industry Cash Flow. The aim here is to find an indicative value as most of these companies do not have substantial assets – not enough to produce a value.

fig 9.7 :: DE-EZ: industry cash flow

JSE-listed real estate companies	Latest Year	2005	2004	2003	2002	2001	2000	1999	1998	1997	Ave
Asset structure											
Total asset turnover	0.13	0.12	0.21	0.23	0.19	0.21	0.14	0.12	0.13	0.12	0.16
Funding structure											
Total assets to funding	1.06	1.07	1.06	0.97	0.99	1.09	1.08	1.07	1.08	1.09	1.05
Fixed assets as % of funding	93.85	91.78	85.54	79.77	81.52	88.03	52.43	25.95	32.34	34.96	63.82

▷▷

JSE-listed real estate companies	Latest Year	2005	2004	2003	2002	2001	2000	1999	1998	1997	Ave
Solvency and liquidity structure											
Current ratio	1.40	1.36	1.03	0.80	0.64	0.92	0.62	1.27	1.45	1.10	1.03
Quick ratio	1.40	1.32	0.98	0.72	0.59	0.82	0.57	1.25	1.43	1.08	0.98
Debt to assets	0.54	0.53	0.51	0.53	0.50	0.46	0.59	0.23	0.28	0.32	0.44
Debt to equity	1.19	1.11	1.03	0.88	0.82	0.83	1.43	0.29	0.39	0.46	0.81
Interest cover	1.55	1.76	1.95	2.11	2.56	4.86	3.94	4.63	3.61	2.12	3.04
Debt to cash flow	14.32	13.36	10.21	11.12	9.68	3.91	11.71	2.17	3.26	5.56	7.99
Cash flow interest cover	1.79	1.90	2.12	2.28	2.63	5.02	4.10	4.94	3.64	2.20	3.19
Profitability structure											
Operating profit margin (%)	55.87	63.57	39.42	33.63	42.37	66.58	42.67	113.6	86.54	73.29	61.56
Net profit margin (%)	13.06	21.73	13.70	12.21	20.12	49.06	27.46	80.89	54.05	25.53	32.90
Return on assets (%)	7.36	7.65	8.68	7.87	8.18	14.22	6.13	12.14	11.86	9.92	9.60
CPI-adjusted return on assets (%)	7.33	7.54	8.46	7.41	7.97	13.46	5.91	7.16	5.88	4.53	7.57
Return on equity (%)	4.51	6.26	7.34	5.18	6.93	19.30	10.35	12.08	11.73	7.78	9.47

JSE-listed real estate companies	Latest Year	2005	2004	2003	2002	2001	2000	1999	1998	1997	Ave
CPI-adjusted return on equity (%)	4.47	6.06	6.97	4.53	6.62	17.54	9.55	6.36	4.86	2.84	7.08
Leverage factor	-2.20	-3.09	-0.83	0.85	0.96	1.78	-0.92	0.37	0.75	0.85	0.18
Retention rate (%)	67.31	-24.4	24.75	51.07	54.68	78.22	39.87	48.91	40.13	-0.02	44.99
Return on external invest (%)	17.20	11.21	6.99	11.83	11.35	12.33	2.95	14.85	8.72	10.80	10.78
Trading activity structure											
Accounts receivable turnover	10.34	6.43	10.91	5.13	5.71	5.34	6.28	3.46	3.53	3.76	6.05
Share statistics											
Net asset value per share (Rand)	3.12	3.11	3.60	6.66	7.47	4.69	5.28	3.69	4.11	3.45	4.67
Cash flow per share (Rand)	0.43	0.45	0.59	0.59	0.66	1.35	0.85	0.49	0.50	0.29	0.64
Dividend cover	3.06	0.80	1.33	2.04	2.21	4.59	1.66	1.96	1.67	1.00	2.17
Cash flow dividend cover	4.07	0.91	2.09	3.09	2.73	5.10	2.07	2.18	1.72	1.07	2.68
Price/earnings ratio	18.15	16.55	13.01	11.92	12.18	15.93	11.39	10.15	9.73	11.35	12.65
Price/book ratio	1.36	1.27	1.21	0.75	0.82	1.34	0.77	1.45	1.56	2.09	1.26

Source: BCI Database

Note: A comprehensive list of ratios can be found in the appendices.

The JSE Real Estate Industry Cash Flow is 0.64 or 36% discount to share price. If this is the norm for listed real estate companies in South Africa, it is an important indicator for the final valuation for De-ez.

Therefore, the valuation of De-ez is as follows:

fig 9.8 :: valuation od De-ez

End-Feb	ACTUAL		FORECAST			
	2006		2007		2008	
	min	max	min	max	min	max
Pre-tax profit (rands)	R1,0m		R5,2m		R6.16m	
Price earnings ratio (times)	8.5x	12.4x	8.5x	12.4x	8.5x	12.4x
GROSS VALUE: (PE x Profit)	R8.5m	R12.4m	R44.2m	R64.5m	R52.4m	R76.4m
Less Discount 1: ICF (36%)	R3.1m	R4.5m	R15.9m	R23.2m	R18.9m	R27.5m
Value after 1st discount	R5.4m	R7.9m	R28.3m	R41.3m	R33.5m	R48.9m

After the first discount (for Industry Cash Flow), the value of De-ez stands at a minimum of R33.5 million (Year 3) and a max of R48.9 million (Year 3).

Discount 2: Liquidity and tradeability

The next step is to take account of the desire or potential desire of staff, colleagues, directors and the public in general to acquire shares in the business. Experience in international negotiations suggests that this discount can range between 25% and 40%, depending on issues outlined in the following text.

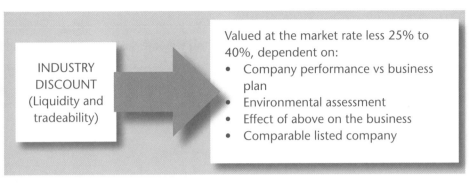

fig: 9.9 :: Discount 2

fig 9.10 :: analysis of De-ez after Discount 2

	ACTUAL		FORECAST			
End-Feb	**2006**		**2007**		**2008**	
	min	max	min	max	min	max
Pre-tax profit (rands)	R1,0m		R5,2m		R6.16m	
Price earnings ratio (times)	8.5x	12.4x	8.5x	12.4x	8.5x	12.4x
GROSS VALUE: (PE x Profit)	R8.5m	R12.4m	R44.2m	R64.5m	R52.4m	R76.4m
Less Discount 1: ICF (36%)	R3.1m	R4.5m	R15.9m	R23.2m	R18.9m	R27.5m
Value after 1st discount	R5.4m	R7.9m	R28.3m	R41.3m	R33.5m	R48.9m
Less Discount 2: Trade/liquid (25%)	R1.4m	R1.9m	R7.1m	R10.3m	R8.4m	R12.2m
Value after 2nd discount	R4.1m	R5.9m	R21.2m	R30.9m	R25.1m	R36.7m

After the second discount (tradeability and liquidity), the value stands at a min of R25.1 million (Year 3) and a max of R36.7 million (Year 3).

Discount 3: Company-specific issues

The final discount accounts for the strength and weaknesses of the directors and owners of a company. However, once the company has been sold, the influence of the previous owners fades. The discount is thus small, between 7% and 10%.

De-ez example: it is assessed that a minimum discount rate of 7% is fair and reasonable.

fig 9.11 :: analysis of De-ez after Discount 3

End-Feb	ACTUAL		FORECAST			
	2006		2007		2008	
	min	max	min	max	min	max
Pre-tax profit (rands)	R1,0m		R5,2m		R6.16m	
Price earnings ratio (times)	8.5x	12.4x	8.5x	12.4x	8.5x	12.4x
GROSS VALUE: (PE x Profit)	R8.5m	R12.4m	R44.2m	R64.5m	R52.4m	R76.4m
Less Discount 1: ICF (36%)	R3.1m	R4.5m	R15.9m	R23.2m	R18.9m	R27.5m
Value after 1st discount	R5.4m	R7.9m	R28.3m	R41.3m	R33.5m	R48.9m
Less Discount 2: Trade/liquid (25%)	R1.4m	R1.9m	R7.1m	R10.3m	R8.4m	R12.2m
Value after 2nd discount	R4.1m	R5.9m	R21.2m	R30.9m	R25.1m	R36.7m
Less Discount 3: Company specific:7%	R0.3m	R0.4m	R1.5m	R2.2m	R1.8m	R2.7m
Value after 3rd discount	R3.8m	R5.5m	R19.7m	R28.8m	R23.4m	R34.1m
EFFECTIVE PE	3.79	5.54	3.79	5.54	3.79	5.54

Two issues can be assessed from the above table:

- The company is valued at between R23 million and R34 million.
- The effective price/earnings ratio is between 4 times and 5.5 times. Note that the PE of the listed company Sable was at a similar level, at 8.5 times.

There are a number of instances when you may need to determine the market value of a business. Certainly, buying and selling a business is the most common reason. Estate planning, reorganisation or verification of your worth for lenders or investors are other reasons.

Valuing a company is hardly a precise science and can vary depending on the type of business and the reason for coming up with a valuation. There is a wide range of factors that go into the process – from the book value to a host of tangible and intangible elements. In general, the value of the business will rely on an analysis of the company's cash flow. In other words, its ability to generate consistent profits will ultimately determine its worth in the marketplace.

Business valuation should be considered a starting point for buyers and sellers.

It's rare that buyers and sellers come up with a similar figure, if, for no other reason, than the seller is looking for a higher price. Your goal should be to determine a ballpark figure from which the buyer and the seller can negotiate a price that they can both live with. Look carefully at the numbers, but keep in mind this caution from Bryan Goetz, president of Capital Advisors Inc., a business appraiser: 'Businesses are as unique and complex as the people who run them and are not capable of being valued by a simplistic rule of thumb.'

PART IV:

VALUATION CASE STUDY

VALUATION
CASE STUDY

In May 2005, I accompanied a client to Bangkok and Singapore to present a business opportunity to a number of venture capitalists. Prior to going there, the businessman had asked me what he needed to ensure that he had a reasonable and fair chance of securing the US$23 million (about R150 million) needed to launch his new business.

I explained that venture capitalists are interested only in the return on their investment. To convince them that your forecasted rate of return is realistic and not just pie in the sky, they will look at the assumptions of your forecasts. In other words, they will assess whether your long-term interest rate is fair, whether you believe that oil prices will rise or not, and so on. How do they determine whether these forecasts are fair? Apart from reports, business plans and due diligence, they need a valuation.

If you want to raise money to make your business successful, you have to undertake due diligence, which is an assessment of a business to determine its viability. But a due diligence assessment, together with a valuation, is less likely to be rejected by a capital provider.

After doing solid research, due diligence and valuation, I was commissioned to assist the businessman to 'sell' his concept to the capital providers in Bangkok.

It took four days to secure and receive the contract. We were on the flight back to South Africa on the fifth day.

When approached by another client (in the following case study) I set out the same scenario. This client, based in Johannesburg, was running a family business that started operating in 1966. It was a great business, with a historically strong cash flow, but it was suddenly finding that its suppliers and clients were no longer providing it with business. The number of contracts was drying up, all during a growth phase in vehicle sales that was by no means anything less than staggering.

So what could be wrong? I conducted a strategic analytical exercise and concluded that the market was suspicious of the client, given that it had no corporate governance structure or Black Economic Empowerment credentials.

Had this firm reached the end of the financial road? All indications were that it had wonderful potential. So the company (I have changed the name) commissioned a valuation that set out some of the research and due diligence issues completed at an earlier stage.

The following report is a summary of the research, due diligence and strategic analysis that substantiate the valuation.

The company also felt that it needed an alternative method of valuation and agreed to complete a Discounted Cash Flow valuation, despite having practically no future cash inflows, given that the company's number of contracts was practically zero.

Due diligence sounds impressive, but it translates into basic common sense. It is a logical process of thinking things through before committing to a project that may be unsuccessful. As parting and closing words, the following are some basic and common mistakes that owners make when running a small business.

- **Incorporating too quickly:** Always wait until your business idea is well formed before taking the plunge. Asking for funds without proper due diligence and a business plan can result in the funders telling you to 'Come back when you are ready!' What chance do you think you have to grab their attention at a later stage? The opportunity is gone. Even worse, someone may steal your idea. Remember, you cannot patent or copyright an idea.

- **Not researching the market:** A frequently overlooked component of business is determining whether a target market is one that is viable and profitable. If it is, assess how sales will affect your profitability.

- **Wanting to over-use consultants:** Attorneys' hourly fees add up extremely quickly and business owners are often shocked by their first few legal bills. The temptation is to involve attorneys in all aspects of business for counsel and drafting of documents. Many business owners quickly learn that it pays to do your own research, draft own documents and call on the expertise of your attorney only to refine your work.

Get the fundamentals right and get them right the first time. There is no second chance in business. I have outlined structures, methods and techniques that will assist you in becoming your own troubleshooter in future. Use them.

fig 10.1 :: indicative strategic valuation for Trucking Engineering Specialists (TES)

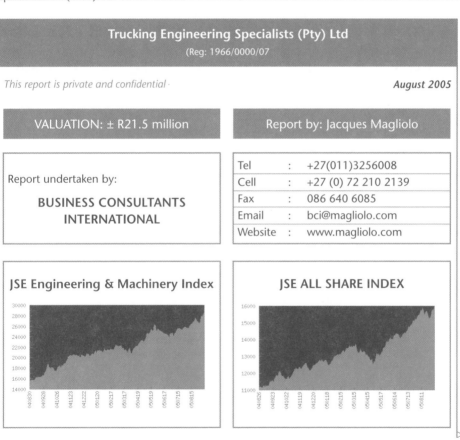

Trucking Engineering Specialists (Pty) Ltd
(Reg: 1966/0000/07)

This report is private and confidential·   ***August 2005***

VALUATION: ± R21.5 million	Report by: Jacques Magliolo

Report undertaken by:

BUSINESS CONSULTANTS INTERNATIONAL

Tel	:	+27(011)3256008
Cell	:	+27 (0) 72 210 2139
Fax	:	086 640 6085
Email	:	bci@magliolo.com
Website	:	www.magliolo.com

JSE Engineering & Machinery Index

JSE ALL SHARE INDEX

▷>

>>

Comment

- **Valuation** during this current bullish market is favourable for Trucking Engineering Specialists (TES).
- **A fair market value** is calculated using comparable listed companies, sector and overall market conditions. This equates to a valuation of between R20.4 million and R22.5 million.
- **Independent** Discounted Cash Flow Analysis *was also undertaken*. It revealed a **value of** R24.5 million.
- Company documentation indicates that **the company needs a BEE partner to expand operations.** Business Consultants International (BCI) believes that the company could raise new capital for expansion via either private equity or a listing on AltX. It is too small for a Main Board listing.
- It is assessed that TES should to enter into an **alliance with a BEE partner** to establish long-term competitive advantage as the South African listed and unlisted market is highly competitive, ie there are eight listed and +270 unlisted companies competing in the same/similar sectors to TES.
- **Research suggests that TES lacks critical mass**, ie it should acquire a smaller competitor to boost balance sheet strength and size of turnover and profit levels. The company also does not currently meet corporate governance issues set out in King II and BEE criteria to make it a long-term viable entity.
- **Correlation analysis:** A strong link exists between TES and GDP growth, Rand/ US$ exchange rate and automotive sector growth. **The latter is crucial and thus outlined in this valuation.** Plans for expansion into Africa are being discussed, given the SADC region and African Alliance growth.
- **The phenomenal motor industry growth is a key value driver for tes's future.**
  Note: TES is well managed with sound financial results and prospects.

BCI's research and advice is thorough, but BCI disclaims all liability for any inaccuracies or omissions.

Directors' Vision

To expand to become a national engineering business and to be the leading BEE re-manufacturer of engines and major engine components in South Africa and ultimately in Africa.

With the sincere desire to offer its customers the best possible value, TES will combine research, extensive education and practical experience to provide clients, investors and shareholders with the greatest possible results.

Group Philosophy

To always apply the highest standards of professional excellence, enthusiasm and integrity to operating a successful business in the world of re-manufacturing.

To do this through developing and facilitating successful business partnerships with designated First World operators throughout South Africa and Africa.

fig 10.2 :: initial investor information

Focus of valuation

- TES is looking to offer shares to a BEE partner to assist it in expanding its business.

- In the event that TES is not able to find a partner that is able to raise funds to acquire 26% of TES, the company is able to accommodate the venture partner – discussions will be held with BCI.

FINANCIALS FOR THE YEAR TO END-FEB 2005:

- **REVENUE = R34.7 million**

- **NET PROFITS = R2.3 million**

TES CURRENT VALUE = R21.5 MILLION

Valuation is based on current financials and a 1-year forecast – see fig 10.17, p. 237.

General information

Full Company Name: Trucking Engineering Specialists (Pty) Ltd

Contact details:

Abbreviation	TES
Contact	A. Jon
Tel	
Fax	
Website	
Email	

General data

Postal address: PO Box X23, Sandton, 2098

Registered address:

Holding company: TES Investment Holdings (Proprietary) Limited (100%)

Company auditors:

Principal bankers: Stanbank Limited

Registration: 1966/0000/07

Current shareholders (equal):   • A Jon   • S. Hall   • D. Alex

Note from Business Consultants International: This assessment is based on available financials and an analysis of the local engineering market. An earnings forecast for the next financial year was assessed and used in the valuation.

This valuation should be read in conjunction with TES's business plan, which outlines strategies and in-depth market and industry analysis. This report is a brief outline and summary of the analysis.

The valuation of TES will thus take the following steps:

- Stage One: *Industry Research and Appraisal*
  - Global and regional analysis of the market
  - An assessment of TES.
- Stage Two: *Industry Discounted Cash Flows and Price Earnings Ratios*
  - Assessment of Industry Discounted Cash Flows
  - Analysis of price earnings ratios:
    - For the **JSE All Share Index**, which reflects the overall state of the South African market.
    - **Assessment of the engineering sector of the JSE:** price earnings ratios
    - **Assessment of the JSE listed engineering companies.**
    - Outline of **Industry Discount rate:** Listed vs unlisted companies.

PROJECT AND RESEARCH METHODOLOGY

In conducting research on the industry, literally hundreds of documents were perused, from World Bank archives to United Nations and IMF research projects to broader South African economic trends. In almost every document, an overwhelming fact emerged:

> For sub-Saharan Africa to satisfy growing economic demand, new businesses are being built, new hotels are springing up, new and second-hand vehicle sales are staggeringly high and productivity is booming. Therefore, a significant increase in demand for re-manufacturing of engines is forecast throughout the African region.

BCI's industrial analysis was a top-down approach – from the global markets to regional (Africa), followed by sub-regional (neighbouring countries) and ending with an analysis of South Africa.

This norm was made more difficult in that major global corporations consider Africa as part of a specific emerging market trading bloc, namely the EMIA – Eastern Europe, Middle East, India and Africa. This part of the research became more valuable when it was determined that South Africa has become a preferred market for the production of new vehicles. The demand for engines is increasing exponentially, with markets coming from European companies (SMEs to multinationals) and from the local industry.

Note: This is not a prospectus and future share price forecasts have not been attempted. The focus of this report was thus to determine the value of TES as a going concern within the South African re-manufacturing and related markets.

There are numerous instances in which latest statistics were not available and thus estimates have been used.

All questions posed to management during the research process were answered with honesty and integrity.

THE FOUR-PHASE APPROACH

The BCI methodology undertaken in this project was based on a four-phase approach, as set out below.

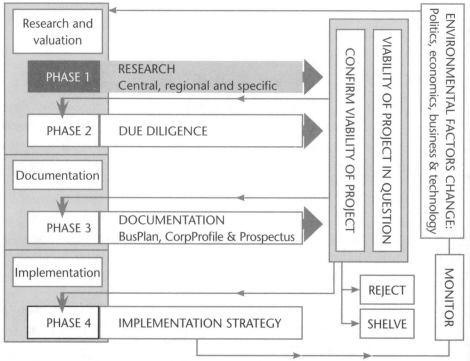

Fig: 10.3 the four-phase approach

NOTE: While this report is essentially a valuation, it was necessary in some instances to highlight trends, prospects and business trend-related issues usually found in research and in-depth business plan documents.

STRUCTURE OF THE PROJECT

The purpose of this valuation is to provide critical information for potential investment or local business interests seeking to explore the potential opportunities for developing/expanding a re-manufacturing business throughout South Africa.

The primary market information on each material is intended to describe the existing and potential markets, both worldwide and in South Africa, ie market size, value and possible segmentation. This will provide the business with the intelligence to estimate the opportunities that exist in its area of interest or for its specific operation.

This valuation is intended to achieve the following:

- To support TES's efforts to market opportunities that exist for re-manufacturers and end-users
- Summarise the information that has been collected to allow potential investors and other interested parties access to information concerning:
  - Existing and developing sources of material
  - Existing, emerging and potential end-use applications for specific materials derived from the South African re-manufacturing business.
- In addition, the information could potentially be used to support strategic planning initiatives – by highlighting market opportunities.

This research is intended to describe the potential markets for re-manufacturers and the opportunities that may be economically and commercially attractive to interested parties.

GENERAL COMPANY PROFILE

Trucking Engineering Specialists was established in 1963. The following is a brief outline of the company.

Current shareholding and directors

At present, the owners of TES are equal shareholders. A full résumé is available on request.

Directors' and BCI's combined experience

In the past, the directors have covered an extensive range of research and development in the field of engineering, re-manufacturing and corporate finance, in addition to market and industry analysis for the South African and regional markets. Future corporate finance and industry trend analysis will be outsourced to the company's financial sponsors.

Combined, the directors' and sponsors' experience cover:

- General strategic, business, marketing and corporate advice
- Competitor analysis
- Industry development, implementation and maintenance
- Creation of financial, economic and business development systems
- Market, trend and sector analysis
- Business plans for start-ups, going concerns and emerging markets
- Listing of businesses on AltX and main board of the Johannesburg Stock Exchange
- International negotiations and market intelligence
- Due diligence and SWOT analysis
- Sector and international market assessment, including global, EMIA and local market analysis.

Together, the directors and BCI intend to place more emphasis on:

- Identifying business opportunities through analytical corporate methods
- Researching the viability of conducting such business deals
- Where viable, to undertake, manage and complete the full spectrum of development, training and advice, in addition to corporate finance work, to complete the circle of the promotion, project management and branding.

Nature of business

This family business has been in operation for 40 years, providing the directors with extensive skills and experience in the specialised field of engine re-manufacturing, establishing the firm as one of South Africa's leading engine re-manufacturers. It produces a phenomenal +2,000 engines per year. The directors have also gained an impressive reputation for reliability, quality and integrity.

TES re-manufactures engines and major engine components for vehicle manufacturers as well as for major fleet users. It is also a multi-engine re-manufacturer and is capable of dealing with individual or mass production requirements. In 1996 the company was awarded the SABS ISO accreditation. Clients can be assured of the highest levels of workmanship throughout the company.

Research indicates that TES's machining productivity for many jobs produces a 50% faster turn around time and an 80% more accurate product when compared to its competitors. In addition, TES offers its clients an engine exchange programme. It has a wide range of engines available to assist in reducing operational downtime and to control productivity.

Where TES does not have a particular unit in stock, it can remanufacture a client's engine within five working days.

All re-manufactured engines come with a full warranty, comprehensive test report and warranty booklet, thus giving clients the assurance that their engines are free of defects resulting from replacement parts being used and shoddy workmanship.

The following is a brief overview of the engine re-manufacturing, machining and production process followed at TES.

• **Stripping and cleaning:** Upon receipt, engines are thoroughly cleaned using a multi-step process. Once stripped, all the components are placed in a specially designed, high-temperature, baking oven. With temperatures inside the oven exceeding 3593°C, all traces of sludge, grease and scale are burnt off. This process ensures that all inaccessible areas, such as oil passages and galleys, are spotlessly clean.

• **Resizing:** TES's state-of-the-art resizing machinery, which includes a cutting facility, enables it to remanufacture to the original equipment manufacturer (OEM) specifications in remarkably short turnaround times. All engines and sub-assemblies undergoing remanufacturing at TES have their bolts replaced.

• **Crankshaft grinding:** Only the latest generation of machine tools and state-of-the-art technology are used to ensure that each crankshaft is remanufactured as close to the original specifications as possible. This maintains the high standards demanded by the OEMs of the engines that TES remanufactures.

All grinding is executed to within the nearest micron of OEM specifications. After grinding, the journals of each crankshaft are polished to ensure longer bearing life. After this is completed, the crankshaft is balanced. This elaborate process helps prolong the overall operating life of the remanufactured engines.

- **Crack testing**: Every camshaft and crankshaft brought to TES undergoes a thorough and detailed magnetic particle crack testing procedure. This allows TES to detect any cracks, especially those invisible to the naked eye, on the shafts.

  If cracks are found, the shaft is immediately scrapped. Any shafts requiring hardening are subcontracted out and when returned are again re-examined in case any other cracking has occurred.

- **Cylinder head work**: All cylinder heads and blocks are pressure-tested utilising the latest hydraulic/pneumatic methods in pressure-testing equipment before any work is commenced.

- **Final assembly**: Only OEM-approved replacement parts are used throughout final assembly. Staff are equipped with specialised tools and work in close conjunction with workshop manuals and procedures.

Current/past customers

The following are some of TES's current and past clients/customers.

- Various Barloworld companies
- Grinaker Group
- GM SA
- Hyundai SA
- SA Breweries
- Various McCarthy group companies
- Various Imperial group companies
- Several large transport and fleet owners
- Some car dealerships, including Citroen, Peugeot, MBSA, Renault.

Future targeted clients/customers

TES believes that with the correct BEE partner it can target the following highly lucrative markets:

SOUTH AFRICA

- The mining sector
- The police (government garages)
- Metro (government garages)

AFRICA

- Construction and logistics companies
- Mining sector
- Agricultural sector

A full assessment of the proposed target markets are outlined in this report.

COMPANY STRUCTURE

During this phase of TES's strategy the company intends to refine the company structure to become more efficient and effective in all facets of TES's business dealings, particularly prior to selling a shareholding stake.

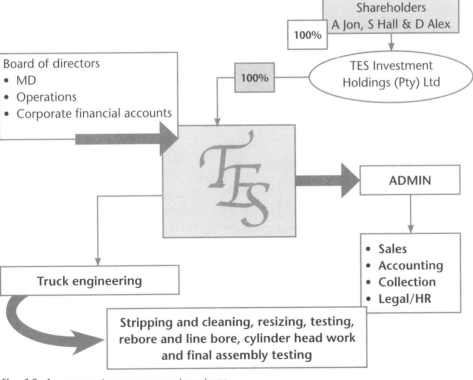

fig 10.4: current company structure

Note: The structure does not comply with King II or general accepted practices of having a broad-based empowerment shareholder structure. These issues are accounted for in the longer-term structure as proposed below.

The aim in the short term is to obtain efficiency.

In the short term, each division is still run from HO, which includes an administration division. This should reduce duplication costs, but over the longer term these factors should become clearer to both clients and investors.

The next stage is to enable the company to grow without restraint. This is the longer term vision, but in reality the medium- and long-term structures are being created almost simultaneously.

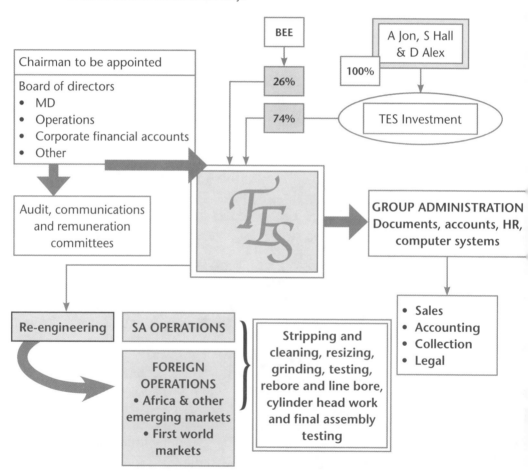

fig 10.5: longer-term company structure

Note: Ultimately, the structure will have an in-house marketing, HR, PR and accounts (admin) team.

Future strategy regarding company structure

The strength of a corporate structure lies in its ability to continually assess current organisational structures, ongoing events and potential risk, while keeping short- to long-term goals in mind. Strategies have to be continuously assessed and re-assessed.

To achieve this, TES intends to implement a Chairman's Office. A team consisting of three directors, namely Business Development (the MD), Operations and Corporate Finance (the strategist) will strategise current and new potential risks and determine the best action to be taken.

The structure (outlined below) provides directors and investors with a multi-level system of checks and balances, financial forecasts, transparency in the accounting system, etc.

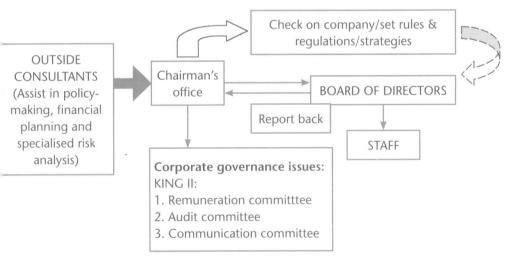

fig 10.6: the chairman's office

The reliability of forecasts lies in the assumptions used to determine them. In turn, these assumptions are based on research, including economic, business, technological and political (legal issues) environments (outlined in this report).

The system of The Chairman's Office enables the continuous assessment of what the company is **doing right and what it is doing wrong** (or about to do wrong). As such, directors can avoid making the mistakes made by others who have ventured into this industry, ie expansion into Africa. Worst-case scenarios can be assessed and solutions drafted. Thereby, the company will always be in a position to act quickly and decisively.

The team

- **Business Development:** The MD is in a solid position to assess new clients, undertake negotiations and report back to the team to broaden the assessment.

- **Operations:** Value-added products must continually be assessed and aligned to existing products and the demand for such products.

- **Corporate analysis:** detailed analysis provides assessment of key market trends, consumer patterns, possible competitive positioning of the major players in the future (profitability of this venture will undoubtedly bring competitors into the environment), economic trends and new product development activity.

- **Accounting:** The accountant would report back to the MD and strategist. Continuous analysis of cash flows, profit margins and cyclical factors pertinent to the re-manufacturing industry within the African environment must be continuously assessed to ensure stability and advancement.

The above scenario creates a corporate filter that enables the directors to determine if and when problems occur, if they will occur and what to do about these potential events.

Research

Global, regional and domestic research is crucial to identify main competitors, trends that could affect supply and demand, pricing, and marketing, financial and operational strategies. The team understands this market, but Africa provides its own unique challenges that must be continuously assessed. Numerous entrepreneurs have tried to enter this market before and have failed. BCI has assessed and addressed these issues accordingly. A clear-cut industry analysis forms the foundation for the company's long-term success.

Due diligence

Research enables the company to be positioned to take care of such issues. A due diligence of the company in relation to the research identifies whether a risk is pertinent to the company or not.

Review

Issues assessed under research are discussed and reviewed with outside consultants to get an objective viewpoint and advice.

Implementation

Changes that need to be implemented are done in the best possible manner, using best methods, skills and investment returns possible.

Monitoring

Once changes are implemented, regular checks are needed to determine whether the desired results are being achieved.

TES'S COMPETITIVE EDGE

TES's competitive edge is its quick response to a customer's request for services. The company will respond within 24 hours of a request by a company.

Most importantly, TES's leadership is a tremendous competitive advantage. The directors' strength is their ability to use the assessment as a sales tool to demonstrate savings and promote the company's services. However, it is a need and desire to expand that has led TES to find a BEE partner to join it in its endeavour.

BROAD-BASED ECONOMIC EMPOWERMENT POLICY

As part of its business and management philosophy, TES is committed to BEE and the advancement and development of previously disadvantaged individuals through business practices and endeavours, without compromising professionalism or quality of service.

TES is committed to the empowerment of all employees, especially previously disadvantaged individuals, in terms of employment equity. It is also committed to the advancement of all employees, by providing leadership, mentorship, education and career opportunities for staff.

The directors understand the community and environment in which they operate. Their belief is that they can build strong communities through the creation of employment and the development of opportunities.

To this extent, TES has adopted the following strategy:

- TES is committed to the economic and social transformation of South Africa
- TES conducts its business with a strong emphasis on human resource development and economic empowerment, which applies to all staff, service providers and suppliers of TES services
- The empowerment framework covers the implementation of empowerment targets and a process to monitor activities aimed at maximising the economic empowerment impact of TES
- Job creation, affirmative action, training and development, wealth creation and harmonious labour relations are key strategic goals.

In essence, TES seeks to:

- Afford opportunities to previously disadvantaged individuals and SMEs
- Conduct training programmes aimed at knowledge and skills transfer
- Maximise the creation of BEE opportunities.

TES targets all broad-based economic empowerment principles, applicable to:

- The creation of employment opportunities for previously disadvantaged individuals
- Appointment of previously disadvantaged consultants and professionals
- The procurement of services from previously disadvantaged suppliers.

TES commits itself to apply BEE benefits to:

- Affirmative Business Enterprises (ABEs)
- Small and Medium Enterprises (SMEs)
- Women and women-owned businesses
- Previously disadvantaged individuals
- Previously disadvantaged trainees.

TES is committed and expects its service providers, suppliers and other stakeholders to also commit to:

- Ensuring that previously disadvantaged individuals and ABEs are afforded opportunities
- Ensuring that the process of awarding work is objective and fair within the context of economic empowerment principles.

TES'S UNDERLYING PHILOSOPHY

TES's mission is always to apply the highest standards of professional excellence, enthusiasm and integrity to operating a successful business in the world of re-manufacturing and related products, and to do this through developing and facilitating successful business partnerships. Its mission is thus to emphasise relationships and to market the company (instead of only service).

Key to success for TES is the following:

- **Good governance:** Setting best-practice benchmarks
- **Strategy:** Managing its business sensibly
- **Capability:** Building the company with competent people
- **Commitment:** Commitment to sustainable growth of business, community and stakeholders.

The foundation of TES's success is its people. It is thus crucial that TES finds the 'right' BEE partner.

TES is proud of the professionalism of its people and it supports a culture of self-development. **Part of the proposed future plan is to invest in a structured approach to training,** linking it with professional bodies for continuous development.

TES intends to build the right team for the challenge. It aims to have sector and service experts experienced in specific problems and in delivering particular project and service types. This enhances the team's performance, allowing clients to benefit from the full power of the group's resources.

The business success will thus be founded on TES's commitment to making clients more profitable and effective.

TES believes that investing in human capital is more than just the management of people. It is about offering clients a unique integrated maintenance solution. Primary responsibilities are to provide a safe and effective workplace for clients in the most efficient way possible.

Therefore, TES believes in:

- **Exceptional service:** Dependable, good value for money, keeping commitments and the courtesy of a personal call.
- **The importance of the individual:** Every member plays a vital role in the success of the company. TES values the worth of every person, diversity, safety and open and direct communication.

- **A passion for service excellence:** Individuals in the company all stakeholders. TES believes service excellence is the cornerstone of the business and the most important key performance indicator in the company.

- **Integrity:** TES and its team are stewards and fiduciaries for its clients and business and require of its members uncompromising honesty, accountability and integrity.

In undertaking an analysis of TES, BCI concluded that TES's competitive strength is primarily vision, people and independence. In a highly intensive, expert-oriented and competitive market such as TES's, consumer choice is vitally important. **This is where TES sees itself as having the edge over competition, in that they are able to supply a competitive service at competitive prices.**

POSITIONING

What became clear to BCI during the course of company and industry analysis was the company's unique positioning with respect to the services it proposes to offer. The company needs the much-desired and in-demand BEE credentials that local and foreign-owned companies require before they can procure state-owned contracts in the future. Judging by recent figures that indicate a growth in motor sales in South Africa, it would appear TES and its team have adopted a winning formula.

Initially, management expects the public to associate and compare TES with other engineering companies. However, important attributes exist that TES will promote in developing its corporate image in future. This tactic will create a positive perception of the network in the minds of the public.

TES's promotional messages to clients will stress the following merits:

- Higher-quality services developed for specific needs
- A highly effective and quick programme to establish a client's specific needs
- The provision of educational and socially responsible technical assistance.

Conclusion:

- **With a BEE partner, TES will be geared for future growth and expansion.**

- **Through its personal one-on-one discussions with clients, the group will position itself and effectively reposition its competition in the BEE market.**

MOVEMENT INTO AFRICA

The company's philosophy must evolve within a continually changing South African environment and African hostile territory. The political and economic climate in countries of the African continent has radically changed in the past decade. These dynamic changes have evoked a better understanding of the benefits to economic co-operation and partnership between the continents' various political divisions.

As new economic and political realities spread, the benefits of economic inter-dependence between the continents' various constituents become more evident.

This has created a need for more efficient and cost-effective methods to promote products and services that cross political and national boundaries.

TES proposes to fill this need by establishing Africa's first inter-continental re-manufacturing network.

The current quality and variety of products in most African countries are inferior to North American and Western European services. Current African technology is comparable to that of the US's technology of the 1980s. The following factors have contributed to this situation:

- Exclusive ownership or control of business by many governments
- Government censorship
- Inferior production equipment
- Poorly trained personnel
- Inadequate operating budgets
- The availability and price of raw materials.

Each of the 54 African countries operates independent policies. There is little – if any – co-operation between countries. Generally, business systems that do exist suffer from inadequate funding by government and semi-government organisations, and are therefore plagued by various problems including:

- Antiquated equipment
- Old systems and programmes, procured from the West and at the turn of the last century
- Lack of skilled technicians and government censorship.

TES will therefore claim the reputation of being the only reliable source of re-manufacturing service in Africa. The directors believe that the company has the advantage of monopolising the cross-continent market. Large multi-national and international corporations as well as indigenous companies are eager to use services offered by TES across Africa.

There is no doubt that price and competitiveness will have to be carefully monitored and adjusted if necessary.

Rates for individual market segments will be competitive. The company may adjust these rates higher or lower depending on its market objective (eg gaining market share, maximising revenue, etc) for any given segment.

However, TES believes that South Africa has the most sophisticated infrastructure and, therefore, intends to continue to use this country as its launching pad for the rest of Africa.

MARKET TARGETS

TES's market strategies have two goals that are designed to achieve the objective of producing revenue for the company.

- The first is to **continue developing, producing and servicing current clients in South Africa**. Simultaneously, the company intends to secure additional contracts in this and other industries and in other regions.

- Secondly, the company aims to **promote and expand its range of engineering (re-engine manufacturing) services** in South Africa and in other African countries.

These strategies are designed to attract clients who have access to investment in every country where the re-manufacturing operations are inaugurated. The company's ability to fulfil orders professionally will be realised by providing clients, entrepreneurs and dealers with support superior to any currently seen in South Africa. As a result, clients will be established with the size and demographic qualities to make TES Africa's foremost re-manufacturing supplier.

TES's market strategy will capitalise on this status by aggressively marketing its ability to reach consumers through methods that are flexible, cost-efficient and highly effective.

Comprehensive plan

The overall plan governing TES's rollout programmes and market development is based on the following fundamentals:

- TES provides the **expertise to design**, set up, implement and maintain re-manufacturing services that are for all markets, whether in Africa or in First World countries
- The company will **monitor client sentiment** and opinion on a continuous basis to help shape an effective and continually improving rollout development programme
- TES will **aggressively market** its capabilities as experts to businesses, organisations and individual entrepreneurs.

GENERAL FACTORS AFFECTING VALUATION

Political factors

TES is relatively unaffected by political factors. The effect of politics on the economy, however, eg how the R/US$ is affected by politics, determines how TES is affected. Government policy on fuel pricing or government tax on fuel will have a substantial effect on business.

The higher the fuel price, the fewer vehicles on the road, and the costs of running fleets is dramatically increasing by the month (see Specific Factors p. 219). Strike action against the government has a delayed effect on TES as the customer has to assess the cost of strikes and downtime before assessing spending with TES. Prudent governance encourages TES's policy towards growth, diversification and capital spending.

Economic factors

The biggest factor that affects TES currently and in future are interest rates, foreign exchange values and inflation. With a low interest rate, consumers and clients are more able to purchase new fleets instead of repairing an old or aging fleet.

With new fleets come maintenance contracts or service plans, which are arranged direct with the dealerships. TES currently has a lot of dealership work that encompasses its warranty work on new fleets. This is mainly on the petrol side of the business. The big money is in big diesel, which is what TES is pursuing on an ongoing basis.

Therefore, TES benefits more by higher interest rates, when clients are more likely to repair older engines or vehicles than purchase new ones. Economic research indicates that the interest rate cycle has bottomed, which is positive for TES.

A strong rand. With the rand at R6/US$ importers of new and used motor components are suited to import. This means the automotive industry is saturated, especially with pirate spares, second-hand motors and components. TES's pricing is geared around the pricing adjustments of suppliers. However, the general public has easy access to cheap, second-hand runners and spares.

Therefore, **TES benefits from a weaker rand against other currencies** as genuine components are then preferred by its clients for quality purposes. At the time of the valuation, **economic research indicated that the exchange rate against major currencies was unlikely to strengthen in the next 18 months.**

Inflation has a direct effect on consumer spending. How the consumer will spend depends on how high or low inflation is and general economic growth. Higher inflation usually sees the customer maintaining vehicles as opposed to buying new ones. The high rate of vehicle sales (new and pre-owned) in South Africa is beneficial for TES.

TES considers all the factors on an ongoing basis to secure the best possible pricing for stockpiling, genuine parts purchasing, upgrading of plant and equipment, tooling and consumables to ensure that its pricing remains competitive, its plant is well maintained and stock has a high turnaround.

Technological factors

TES is a leader in the automotive re-manufacturing industry in Southern Africa. A comprehensive analysis of the motor sector was therefore undertaken, focusing specifically on the engineering (machinery) sector of the JSE.

TES's plant and machinery is state of the art. The company endeavours to continuously upgrade and maintain its machinery to stay in touch with global changes in automotive engineering.

New technology is researched by the directors and staff of TES, who have an excellent relationship with the retail motor industry (RMI) and the biggest suppliers of automotive engineering machinery in Africa.

Their research is extensive and technological innovation in the motoring sector is well anticipated by TES, which enables them to stay one step ahead of its competitors in the industry. The supply is generally pre-empted by TES so that when the demand for high-tech automotive reporting, evaluation and repair is required, TES can accommodate it.

Business trends and future growth

TES's future growth strategy will be largely dependent on BEE. Current customers and suppliers in the larger groups are currently BEE or are in the process on becoming BEE. With BEE status, TES will be in a better position to target markets that it cannot currently access. This is mainly the mining sector, government garages and Metro bus fleets.

TES aims to target gold, platinum, coal and other mining sectors. These sectors are hugely involved in 'big diesel engines', in which TES specialise. Their vehicle fleets and underground diesel engines could have the effect of doubling TES's turnover initially and result in an ongoing increase in turnover and profits in big increments for years to come. With BEE status, TES will be able to get a foot in this door and gain clout in the tendering process.

A 10% growth rate was taken as the 2005/6 financial year headline earnings. This was used in the valuation.

TES also want to penetrate across-border clients. Currently TES does work with some organisations in Botswana and Zambia. Risk analysis is being conducted and strategies are being determined looking at the best way to implement an African expansion.

SPECIFIC SECTOR FACTORS AFFECTING VALUATION

- Changes to motor industry strategies: The slowing of the rate of growth in vehicle and component exports reflects South Africa's vulnerability to global trends under the Motor Industry Development Programme (MIDP). The MIDP has an emphasis on rationalisation of production, increasing unit volumes, coupled with export incentives that open up the domestic market to imports.
- Global, regional and national influences: South Africa is the only significant automotive manufacturing nation in the sub-Saharan Africa region and accounts for about 80% of the sub-continent's output, with still unexploited opportunities to develop, produce and market vehicles appropriate to African operating requirements.

By some informed estimates, the global OEMs will have to close as many as 45 assembly plants internationally to cope with the pressures on sales, pricing and the over-capacity issue. This and the industry's interest in growth prospects in emerging markets in Eastern Europe, India and China rather than Africa will make it increasingly difficult to attract further investment.

Toyota, BMW, DaimlerChrysler, Volkswagen are already – and General Motors, Ford and Nissan should soon be – significant exporters of vehicles that have enabled the industry to be accepted internationally for quality and reliability of supply from a comparatively low-cost base.

- **Political considerations:** Statements by President Thabo Mbeki and other political and economic opinions confirm that South Africa is not impressed by the contributions that global corporations – which must include those in the motor sector – are making to the nation, despite the generous concessions made to business since 1994.

  In 2004, **Toyota had to pay R12 million in penalties** related to price fixing on the new Corolla. Other importers and assemblers are being subjected also to what promise to be extended investigations into how they conduct their affairs in this and other emerging market territories.

- **Industry globalisation:** The takeover of Delta Motor Corporation by General Motors marked the end of South African-owned car assemblers. South African auto workers are now firmly tied into the global network of auto production.

  Over-supply of cars resulting in the under-utilisation of capacity in car-producing plants has been the prime factor motivating car producers to focus on cutting production costs by whatever means possible.

- **Ban on used vehicle imports:** Only South Africa in sub-Saharan Africa is trying to compete globally in motor manufacturing, while the rest of the sub-continent sees better prospects from opening up its markets to the now easily available and low-priced used vehicles obtainable from both right- and left-hand drive industrialised nations in Europe, Japan and North America. **Such imports are banned in South Africa,** enabling the industry to maintain high new vehicle prices and fuelling the argument that having a vehicle manufacturing industry is socially and economically a mixed blessing.

OTHER FACTORS AFFECTING VALUATION

TES offers a full service, which is supported by well-established brands that are world-class quality products, with ISO accreditation.

The management team is **experienced and highly capable**. This has been proven and highlighted in the company's sound historic financial performance / position and controls with low staff turnover ratio.

Opportunities do exist to expand into Africa, based on TES's technologies, experience and skills.

However, there are a number of weaknesses within the business and its environment that could affect the valuation:

- As a family business, the enterprise is too tightly held by too few people
- KING II: TES needs to explore the guidelines of KING II criteria for corporate governance and incorporate these in its approach to find a BEE partner
- Increased competition within the industry and resultant pressure to remain competitive through ongoing R&D costs
- Changes in technology are costly
- Retaining technical staff/engineers is always a problem, when they could be poached by competitors
- Uncertainty regarding the exchange rate
- **Potential loss of clients/customers if a BEE structure is not implemented in the short to medium term.**
- The company's growth is linked (correlated) to the motor/engineering cycle.

In order to remain competitive and to enhance the benefits provided to its customers, TES has focused on cost reduction and increased efficiencies, stable pricing policies and ongoing R&D in order to continue to provide customers with advanced service.

RISK ANALYSIS REGARDING PROFILE

In an environment (Africa) that has significantly differing levels of statistics (officially and unofficially), forecasts become difficult to reliably confirm. As such, the company has adapted a principle that it can only use statistics and general information that are confirmed by at least two other official documents, preferably from recognised global institutions, such as the United Nations, World Bank, IMF, etc.

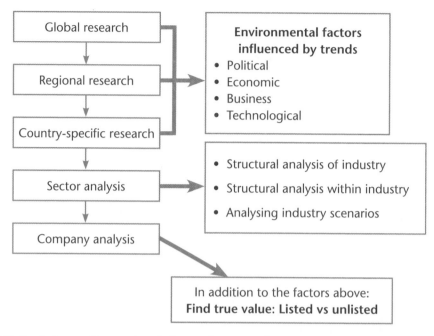

Research is used to determine the viability of any future change in risk profile. As such due diligence on the company would be carried out in relation to the research. Environment and social issues represent one of the most complex challenges facing management. TES aims to ensure that its team always has a high level of technical, market and regulatory understanding that encompasses the highly technical elements of the re-manufacturing business.

Risk is always assessed by:

- Structural analysis of the industry
- Structural analysis within the industry
- Analysing industry scenarios.

Structural analysis of the industry

This research is more general, looking at TES within its engine re-manufacturing environment. Although the relevant environment is broad, encompassing factors such as socio-economic forces, as well as political, business and technological factors, the key aspect of the firm's environment is the industry or industries in which it competes. Industry structure has a strong influence in determining the competitive rules as well as strategies potentially available to the firm.

Competition in an industry is rooted in its underlying economic structure and goes well beyond the behaviour of current competitors. The state of competition in an industry depends on a number of basic competitive forces which determine the ultimate profit potential in the industry. Here, profit potential is measured in terms of return on invested capital.

It is the key structural features of industries that determine the strength of the competitive forces and hence profitability.

The goal of competitive analysis for a business is to find a position in the industry where the company can best defend itself against these collective forces – ie the threat of new entrants into the market, the threat of substitutes, competitive rivalry, the bargaining power of buyers and the bargaining power of suppliers – or can influence them in its favour. Since the collective strength of the forces may well be painfully apparent to all competitors, the key for developing strategy is to delve below the surface and analyse the sources of each.

Knowledge of these underlying sources of competitive pressure highlights:

- The critical strengths and weaknesses of the company
- The areas where strategic changes may yield the greatest payoff
- The areas where industry trends promise to hold the greatest significance as either opportunities or threats.

Structural analysis applies to diagnosing industry competition in any country or in an international market, although some of the institutional circumstances may differ.

BCI has undertaken such analysis and The Chairman's Office roots out possible risks by ensuring succession, analysis and independent assessment of the board's performance and future prospects, while continually assessing changing market and industry supply and demand factors.

SWOT analysis

This is a summary of TES's most important strengths, weaknesses, opportunities and threats.

Strengths

- Good reputation of the directors and owners
- Business provides succession. High expectations of management

- Owns all assets, nothing is financed or encumbered. As such, it has a strong financial position and no bad debts (controls)

- Very little staff turnover, especially skilled journeymen. Staff is dedicated, skilled and well motivated. High-calibre journeymen, who are continually training on site

- Exceptional analytical and technical skills in global market strategy, analysis of domestic, business and political environments

- Good technical support staff

- Locality to clients and suppliers (central position)

- Ability of directors and consultants to work independently or in a team. This includes availability of labour and skills in operational management

- Ability of directors and consultants to work under high pressure

- Excellent communication skills. TES provides management with the opportunities to share information and technology with suppliers

- Good ability to analyse and develop market information

- Competitive edge, as TES is up to date with the latest technology. Quality and service (SABS) has been TES's forte

- TES's non-affiliation with any African government will ensure its political neutrality, creating confidence in the integrity of the company's rollout programme. There is also no major threat from unions

- The company will be able to establish a leading position in the marketplace before potential competitors attempt to replicate TES's concept.

Weaknesses

- Lack of a strong brand name in and outside South Africa. It will take extensive marketing in order to establish the company in the market. As such, TES is not marketed sufficiently/effectively. The company needs better exposure

- TES is not into certain strategic areas eg – mines, government workshops or big logistic companies

- Bureaucratic business processes with inflexible rules

- Subject to fluctuations in business and economic cycles

- Decline in matric standards and potential intake of undesirable/under-educated prospective staff

- The company's rights in individual countries may become jeopardised by political issues from time to time

- Needs more skilled workers in its operations, which are difficult to get and expensive
- Cash flow problems are inherent in small companies. It must be noted that TES has no gearing
- It does not have a Big Brother with financial muscle to support it in its ventures
- HIV/Aids and absenteeism
- The engineering sector is highly competitive
- TES needs to restructure to account for KING II and BEE.

Opportunities

- The industry is confronted by vast opportunities, especially as a result of bi-lateral / multi-lateral trade agreements
- A relatively weak exchange rate has made South African-produced goods and services particularly attractive internationally
- Strong potential to compete in niche markets. While South African service providers have, in the past, not often been able to achieve significant economies of scale, they have successfully penetrated niche markets with higher value-added products.
- Regional and international trade agreements will open new opportunities in supply chain optimisation and sourcing, as well as new opportunities to market re-manufacturing services capabilities
- Technical skills are extremely limited in Africa
- South Africa's restructuring and public sector commercialisation programmes could offer extensive opportunities in the long term as all new contracts/ tenders have to have a BEE element. TES aims to provide the multinationals the opportunity to secure contracts on an association basis
- The company intends to exploit the fact that South Africa has a very poor service record. This is in view of several other value-added markets that would boost TES's revenue.

Threats

- South African industry is no longer able to hide behind protectionist barriers, and its exposure to the 'world economy' has led to the free flow of competing products and services into the Southern African market
- Labour market legislation, while mostly good in its intentions, is often seen to be unsuitable to developing country conditions, especially in the light of a

generally abundant labour supply. This has made the formal labour market inflexible, and has constrained formal employment growth

- China's accession to the WTO in December 2001 gives that country significant access to international markets. China is seen as a significant threat across all sectors and its WTO membership means that it may not be (unduly) discriminated against in terms of market access by other WTO member countries (including South Africa)

- The current fluctuations in the R/US$ exchange rates make any project risky

- The normal risk factors inherent in any business venture can be minimised by a capable management team. The management team assembled by TES has the experience necessary to compensate for these risks.

- As part of TES's policy of being a market-driven company, industry and market research will be conducted on a continuing basis. This will alert management to any changes needed in strategy, and allow the necessary corrections to be implemented.

- Newer technologies render current equipment and systems deficient or obsolete

- A price war could result in undercutting by the multinationals, who can afford to poach key technicians and staff

- Being strongly environmental, government interference (such as price hikes and tariffs) could occur.

Comment

TES needs to broaden its scope on business targets. Considering the company's relative strengths and weaknesses, the opportunity for success is readily apparent. This potential exists because of the factors discussed in this and other sections of this business plan. Simply listed, they are:

- The political and economic changes currently taking place in Africa (African Union, Nepad, etc) provide a more stable environment for commercial activities

- Technological advances in broadcasting allow entrepreneurs access to larger markets on a cost-efficient basis

- An emerging market that is ready to embrace a new concept, while empowering its own people, can become self-sufficient.

GROWTH STRATEGIES

The following is a brief outline of TES's growth strategies, which the company wishes to partner with new investors.

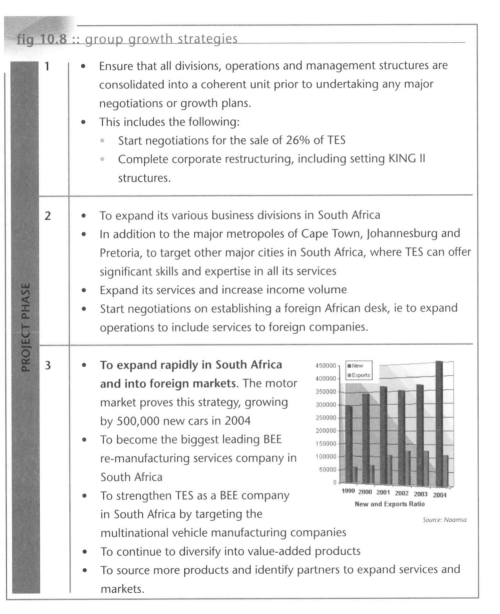

fig 10.8 :: group growth strategies

PROJECT PHASE

1
- Ensure that all divisions, operations and management structures are consolidated into a coherent unit prior to undertaking any major negotiations or growth plans.
- This includes the following:
  - Start negotiations for the sale of 26% of TES
  - Complete corporate restructuring, including setting KING II structures.

2
- To expand its various business divisions in South Africa
- In addition to the major metropoles of Cape Town, Johannesburg and Pretoria, to target other major cities in South Africa, where TES can offer significant skills and expertise in all its services
- Expand its services and increase income volume
- Start negotiations on establishing a foreign African desk, ie to expand operations to include services to foreign companies.

3
- **To expand rapidly in South Africa and into foreign markets.** The motor market proves this strategy, growing by 500,000 new cars in 2004
- To become the biggest leading BEE re-manufacturing services company in South Africa
- To strengthen TES as a BEE company in South Africa by targeting the multinational vehicle manufacturing companies
- To continue to diversify into value-added products
- To source more products and identify partners to expand services and markets.

New and Exports Ratio

Source: Naamsa

LATEST SECTOR NEWS

More and more vehicles: South African manufacturers recorded just short of 450,000 new vehicle sales in 2004 thanks to record low interest rates, subdued inflation and a bullish rand. Vehicle sales are one of the leading indicators of domestic economic growth, showing high levels of employment and expansion. Automobile makers are thriving in South Africa's conducive production environment.

2005: Second quarter passenger car sales of 89,282 units recorded a further substantial improvement of 22,335 units or 33.3% compared to the 66,947 new cars sold during the corresponding quarter for 2004. Combined commercial vehicle sales during the second quarter of 2005 at 47,109 units reflected a gain of 12,842 units or an improvement of 37.5% compared to 34,267 units sold during the corresponding quarter of 2004.

Remember that every vehicle has an engine that will ultimately have to be reconditioned. These statistics provide for a solid financial future.

The industry's 2005 second quarter performance represented the best ever quarterly new vehicle sales recorded.

Ford to double production: The Ford Motor Company of Southern Africa is set to double its production at its Silverton production plant in Pretoria. The development will help sustain employment in the company and should also inevitably lead to some extra staff recruitment. Ford's fully built-up export programmes started in 2004 with the export of commercial vehicles.

Exports to existing and new markets were set to increase in 2005 from 40,000 to 80,000 vehicles. Ford is continually searching for new export opportunities and could even consider producing left- and right-hand drive vehicles for export in the near future.

INDUSTRY INVESTMENT NEWS

- Volkswagen SA will invest R1.2-billion in South Africa over the next three years. The company hopes to grow its exports of fully built-up cars by 45% and its component export revenue by 8% this year
- Toyota SA is to invest R1-billion in a state-of-the-art, water-based paint plant, as part of its ongoing production facilities investment

- Daimler-Chrysler SA is committing R1-billion into its plant in South Africa, after being selected as one of three plants to produce the new Mercedes-Benz C-Class

- General Motors SA invested R300-million into facility upgrades at its Port Elizabeth assembly plant so as to better compete for lucrative vehicle export contracts

- Nissan SA spent more than R250-million on equipment at its plant near Pretoria. This led to a R1-billion contract from Nissan Japan to export locally assembled vehicles

- BMW SA completed a R2-billion investment in its manufacturing plant near Pretoria.

South Africa's motor manufacturing industry is starting to take greater advantage of the potentially enormous opportunities offered by the African Growth and Opportunity Act, which opens up the US market to South Africa's automotive exports.

Many of these vehicles are second hand and have to have remanufacturing completed to industry standards.

VALUATION METHOD: INDUSTRY CASH FLOWS AND PRICE EARNINGS RATIOS

The BCI method of determining a company's value is a combination of price earnings and discount rates to determine a fair and realistic valuation. Price earnings is determined by comparing companies of similar size, track record, growth prospects and risk profile.

Stage one: Brief overview of the South African engineering industry

The previous month saw a stream of good data releases: consumer and producer inflation came in lower than expected; there was a sharp rebound in economic growth; the foreign trade balance improved; government finances looked healthy; and, best of all, half a million net new jobs were created over the previous year.

This data supports BCI's view that the economy will surprise many economists over the next few years. With both inflation indicators surprising on the downside over the past month and the rand firming moderately again, BCI continues to believe that the current interest rate outlook is benign.

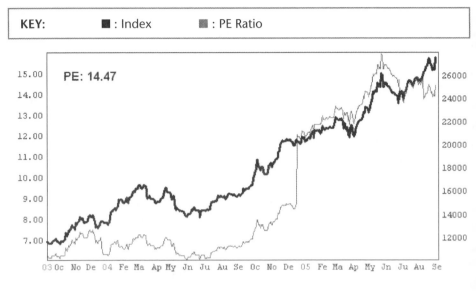

KEY: ■ : Index   ■ : PE Ratio

fig 10.9:: South Africa's engineering sector

The financial performance of companies in this sector during the past year reflected unfavourable currency exchange rate movements as well as important developments in the markets served by group businesses. Currency exchange rate movements influenced the **competitive dynamics** within certain markets, **reduced some company's margins** and resulted in net foreign exchange losses. The global engineering (machine) market **continued to evolve**, while South Africa's businesses enjoyed robust demand.

The significant and sustained strength of the rand **enabled competitors to import motors** at prices substantially lower than locally manufactured products. It also had a detrimental effect on the export of products of original equipment manufacturers utilising motors manufactured by South African companies.

For numerous companies, this **resulted in lower revenues for the year** as well as significantly reduced margins. Strategies were implemented to enable profitable trading in the current market conditions, which included:

- Achieving flexibility in importing or manufacturing product in response to movements in the local currency
- Rationalisation of the manufacturing process by inter alia outsourcing non-core production processes
- Rationalisation of the product range stocked

- Right-sizing of operations in line with the above strategies. Due to the substantial drop in market prices, some companies had to write down inventories to net realisable values and also incurred certain costs in right-sizing the business.

As a result, companies must undertake a number of **critical risk management processes**:

- **Credit risk management:** Potential areas of credit risk consist of trade accounts receivable and short-term cash investments. Trade accounts receivable consist mainly of a large, widespread customer base. Group companies should monitor the financial position of their customers on an ongoing basis.

- **Liquidity risk management:** The group manages liquidity risk by monitoring forecast cash flows and ensuring that adequate unutilised borrowing facilities are maintained. **Of crucial note, TES has no gearing.**

- **Foreign currency exposure:** The higher the amount of foreign income that is generated via offshore branches, the greater the need for the company to adopt a risk measurement to keep foreign income under control.

TES in the engineering sector

TES has grown significantly since its inception. However, its net attributable profit was only 7%, given the lack of a BEE component to the business.

Management claim that the company is committed to remaining a world-class leader in South Africa and dominating the local industry. Their philosophy is to produce a world-class service that can compete successfully in the international arena. The ultimate success of the company will be its ability to become a world player, although in niche markets.

Market Share: In relation to the engineering sector, TES is based in the sub-sector of machine and equipment. In this field it excels and management believe that they have a dominant market share. As such, their philosophy has been to concentrate on offering existing clients excellent service and focusing on optimising the profitability of existing products.

Latest issues: Management and financials confirm that the company has recently focused on input costs and improving productivity. They have invested in capital equipment, which has enabled the company to improve on techniques and reduce costs.

While the market is competitive, BCI believes that lies in the fact it is a world class operator focused on the local market. Another of TES's strengths is technology.

Stage Two: Industry cash flows and price earnings ratios

TES financials

	2005 R	2004 R
Turnover	34 682 106	42 957 059
Cost of sales	25 740 404	34 689 294
Gross margin	8 941 702	8 267 765
Other operating costs	5 849 464	5 449 390
Operating profit	3 092 238	2 818 375
Income from investments	110 502	172 410
Profit before taxation	3 202 740	2 990 785
Taxation	910 362	855 588
Net profit for the year	2 292 378	2 135 197

fig 10.10:: TES income statement

	2005 R	2004 R
CASH FLOWS FROM OPERATING ACTIVITIES	2 399 022	2 503 867
Cash generated from operations	3 988 522	4 382 903
Interest received	110 502	172 410
Dividend paid	(1 000 000)	(1 500 000)
Taxation paid	(700 002)	(551 446)
CASH FLOWS FROM INVESTING ACTIVITIES	(224 670)	(2 874 721)
Purchase of tangible assets	(280 920)	(3 090 350)
- Replacements		
Proceeds on disposal of tangible assets	56 250	215 629
NET INCREASE (DECREASE) IN CASH AND CASH EQUIVALENTS	2 174 352	(370 854)
Cash and cash equivalents at the beginning of the year	978 819	1 349 673
Cash and cash equivalents at the end of the year	3 153 171	978 819

fig 10.11:: TES cash flow

	Notes	2005 R	2005 R
ASSETS			
Non-current assets	2	2 852 883	4 102 463
Tangible assets			
Current assets		7 700 228	6 285 650
Inventories	3	1 500 000	915 000
Trade and other receivables		3 047 057	4 352 235
Taxation		-	39 596
Cash at bankers and on call		3 153 171	978 819
Total assets		10 553 111	10 388 113
EQUITY AND LIABILITIES			
Equity capital and reserves		7 239 460	5 947 082
Share capital	4	100	100
Non-distributable reserve	5	390 467	390 467
Distributable reserve		6 848 893	5 556 515
Non-current liability			
Deferred taxation	6	244 763	125 128
Current liabilities		3 068 888	4 315 903
Taxation		51 129	-
Trade and other payables		1 277 759	2 165 903
Provision for warranties		1 740 000	2 150 000
Total equity and liabilities		10 553 111	10 388 113

fig 10.12:: TES balance sheet

At present, there are no directly comparable companies listed on the JSE and therefore the JSE's Engineering and Machinery index is used (in combination with the PE ratios of sector-listed companies) to provide broad comparative benchmarks. Major differences include:

- The size of TES's operations compared to listed engineering companies

- The current marketability and tradeability of TES's shares compared to those of listed companies. This is derived by using the **Industry Cash Flow.**

- TES's operations/products/assets compared to listed peers

- Relevant risk factors particularly attributable to TES (**derived by using a market standard risk rate, ie listed vs. unlisted companies**).

Industry cash flows

An assessment of all JSE-listed companies' cash flow per share is outlined:

JSE Sector: ENGINEERING AND MACHINERY

	Latest year	2004	2003	2002	2001	2000	1999	1998	1997	1996	Average
Asset structure											
Total asset turnover	2,06	2,01	1,86	1,53	1,52	1,62	1,76	1,81	1,70	1,67	1,73
Funding structure											
Total assets to funding	1,87	1,87	1,87	1,74	1,63	1,52	1,88	2,01	1,73	1,87	1,79
Fixed assets as % of funding	19,28	18,64	18,54	18,17	15,52	15,53	13,97	29,38	28,04	34,07	21,39
Long-term loans as % of total debt	7,08	6,46	5,77	7,26	10,27	14,77	9,99	11,70	18,76	17,19	11,42
Solvency and liquidity structure											
Current ratio	1,79	1,79	1,82	1,96	2,15	2,49	1,91	1,61	1,66	1,64	1,89
Quick ratio	0,73	0,73	0,73	0,89	1,02	1,28	0,90	0,69	0,77	0,76	0,86
Debt to assets	0,52	0,52	0,52	0,48	0,43	0,41	0,52	0,59	0,62	0,60	0,52
Debt to equity	1,05	1,03	1,03	0,88	0,76	0,68	1,09	1,38	1,34	1,38	1,07
Interest cover	5,71	5,42	6,00	6,38	6,10	3,67	2,85	3,17	4,07	3,27	4,58
Debt to cash flow	3,80	3,82	4,06	4,98	3,70	3,83	7,57	5,68	5,09	7,61	5,15
Cash flow interest cover	4,86	4,57	5,06	5,56	5,61	4,05	2,75	3,10	4,16	3,17	4,26
Profitability structure											
Operating profit margin (%)	9,89	10,24	10,10	8,73	10,16	7,89	6,36	8,24	9,19	7,10	8,63
Net profit margin (%)	5,66	5,73	5,49	4,83	6,59	4,90	2,66	4,19	5,18	3,53	4,78
Return on assets (%)	20,38	20,62	18,82	13,36	15,45	13,05	11,21	15,28	15,93	11,85	15,04
Inflation-adjusted return on assets (%)	19,59	19,79	17,80	12,71	14,82	12,32	10,56	14,46	14,78	10,54	14,18
Return on equity (%)	23,43	22,98	20,34	13,69	17,59	13,88	9,78	18,60	19,72	13,54	16,73
Inflation-adjusted return on equity (%)	21,79	21,29	18,27	12,49	16,46	12,64	8,48	16,60	17,09	10,52	14,93
Leverage factor	1,35	1,26	1,25	1,12	-2,80	-1,17	0,76	1,28	1,59	-0,47	0,32
Retention rate (%)	50,27	53,01	61,94	81,61	73,25	62,59	67,15	81,66	84,50	62,33	69,48
Return on external investments (%)	85,09	84,46	172,22	60,70	61,08	99,05	51,00	89,07	121,13	114,83	94,91
Trading activity structure											
Accounts receivable turnover	9,21	8,83	6,82	5,20	5,54	5,88	6,40	6,09	5,31	5,39	6,20
Share statistics											
Net asset value per share (Rand)	3,37	3,29	3,03	2,86	3,18	2,87	3,12	2,26	2,20	1,66	2,73
Cash flow per share (Rand)	0,93	0,89	0,77	0,51	0,65	0,51	0,45	0,55	0,58	0,30	0,58
Dividend cover	2,01	2,13	2,63	5,44	3,74	2,67	3,04	5,45	7,15	3,18	3,92
Cash flow dividend cover	2,62	2,80	3,87	6,66	4,52	3,95	4,62	7,29	11,15	4,46	5,46
Price/earnings ratio	6,67	6,29	5,83	6,27	5,93	6,86	7,35	8,57	10,47	12,89	7,87
Price/book ratio	1,27	1,19	1,11	0,92	0,83	0,78	0,86	1,94	2,05	2,28	1,34

Source: Business Consultants International database, 2005

fig 10.13:: average 2005 JSE-listed companies' cash flow per share

Under 'Share statistics' a ratio of 0.93 cents indicates that listed engineering companies' cash flow per shares is trading at a 7% discount to share prices. At the time of market analysis, BCI determined that the general trend was that no listed company achieved a scenario of attaining a ratio of 1. This is due to positive investor sentiment in South Africa, which has pushed share prices above the 'true' cash flow per share valuation.

The engineering (machinery) sector's cash flow forms part of general industries. Their cash flow per share is trading at discounts of 7% to share price.

This is the norm for listed companies in South Africa and is thus an important indicator for the final valuation or TES.

Price / earnings ratios

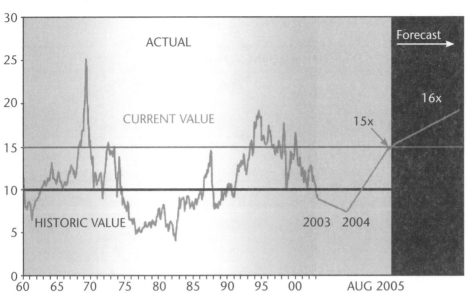

fig 10.14:: PE ratios of listed companies, August 2005

Note: The historic PE ratio for the All Share Index is at 10 times, while the current market ratio is at close to 15 times. This indicates that the market is 'expensive' and the forecast 'growth' line is indicative that the market is expected to continue to grow between 2005 and 2007.

However, it can be said that the 'minimum' PE ratio to be used in a valuation is 10 times while the norm would be 15 times.

A sector PE ratio would thus hone that valuation closer to a **fair and realistic** value. This would be further honed down by an assessment of listed engineering companies' PE ratios.

fig 10.15 :: specific price earnings ratios

SHARE	PE RATIOS
ENGINEERING & MACHINERY	
Bell	209 times
Howden	11 times
Hudaco	11.2 times
Invicta	9.27 times
Kairos	9.44 times
SECTORS	
All Share Index	15.0 times
Industrial Index	13.95 times
Engineering & Machinery	14.74 times

Conclusion:

- The PE ratio of Bell is ignored as it is a ridiculous level.

- Given this industry's market potential, the current All Share Index PE of 15 times is possible to use a maximum valuation.

- Note that the Engineering & Machinery (E&M) sector is trading at close to this level (on 14.74 times).

- BCI will use the sector PE as a fair & realistic measure of valuation.

Industry discount rates: Listed vs. unlisted companies

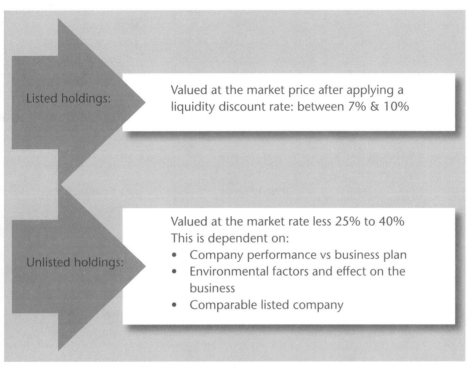

Listed holdings: Valued at the market price after applying a liquidity discount rate: between 7% & 10%

Unlisted holdings: Valued at the market rate less 25% to 40%
This is dependent on:
• Company performance vs business plan
• Environmental factors and effect on the business
• Comparable listed company

fig. 10.16:: conservative evaluation principles

NOTE: Given the high competitive nature of this market, the size of this company, lack of transparency and BEE, but solid history, management and future prospects, BCI has used a discount rate of 35%.

fig 10.17 :: fair value calculation

INCOME STATEMENT	ACTUAL	FORECAST
	2005	2006
Attributable income	R2,292,378	R2,521,615

INDICATIVE VALUATION				
VALUATION	**CURRENT VALUE**		**ONE YEAR FORECAST VALUE**	
PE ratio (attributable x PE)	14.74x	R33,789,651	14.74x	R37,168,61
LESS: Cash flow rate	7%	R31,424,376	7%	R34,566,813
LESS: a 35% Discount Industry Rate was used given that the company is small relative to its listed competitors	**R20,425,844**		**R22,468,428.91**	
FAIR VALUE (MID-POINT)	**R21,447,136**			

Note: The PE ratios reflect the E&M sector ratios. These were used as they represent similar company's price earnings and confirmed by the current sector ratio.

Cash flow discount rates reflect E&M sector (outlined above); standard industry rates.

The international minimum discount rate for liquidity and tradeability (listed vs. unlisted) of 35% was used as the company is expected to continue producing solid results; with a BEE partner.

BCI places a value of R21.5 million on TES, which is reasonable and fair.

This view may be reviewed/confirmed if a decision is taken to proceed with a corporate deal, ie BEE partnership. This would be done by analysing the underlying income/cash flows of the company.

Of importance:

- TES needs to formalise an alliance with a BEE company with regard to expansion plans, local industries and foreign expansion
- A restructuring of shareholding should be carried out via a staff incentive scheme and by implementing a BEE structure
- The new management structures should take into account KING II criteria for corporate governance.

Discounted cash flow analysis

As a second check on value, BCI's analysis concluded that the value of TES is R24.5 million. This analysis is set out below.

Income Statement Analysis (R'000)

	2006	2007	2008	2009	2010
Revenue	43,422	54,364	68,064	85,216	106,691
EBITA	4,125	5,165	6,466	8,096	10,136
Cash taxes on EBITA	1,485	1,859	2,328	2,914	3,649
NOPAT	2,640	3,305	4,138	5,181	6,487
Interest (paid) / received	141	143	146	149	152
Other income	0	0	0	0	0
Tax shield on interest and other income	51	-52	-53	-54	-55
Headline earnings & attributable income	2,730	3,397	4,232	5,276	6,584
No. shares	10,000	10,000	10,000	10,000	10,000
HEPS	27.3	34.0	42.3	52.8	65.8

Balance Sheet Analysis (R'000)

	2005	2006	2007	2008	2009	2010
Fixed assets	2,853	3,386	4,053	4,889	5,935	7,245
Other operating assets	0	0	0	0	0	0
Net working capital	1,478	1,810	2,226	2,747	3,398	4,215
Net invested capital	4,331	5,196	6,280	7,636	9,334	11,460
Excess cash	3,153	3,202	3,256	3,317	3,385	3,464
Marketable securities	0	0	0	0	0	0
Total investor funds	7,484	8,398	9,536	10,953	12,719	14,924
Debt	0	0	0	0	0	0
Non interest bearing liabilities	0	0	0	0	0	0
Minorities	0	0	0	0	0	0
Shareholders interest	7,484	8,398	9,536	10,953	12,719	14,924
Attributable income	2,292	5,023	10,620	12,318	14,436	17,080
Dividends	1,525	1,816	2,260	2,815	3,510	4,380
Dividend cover	1.42	1.50	1.50	1.50	1.50	1.50

Balance Sheet Analysis (R'000)

	2006	2007	2008	2009	2010
NOPAT	2,640	3,305	4,138	5,181	6,487
NI	665	1,083	1,356	1,698	2,126
FCF	1,775	2,222	2,782	3,483	4,361
Discount rate	1	1	1	0	0
NPV of FCF	1,479	1,543	1,610	1,680	1,753
5 Year value of NPV of FCF	1,479	3,022	4,632	6,312	8,064
Residual value and % of operational value				1	13,269
Operational value					21,333
Add cash/mkt occ					3,153
Less debt/minorities					0
Equity value					24,487
Shares in issue					10,000
Value per share (cps)					245

fig: 10.17:: discounted cash flow analysis

On a discounted cash flow basis, TES is valued at R24.5 million.

:: ::

APPENDICES

APPENDIX 1: TRENDS DIFFERENTIATING THE PAST FROM THE FUTURE

There are a number of general trends that business owners should be aware of:

- **Globalisation:** Organisations, of any size, today operate in the global arena. They are no longer restricted to their country or origin, nor are competitors. Many organisations start up with the sole intention of operating worldwide – these have been called 'born globals'. If global sounds too ambitious, it is nonetheless increasingly important not to confine a business to too limited a location.

- **Technological advancement:** The explosion of the Internet in recent years is changing how businesses operate, particularly in the areas of communication and information transfer.

- **Societal change:** A profound shift has occurred in the West from being a manufacturing-based society to an information and knowledge society. Organisations are now competing on knowledge and information. Your competitive advantage depends on what you know and how you put your knowledge to use.

- **The organisation as a collection of shareholders:** It is now accepted that organisations are much more than a group of employees. Progressive organisations involve their suppliers, customers and shareholders, as well as their employees, in their strategy. These groups of people have a 'stake' in the organisation, hence the term 'stakeholders'.

- **The reliance on innovation for success:** Organisations that refuse to change their product line or service while the environment around them changes are on course for failure. Innovation, doing new and different things, is what provides an organisation with an advantage over its competitors.

- **The nature of competition:** No longer do industry giants have an unchallenged monopoly. Small companies such as Netscape and Amazon can now compete directly with the major industry players.

- **A more diverse workforce:** It now includdes older workers, women and those from ethnic minorities. Diversity both impacts on, and enriches, the working practices and services that organisations can offer.

- **Changing organisational structure:** Where organisations use outsourcing, empowerment and communications technologies, they can be more flexible and responsive to market opportunities.

- **The need for lifelong learning:** Skills need to change with the requirements of the environment. It has been said that learning is the real key to competitive advantage in the future.

- **The increasing speed of change:** It's getting quicker.

- **Changing customers' attitudes and demands:**
  - Will the critical success factors of today hold good for tomorrow?
  - How well do you think your organisation's current strategy will fit into the future?
  - How quickly could your organisation change to take advantage of opportunities and defend against threats?
  - Do you have the flexibility to change direction rapidly?
  - How is technology changing what you do?
  - What key skills do you need to develop?
  - Do you have a learning workforce, or an obedient one?

APPENDIX 2: DOCUMENTS NEEDED WHEN PERFORMING IN-DEPTH DUE DILIGENCE

Financial

- Detailed statements of income and balance sheets per half-year (including annual reports) for the past three years and the current year to date.

- All supporting schedules to the above financial statements for the periods listed (eg manufacturing and overhead detailed accounts, selling, general and administrative accounts).

- These schedules should be split by major product line, if available. There should be separate schedules for local and international markets.

- Accounts receivable per customer for the past three years.
- Physical inventory summary or detailed breakdown of inventory (raw materials, work in process, labour and overheads) for the past three years.
- Accounts payable by vendor for the past three years.
- Listing of accrued expenses for the past three years.
- Tax returns for the past three years.

Property

- List of real and material personal property owned by the company.
- Documents of titles, mortgages, deeds of trust and security agreements pertaining to the properties listed.

Marketing

- Customer order reports. These are split per customer and product line for a period of at least three years.
- Listing of shipments by customer and product line for each month for the past three years and the current year to date.
- Listing of outstanding customer contracts and outstanding customer bids for the domestic, export and international divisions.
- Description of all manufacturer's representative organisations, agreements and commission schedules.
- List of buying sources: domestic, export and international.

Personnel

- All employment contracts or agreements.
- All bonuses, deferred compensation, share-option schemes, profit-sharing and retirement programmes.
- All pension plan documentation, including actuarial reports, tax returns and funding requirements for the past three years.
- Schedule of hourly wage rates and number of personnel at each rate.
- Organisation chart of salaried personnel, by location, showing function, responsibility, tenure, age, salary, name and title.
- A management organisation chart and biographical information.
- Summary of any labour disputes.

- Correspondence, memoranda or notes concerning pending or threatened labour stoppage.
- List of negotiations with any group seeking to become the bargaining unit for any employees.
- Schedule of all compensation paid to officers, directors and key employees for the most recent fiscal year showing, separately, salary, bonuses and non-cash compensation (ie use of cars, property, etc.).
- Summary of employee benefits and copies of any pension, profit-sharing, deferred compensation and retirement plans.
- Summary of management incentive or bonus plans not included above, as well as other non-cash forms of compensation.
- Confidentiality agreements with employees.
- Description of all related party transactions which have occurred during the last three years (and any currently proposed transaction) and all agreements relating thereto.

Contracts and Agreements

- All contracts or agreements with:
  - Vendors and customers
  - Employees
  - Unions
  - Other third parties
- All recent (within three years) appraisals of property, machinery and equipment.
- A list of machinery and equipment.
- All outstanding insurance claims.
- All patents, copyrights and license agreements.
- All lease or purchase agreements for machinery and equipment, vehicles and property.
- Legal descriptions of all property, including deeds, title reports and title insurance documentation, together with documentation of any lien thereon.
- List and description of all outstanding litigation or anticipated litigation.
- Is the union contract transferable? If yes, then a description of the mechanics of making a transfer, such as required approvals.

APPENDIX 3: RATIO ANALYSIS: COMMON CALCULATIONS

AREA	RATIOS	CALCULATION OF RATIO
Solvency	• General solvency check	[(Fixed assets + investments + current assets) × (Long term loans + current liabilities)] × 100
Liquidity	• Current asset ratio	Current assets × current liabilities
	• Quick ratio (acid test)	(Current assets - stock) × current liabilities
	• Stock to working capital ratio	(Stock × net current assets) × 100
	• Defensive interval ratio	Defensive assets × projected daily operating expenses
Profitability	• Profit margins	(Any profit figure × turnover) × 100
	• Return on shareholders' equity	(Attributable profits × shareholders' funds) × 100
	• Return on net assets	(Attributable profits × net assets) × 100
	• Return on capital employed	(Operating income × capital employed) × 100
Efficiency	• Stock turn	Group turnover × average stock
	• Accounts receivable days	Accounts receivable × (turnover × 365)
	• Accounts payable days	Accounts payable × (turnover × 365)
Leverage	• Debt : equity (gearing)	[(Long- and short-term loans + overdraft - cash) × Ordinary shareholders' funds] × 100

AREA	RATIOS	CALCULATION OF RATIO
	• Proportional debt ratio	Long-term loans × total assets
	• Ordinary shareholders' interest	(Ordinary shareholders' funds × loans) × 100
	• Long-term debt to capital employed	(Long-term loans × capital employed) × 100
	• Interest cover	Pre-tax income × interest paid
	• Average interest rate	(Interest expense - accounts payable) + liabilities
	• Gross cash flow to total debt ratio	[Gross cash flow (prior dividends) × loan] × 100
	• Cash flow to assets	Cash from operations + total assets
Investment performance ratios	• Earnings per share	(Attributable profit × issued ords) × 100
	• Dividend per share	(Dividends payable × issued ords) × 100
	• Dividend cover	Earnings per share × dividend per share
	• Earnings yield	(Earnings per share × share price) × 100
	• Dividend yield	(Dividend per share × share price) × 100
	• Dividend payout ratio	Yearly dividend per share + EPS
	• Price : earnings ratio	Inverse of earnings yield
	• Price : earnings growth (PEG)	Price : earnings + company's projected year-over-year earnings growth rate

>>

AREA	RATIOS	CALCULATION OF RATIO
	• Book value per share	(Shareholders' equity - preferred stock) + average outstanding shares
	• Debt / asset ratio	Total liabilities + total assets

APPENDIX 4: JSE AND ALTX LISTING REQUIREMENTS

Listing requirements	Main board	VCM	DCM	AltX
Share capital	R25 million	R0.5 million	R1 million	R2 million
Profit history	3 years	None	1 year	None
Pre-tax profit	R8 million	N/A	N/A	N/A
Shareholder spread	20%	10%	10%	10%
Number of shareholders	500	75	75	100
Sponsor/DA	Sponsor	Sponsor	Sponsor	Designated advisor
Publication in the press	Compulsory	Compulsory	Compulsory	Voluntary
Number of transaction categories	3	3	3	2
Special requirements	N/A	N/A	N/A	Financial director

Listing requirements	Main board	VCM	DCM	AltX
Annual listing fee	0.04% of average market capitalisation with a minimum of R26 334 and a maximum of R121 700 (including VAT).	0.04% of average market capitalisation with a minimum of R26 334 and a maximum of R121 700 (including VAT).	0.04% of average market capitalisation with a minimum of R26 334 and a maximum of R121 700 (including VAT).	R20 000 (including VAT)
Education requirements	N/A	N/A	NA	All directors to attend directors' induction programme

Source: JSE Securities Exchange

Note that the VCM and DCM are 'closed' to any new listings.

GLOSSARY

Acceleration clause: Clause causing repayment of a debt, if specified events occur or are not met.

Acceptance date: Time limit given to a prospective shareholder to accept an offer of shares in a rights issue.

Account: A trading period whose dates are fixed by the stock exchange authorities.

Accounting policies: Principles, bases, conventions, rules and procedures adopted by management in preparing and presenting financial statements.

Accounts payable: Bills which have to be paid as part of the normal course of business.

Accounts receivable: Debt owed to your company from credit sales.

Accumulated depreciation: Total accumulated depreciation reduces the book value (formal accounting value) of assets. The value of an asset is reduced each month by a predetermined amount and time frame. An asset worth R100, depreciated by R10 per month, would be written off over 10 months.

Acid test: A ratio used to determine how liquid a company is. It is determined by subtracting short-term assets from accounts receivable and inventory, which is then divided by short-term liabilities.

Aftermarket performance: A term typically referring to the difference between a stock's offering price and its current market price.

Agent: A person who acts on behalf of a client and has no personal interest in the order.

AIM: The UK-based AltX version, called the Alternative Investment Market.

All or nothing: Means the full order must be executed immediately or, if it is not possible to do so, the order must be routed to the special terms order book.

Allotment letter: Formal letter sent by a company to the investor to confirm that it will allocate him or her shares in a new issue.

AltX: The new Alternative Exchange launched in South Africa in October 2003.

American depositary receipts (ADRs): These are offered by non-US companies who want to list on a US exchange. Rather than constituting an actual share, ADRs represent a certain number of a company's regular shares.

Arbitrage: A purchase or sale by a member on his/her own account of securities on one stock exchange with the intent to sell or buy those securities on another stock exchange to profit by the difference between the prices of those securities on such stock exchanges.

Asset swap: A transaction which complies with all the requirements of the South African Reserve Bank in respect of an asset swap.

Asset turnover: Sales divided by total assets. Important for comparison over time and to other companies of the same industry.

At best: An order to be transacted in a manner that will, at the discretion of the member executing the order, achieve the best price for the client.

At market: An order to be transacted immediately against the best opposite order in the order book at the time of making such entry.

Authorised/issued share capital: While the authorised share capital is the maximum number of shares a company is permitted to issue over time, the issued share capital is the actual number of shares in issue. These figures are specified in pre-incorporation agreements (memorandum and articles of association). Investors can find these figures in a company's annual report.

Bad debts: An amount payable by debtors, which the firm determines is irrecoverable.

Balance sheet: A statement that shows a company's financial position on a particular date.

Bankers acceptances: A bill of exchange, or draft, drawn by the borrower for payment on a specified date and accepted by a chartered bank. Upon acceptance, the bill becomes, in effect, a post-dated certified cheque.

Bankruptcy: A legal procedure for formally liquidating a business carried out under the jurisdiction of courts of law.

Bear sales: The sale of listed securities of which the seller is not the owner at the date of sale.

Bear trend: When supply of shares outstrips demand and prices start to fall. If this trend continues for a number of weeks, the general sentiment becomes bearish and prices continue to fall.

Best efforts: This term is used to describe a deal in which underwriters only agree to 'do their best' in selling shares to the public. An IPO is more commonly done on a bought or firm commitment basis in which the underwriters are obligated to sell the allotted shares.

Bid (buyer's price): An offer to buy a number of securities at a certain stated price.

Bid, not offered: When shares are sought, but none are available. The opposite would be 'offered, not bid'.

Blank cheque: A company that indicates no specific industry, business or venture when its securities are publicly offered for sale and the proceeds of the offering are not specifically allocated.

Bond: Usually a fixed-interest security under which the issuer contracts to pay the lender a fixed principal amount at a stated date in the future and a series of interest payments, either semi-annually or annually. Interest payments may vary throughout the life of the bond.

Book value: The net amount of an asset shown in the books of a company, ie the cost of purchasing a fixed asset less the depreciation on that asset.

Bookkeeping: The process of collecting, classifying, recording and summarising a business's financial transactions in what are known as journals and ledgers.

Break-even point: The unit sales volumes or actual sales amounts that a company needs to equal its running expenses rate and not lose or make money in a given month. Break-even can be based on regular running expenses, which is different from the standard accounting formula based on technical fixed expenses.

Broker: The name given to a natural person recognised by the official stock exchange. Institutions will, from 1995, be able to become corporate members.

Brokerage: The commission charged by a member for the purchase or sale of securities.

Broker's note: A note which a member is required to send to a client recording the details of a purchase or sale of securities.

Bull trend: When demand for shares outstrips supply and prices start to rise. If this trend continues for a number of weeks, the general sentiment becomes bullish and prices continue to rise.

Burden rate: Refers to personnel burden, the sum of employer costs over and above salaries, including employer taxes and benefits.

Capital assets: Long-term assets, also known as fixed assets (plant and equipment).

Capital expenditure: Spending on capital assets (also called plant and equipment, or fixed assets).

Capital input: New money being invested in the business. New capital will increase your cash, and will also increase the total amount of paid-in capital.

Capital structure: Usually refers to the structure of ordinary and preference shares and long-term liabilities.

Capital turnover: Annual sales divided by average stockholder equity (net worth) (ie total sales for each R1 of equity).

Capital: This is also known as total shares in issue, owner's equity or shareholders' funds.

Capitalisation: The total amount of debt and equity issued by a company.

Cash budget: A plan or projection of cash receipts and disbursements for a given period of time. It is essential for the determination of cash deficiencies or excess cash balances.

Cash conversion cycle: The period of time it takes for a company to pay cash for a product, add its value to the product and then receive cash from the sale of that product.

Cash equivalents: Instruments or investments of such high liquidity and safety that they are virtually equal to cash.

Cash flow: A statement which shows the net difference between cash received and paid during the company's operating cycle.

Cash: The bank balance, or cheque account balance, or real cash in bills and coins.

Cash-flow forecast: An estimate of the timing and amount of a company's inflow and outflow of money measured over a specific period of time, typically, monthly for one to two years, then annually for an additional one to three years.

Closing price: The last sale price or a higher bid or lower offer price for a particular security.

Collection period (days): The average number of days that pass between delivering an invoice and receiving the money.

Collection days: See Collection period.

Commission: The brokers charge a fee for buying and selling shares, which is brokerage or commission earned on a deal.

Commission percent: An assumed percentage used to calculate commissions expense as the product of this percentage multiplied by gross margin.

Convertible and redeemable - preference shares: An alternative mechanism to ordinary shares. It enables companies to issue other shares which can either be bought back from investors or converted into ordinary shares at a later date.

Corporate finance transaction: A transaction which is entered into in writing and requires public notification in the press in terms of the listings requirements of the JSE.

Cost of sales: The costs associated with producing the sales. In a standard manufacturing or distribution company, this is about the same as the costs for people delivering the service, or subcontracting costs.

Credit risk: Risk that a borrower may default on obligations, thus a danger that repayment will not take place.

Creditors: People or companies that you owe money to. This is the old name for accounts payable.

Crossed market: Where a bid price is higher than the offer price for a security.

Cum or ex-dividend: After a company has declared a dividend, it would close its books to start paying dividends. The share will be marked ex-div, which means that any new shareholder will be omitted from the past year's dividend payout. Before the company declares a dividend payout, the share will be assumed to include possible dividends or to be cum-div.

Current assets: Those assets that can be quickly converted into cash and include accounts receivable, stock and debtors book. These are often called liquid assets.

Current debt: Short-term debt, short-term liabilities.

Current liabilities: A company's short-term debt, which must be paid within the firm's operating cycle, ie less than one year.

Deal breaker: A significant issue relating to proposed financing between the prospective investor and the business owner that must be resolved in order to close the deal.

Debentures: A bond which is not secured by fixed assets.

Debt and equity: The sum of liabilities and capital. This should always be equal to total assets.

Debtors: People or companies who owe your company money. It is the old name for accounts receivable.

Demand loan: A loan that must be repaid in full on demand.

Depreciated replacement value: The value of an asset with reference to the cost of replacing the asset with a new asset of similar utility minus an amount reflecting the depreciation of the existing asset.

Depreciation: An accounting and tax concept used to estimate the loss of value of assets over time – for example, cars depreciate with use.

Dilution: Reduction in per share participation in net earnings and ownership through an increase in issued stock.

Discount rate: A rate of return used to convert a monetary sum, payable or receivable in the future, into present value.

Discounted cash flow (DCF): Techniques for establishing the relative worth of a future investment by discounting (at a required rate of return) the expected net cash flow from the project.

Discounting: The process of finding the present value of a series of future cash flows. Discounting is the reverse of compounding.

Divestiture: Sale of part of a company. It is the opposite of merger.

Dividend coverage: Number of times a company's dividend is covered by earnings available to pay it.

Dividend yield: The ratio of the latest dividend to the cost or market price of a security expressed as a percentage.

Dividends: Money distributed to the owners of a business as profits.

Double top: This technical assessment is formed when a stock advances to a certain price level only to retreat from that level, and then rally again back to that level. The up moves are accompanied by high volume and the recession from the top comes on receding volume.

Due diligence review: The investigatory and review procedures carried out by strategists, accounts and lawyers,

Due diligence: A reasonable investigation conducted by the parties involved in preparing a disclosure document to form a basis for believing that the statements contained therein are true and that no material facts are omitted.

Earnings yield: The ratio of net earnings per security to the market price expressed as a percentage.

Earnings: Also called income or profits, earnings are the famous 'bottom line': sales less costs of sales and expenses.

Earnout: A method of structuring a transaction whereby the ultimate purchase price depends in part on the future performance of the business being acquired.

EBIT: Earnings before interest and taxes.

EBITDA: Earnings before interest, income taxes, depreciation and amortisation.

Economic value added (EVA): After-tax net operating profit minus cost of capital.

Empirical approach: Valuation approach whereby the value of a company is determined by reference to open market transactions involving similar companies or by reference to value relationships implied in the stock price of publicly traded companies.

Equity buyback: The investors' percentage ownership of a company that can be re-acquired by the company, usually at a predetermined amount.

Equity kicker: The term usually refers to the situation where an investor has subordinated debt in a company and, in return for a lower interest rate, the investor is given the option to convert some of the debt into equity at a future date.

Equity: Business ownership; capital. Equity can be calculated as the difference between assets and liabilities.

Escrow: An agreement put into the custody of another party until certain conditions are fulfilled.

Exchange risk: The risk associated with an asset or liability denominated in a foreign currency. It is vulnerable to the movement of exchange rates.

Executive summary: A concise summary of an investment proposal that describes a company's background, products or services, financial needs, financial requirements, management capabilities, market description and financial data.

Exit options: A variety of options available to investors to recover their invested capital and the return on their investment.

Expected return: The total amount of money (return) an investor anticipates to receive from an investment.

Fill or kill: The full order must be executed immediately or otherwise cancelled.

Financial notes: Information explaining financial figures (balance sheet, income statement and cash flow).

Fiscal costs: Running costs that take time to wind down, usually rent, overheads, some salaries. Technically, fixed costs are those that the business would continue to pay even if it went bankrupt. In practice, fixed costs are usually considered the running costs.

Fiscal year: Standard accounting practice allows the accounting year to begin in any month. Fiscal years are numbered according to the year in which they end. For example, a fiscal year ending in February of 1992 is fiscal year 1992, even though most of the year takes place in 1991.

Fixed assets: Includes all fixed (immovable) assets, namely property, vehicles, machinery and equipment. It cannot usually be converted into cash within the firm's operating cycle.

Fixed expenses: Cost of doing business, which does not change with the volume of business. Examples might be rent for business premises, insurance payments, heat and light.

Fixed rate loan: Loan for a fixed period of time with a fixed interest rate for the life of the loan.

Flipping: This is when an investor has acquired an IPO at its offering price and sells it immediately for a quick gain soon after it starts trading on the open market. It is a practice discouraged by underwriters, and can lead such investors to unfavourable relationships with their underwriters with future IPOs.

Floating charge: Charge or assignment on a company's total assets as security for a loan on total assets without citing specific assets.

Floating rate: A situation where the interest rate or rate of exchange is determined solely by market forces.

Forecast: Future-oriented financial information prepared using assumptions, all of which reflect the entity's planned courses of action for the period covered, given management's judgement as to the most probable set of economic conditions.

Foreign exchange: Claims in a foreign currency payable abroad, including bank deposits, bills, cheques. Foreign exchange rates refer to the number of units of one currency required to buy another.

Front-end fees: Fees paid when, for example, a financial instrument such as a loan is arranged.

Front-end loading: Charges or fees that are greater at the start of a loan or investment contract than in its later stages.

Funding consolidation: The process of replacing short-term debt with long-term securities (shares or bonds).

Funding costs: The price of obtaining capital, either borrowed or equity, with intent to carry on business operations.

Going concern: A company which is operating, ie has not stopped producing goods or providing a service and one which has not been placed under liquidation or curatorship.

Goodwill: An intangible asset reflected in balance sheets, which indicate an excess over market value for assets paid by the firm.

Gross geographic product: A statistic which shows the remuneration received by the production factors (land, labour, capital and entrepreneurship) for their participation in production of goods and services in a defined area.

Gross margin percent: Gross margin divided by sales, displayed as a percentage. Acceptable levels depend on the nature of the business.

Gross margin: Sales less cost of sales.

Head and shoulders: This technical pattern is typically characterised by one intermediate top (left shoulder), followed by a second top higher than the previous top (head), and a third rally that fails to exceed the head (right shoulder). The neckline is drawn connecting the reaction lows (support). The pattern is completed when prices break below the neckline and the sell signal is given.

Horizontal analysis: The process of comparing consecutive financial statements by examining the increases or decreases between the periods in terms of absolute rands and percentages.

Hurdle rate: A predetermined benchmark rate of return. If the rate of return expected from the project or investment falls below the benchmark, the projected investment will no longer be accepted. The hurdle rate should be the marginal cost of capital adjusted for the project's risk.

Hypothecation: The pledge of property and assets to secure a loan. Hypothecation does not transfer title, but it does provide the right to sell the hypothecated property in the event of default.

Immediate deal: A transaction in a listed security where settlement is to take place the next business day.

Income statement: A statement showing net income or loss for a specified period.

Interest expense: Interest is paid on debts, and interest expense is deducted from profit as expenses.

Inventory turnover: Sales divided by inventory. Usually calculated using the average inventory over an accounting period, not an ending-inventory value.

Inventory turns: Inventory turnover (above).

Inventory: This is another name for stock; goods in stock, either finished goods or materials to be used to manufacture goods.

Jobbers: These are the market's share merchants. They deal only with brokers and other jobbers (ie not with dealers) and their main function is to maintain a market by quoting a price.

Labour: In business plans the word 'labour' often refers to the labour costs associated with making goods to be sold. This labour is part of the cost of sales, part of the manufacturing and assembly. In economic terms, labour often denotes the sale of a skill to produce a good or service.

Letter of acceptance: The investor may receive such a letter if the company accepts his application for shares.

Leverage ratio: A financial ratio that measures a firm's debt burden. The debt, times interest earned and fixed charges coverage ratios are leverage ratios.

Leverage: The relationship between interest-bearing debt and equity in a company (financial leverage) or the effect of fixed expense on after-tax earnings (operating leverage).

Liabilities: Debts; money that must be paid. Usually, debt on terms of less than five years is called short-term liabilities, and debt for longer than five years is called long-term liabilities.

Limit order: An order which may be effected only at prices equal to or better than the price on the order.

Liquidity: A company's ability to pay short-term debt with short-term assets.

Listing: The official granting of a listing of a company's shares on the JSE.

Local counter-party transaction: A transaction in which a member trades as a principal with a person in South Africa other than a member.

Long-term assets: Assets like plant and equipment that are depreciated over terms of more than five years, and are likely to last that long too.

Long-term interest rate: The interest rate charged on long-term debt. This is usually higher than the rate on short-term debt.

Long-term liabilities: This is the same as long-term loans. Most companies call a debt long term when it is on terms of five years or more.

Management leveraged buyout: The situation when the management of a company purchases all the company's shares or assets. Usually, the company's assets become security for the loans necessary to make the purchase.

Management of investments: The management of investments on behalf of a client, by a member or an approved person.

Management: Individuals in an entity that have the authority and the responsibility to manage the entity. The positions of these individuals, and their titles, vary from one entity to another and, to some extent, from one country to another depending on the local laws and customs. Thus, when the context requires it, the term includes the board of directors or committees of the board that are designated to oversee certain matters (eg audit committee).

Market capitalisation: Used to denote a company's size and is calculated by multiplying a company's issued share capital by its current share price.

Market indicators: Statistics that give an overall picture of how the market is performing.

Market maker: A member who negotiates dealings in blocks of securities.

Market risk: The part of a security's risk that cannot be eliminated by diversification.

Marketable securities tax (MST): The tax imposed in terms of the Marketable Securities Act of 1948 in respect of every purchase of marketable securities through the agency of or from a member at the rate of 0.25% of the consideration for which the securities are purchased.

Marketable securities: All instruments legally permitted to trade on the JSE. These include shares (ordinary and preference), gilts, futures and options.

Materials: Included in the cost of sales. These are not just any materials, but materials involved in the assembly or manufactured of goods for sale.

Maturity date: Date on which a debt is due for payment.

Mentor: A close personal contact, usually in your industry, who has a network of contacts in the investment community and can assist in achieving your objectives.

Mezzanine debt: Non-conventional debt that has a greater element of risk than secured debt, but less risk than equity.

Minority shareholders: Shareholders who by virtue of their percentage ownership of the company do not have voting control of the company.

Monopoly: When one company controls and dominates a particular company.

Mortgage: Debt instrument by which the borrower (mortgagor) gives the lender (mortgagee) a lien on property as security for the repayment of a loan.

Negative covenant: A promise not to do certain things.

Net cash flow: This is the projected change in cash position, an increase or decrease in cash balance.

Net income: The level of profit in a business after the deduction of income taxes, depreciation, operating expenses and other expenses. It is also known as after-tax profit or net profit.

Net present value (NPV): A method of ranking investment proposals. NPV is equal to the present value of future returns, discounted at the cost of capital, minus the present value of the cost of the investment.

Net profit: The operating income less taxes and interest. The same as earnings, or net income.

Net realisable value: Selling price of an asset minus the expenses of bringing the asset into a saleable state and expenses of the sale.

Net working capital: Current assets minus current liabilities. Often simply referred to as 'working capital'.

Net worth: This is the same as assets minus liabilities, and the same as total equity.

Networking: Making use of contacts, associates and friends.

Non-assignable: Restriction in a contract limiting the ability of a shareholder to transfer the rights, benefits or obligations pursuant to that contract.

Non-compete: Generally refers to a clause in a contract that restricts a person from starting a similar business or working for a competitor. It is normally time- and area-specific.

Odd lot: Any quantity of securities which is less than a round lot (Krugerrands do not have odd lots).

Offer (seller's price): The price at which a dealer is prepared to sell securities on the market.

Offering price: This is the price set by the sponsor, at which the company's stock is sold to the first round of investors.

Offering range: This is the price range at which the company expects to sell its stock. This can be found on the front page of the prospectus. As with everything traded, market conditions and demand dictate the final offering price.

Oligopoly: When a few companies control and dominate a particular market.

Opening price: This is the first price that the company's stock trades on its first day of trading.

Order: An instruction.

Ordinary shares: Commercial paper issued to investors to raise capital. Investors hold these shares as part owners in the firm.

Other short-term assets: These are securities and business equipment .

Other short-term liabilities: These are short-term debts that don't cause interest expenses. For example, they might be loans from founders or accrued taxes (taxes owed, already incurred, but not yet paid).

Overheads: Running expenses not directly associated with specific goods or services sold, but with the general running of the business.

Over-the-counter market (OTC): A market made up of dealers who make a market for those securities not listed on an exchange. The over-the-counter market is made between buyers and sellers over the telephone, rather than the electronic market found on the JSE.

Paid-in capital: Real money paid into the company as investments. This is not to be confused with par value of stock, or market value of stock. This is actual money paid into the money as equity investments by owners.

Paper profit: A surplus income over expense, which has not yet been released, ie share prices which have increased above the price at which they were bought, but not yet sold.

Par value: The nominal value of a share and is an arbitrary amount placed on the share by the company.

Payment days: The average number of days that pass between receiving an invoice and paying it.

Payroll burden: Payroll burden includes payroll taxes and benefits. It is calculated using a percentage assumption that is applied to payroll. For example, if payroll is R1,000 and the burden rate 10 percent, then the burden is an extra R100. Acceptable payroll burden rates vary by market, by industry and by company.

Plant and equipment: This is the same as long-term assets, or fixed assets, or capital assets.

Portfolio: A schedule, normally computer-generated, listing the relevant details in respect of the securities held by an investor.

Price earnings (PE) ratio: The market price of securities divided by its earnings. It expresses the number of years' earnings (at the current rate) which a buyer is prepared to pay for a security.

Primary market: Where shares are distributed at the offering price to investors.

Principal transaction: A member trades with a counter-party or another member.

Private placement: An offering of a limited amount of shares or units, in which the recipients receive restricted stock from the issuer.

Product development: Expenses incurred in development of new products; salaries, laboratory equipment, test equipment, prototypes, research and development, etc.

Profit before interest and taxes: This is also called EBIT, for Earnings Before Interest and Taxes. It is gross margin minus operating expenses.

Projection: Future-oriented financial information prepared using assumptions that reflect the entity's planned courses of action for the period.

Prospectus: This document is an integral part of a documentation that must be filed with the JSE. It defines, among many things, the company's type of business, use of proceeds, competitive landscape, financial information, risk factors, strategy for future growth, and lists its directors and executive officers.

Published financials: Financial statements and financial information made public.

Purchase agreement: A legal document recording the final understanding of the parties with respect to the proposed transaction.

Ratchet clause: A clause in a contract that adjusts the rights of the parties to the contract on the completion of mutually agreed upon performance criteria.

Rate of return: Return on invested capital (calculated as a percentage). Often an investor has, as one investment criterion, a minimum acceptable rate of return on an acquisition.

Real property: Real estate, including land and buildings.

Receivable turnover: Sales on credit for an accounting period divided by the average accounts receivable balance.

Recourse: The right to receive payment in the event a person defaults on a loan. Recourse could give the lender the ability to take possession of the borrower's assets.

Redundant assets: Assets that are not required for the ongoing operation of the business and could be withdrawn without affecting future earning potential.

Registration: A new shareholder is registered when his or her name is placed on the role of shareholders for that specific company.

Renunciation date: The company sets a date by which the shareholder has to decide whether he or she will take up the rights issue.

Replacement value: Cost of acquiring a new asset to replace an existing asset with the same functional utility.

Representations: Statements made by either party with respect to certain elements of the proposed transaction that, if proven untrue, may give the other party the right to claim for damages from the party making the warranty.

Research and development incentives: Government programmes to promote research and development.

Residual value: Typically estimated based on the present value of the after-tax cash flow expected to be earned after the forecast period.

Resistance: When stocks go up, they tend to reach a point where investors think they are overvalued and sellers of the stock outnumber buyers. This causes the price of the stock to stop dead in its tracks. It cannot go higher because there are no buyers. This point is called 'resistance'.

Restricted liquidity: Inability of an individual or company to convert an asset into cash, or cash equivalent, without significant cost.

Retained earnings: A figure which shows the sum of a company's net profit less dividends paid to shareholders.

Return on assets: Net profit dividend by total assets. A measure of profitability.

Return on equity: A ratio used to show how profitable a business is to the shareholders.

Return on investment: Net profits dividend by net worth or total equity, yet another measure of profitability. Also called ROI.

Return on sales: Net profits dividend by sales, another measure of profitability.

Reverse head and shoulders: This is the same pattern as a head and shoulders except that it has been turned upside down and indicates a trend change from down to up. A buy signal is given when prices carry up through the neckline.

Rights issues: There are a number of methods a company can use to increase the size of its share capital. If it decides to offer its existing shareholders first option on the issue, it is called a 'rights' issue. The dealers would note that such an issue is in progress as it would be quoted as cum-capitalisation and after completion of the issue it would be noted as ex-capitalisation.

ROI: Return on investment; net profits dividend by net worth or total equity, yet another measure of profitability.

Round lot: the standard unit of trade – in all equities: 100 shares.

Sales break-even: The sales volume at which costs are exactly equal to sales.

Sales on credit: Sales on credit are sales made on account, shipments against invoices to be paid later.

Scrape value: An amount left after an asset has been fully depreciated, ie if an asset of R115 is depreciated by R10 per month over 11 months, the scrape value would be R5.

Secondary market: Better known as the Stock Market, where shares are openly traded.

Securities: Includes stocks, shares, debentures (issued by a company having a share capital), notes, units of stock issued in place of shares, options on stocks or shares or on such debentures, notes or units, and rights thereto, and options on indices of information as issued by a stock exchange on prices of any of the aforementioned instruments.

Seed financing/capital: Generally refers to the first contribution of capital towards the financing requirements of a start-up business.

Sensitivity analysis: Technique used to determine the effects on net income or cash flow due to changes in assumptions (ie 'what if' analysis).

Settlement value: Rand amount of the final payment in a lease.

Settlement: Procedure for brokers to close off their books on a particular transaction. The client is expected to pay for his or her new shares on or before the settlement date and he or she, in turn, can expect to be paid (on selling shares) within the same period (also called the Settlement Period).

Share capital: Total shares authorised to be issued, or actually issued, by a company.

Shareholders: Owners of one or more shares in a company.

Short-term assets: Cash, securities, bank accounts, accounts receivable, inventory, business equipment, assets that last less than five years or are depreciated over terms of less than five years.

Short-term notes: This is the same as short-term loans. These are debts on terms of five years or less.

Short Term: Normally used to distinguish between short-term and long-term, when referring to assets or liabilities. Definitions vary because different companies and accountants handle this in different ways. Accounts payable is always short-term assets. Most companies call any debt of less than five-year terms short-term debt. Assets that depreciate over more than five years (eg plant and equipment) are usually long-term assets.

Shotgun: A clause in a shareholders' agreement whereby if one party offers to buy out the other at a certain price, the other party has, within a limited period, the right either to accept the price or buy the offeror out at the same price.

Sinking funds: A required annual payment designed to amortise a bond or an issue of preferred shares. The sinking fund may be held in the form of cash or marketable securities, but generally the money put into the fund is used to retire some of the securities in question each year.

Splitting of shares: At times a share could become too expensive for the private investor, at which time the company may decide to split or sub-divide the shares into smaller denominations. The aim is often to make the shares more tradeable and, at times, this increases the share price on positive sentiment.

Spread: The differential between a bid and an offer price.

Stag: An investor who buys shares in a pre-listing or rights offer with the intention of selling those shares at a profit as soon as trading starts.

Standby fee: A fee charged on the unused portion of the credit under a revolving credit or line of credit arrangement.

Starting year: A term to denote the year that a company started operations.

Statement of changes in financial position: A financial document that presents the increases or decreases in funds of a business for all its accounts broken down under three major headings: operating activities, financing activities and investing activities.

Statement of retained earnings: A financial document that shows how much of the net income of a business has been retained over a given period of time, and how much has been paid out to the owners.

Stock dividend: A dividend paid in shares as opposed to cash.

Stock Exchanges Control Act of 1985 (as amended): An Act of Parliament in terms of which stock exchanges in South Africa are governed. The Act is administered by the Financial Services Board.

Subordinated debt: A non-conventional financing instrument where the lender accepts a reduced rate of interest in exchange for equity participation.

Support: Over time, a stock tends to become attractive to investors at specific prices. When a stock starts to decline to one of these prices, investors tend to come in and purchase the stock, thereby halting its decline. When buyers outnumber sellers, the price of the stock tends to go up. This point at which buyers enter the market is called 'support'.

Sustainable growth rate: The rate of increase in sales a company can attain without changing its profit margin, assets to sales ratios, debt to equity ratio or dividend payout ratio. It is the rate of growth a company can finance without excessive borrowing or a new stock issue.

Syndication: A method of selling an investment through the use of a group of companies or investors.

Tax rate percent: An assumed percentage applied against pre-tax income to determine taxes.

Taxes incurred: Taxes owed but not yet paid.

Tick size: The specified parameter or its multiple by which the price of a security may vary when trading at a different price from the last price, whether the movement is up or down from the last price.

Undepreciated capital costs: The tax definition of the value of an asset that is eligible for tax depreciation.

Undercapitalisation: A situation in which a business does not have sufficient equity in its capital structure.

Unencumbered: Property free and clear of all liens (creditors' secured claims).

Unit variable cost: The specific labour and materials associated with a single unit of goods sold. Does not include general overheads.

Units break-even: The unit sales volume at which the fixed and variable costs are exactly equal to sales.

What-if scenarios: Analysis of the economic effect of possible future situations, such as economic downturns, loss of key customers, changes in interest rates or price levels, or new competitors or technologies.

Withdrawn/postponed: From time to time a company will decide that market conditions are out of favour and not conducive to a successful IPO. There are many reasons why a company will decide to withdraw its IPO. Among these reasons are: a simple lack of willing investors at that time, market volatility or the emergence of a bear market.

Working capital: The excess of current assets over current liabilities. This represents the amount of net non-fixed assets required in day-today operations.

Write-off: Debt that cannot be collected and finally written-off as bad. The debt is a loss to the company, and the greater the level of bad debts, the less likely a business owner will be able to obtain bank financing. Maintaining bad debts to a minimum is seen as the ability of a company to run efficiently and to have efficient systems in place.

REFERENCES

Alford, A.W. 1992 'The Effects of the Set of Comparable Firms on the Accuracy of the Price Earnings Valuation Method'. *Journal of Accounting Research.*

Ansoff, H. 1965 *Corporate Strategy.* McGraw-Hill.

Armen, A. and Allan, W.R. 1972 *University Economics* (3rd ed.) Wadsworth Publishing Company.

Brigham, E. 1983 *Essentials of Management Finance* (3rd ed.). Chicago: Dryden Press.

Britzuis, O. 1988 *South African Company Practice.* Juta & Co.

Dropkin M. & La Touch, B. 1998 *The Budget Building Book for Non profits: A Step-by-Step Guide for Managers and Boards* San Francisco: Jossey-Bass.

DuCharme, L. L., Malatesta P. H. and Sefcik S. E. 2000 *Earnings management, stock issues, and shareholder lawsuits.* Working paper, University of Washington.

Ernst & Whinney. 1982 *Preparing a Business Plan: A Guide for the Emerging Company.* Ernst & Whinney.

Fowler, B. A. 1989 'What do Venture Capital Pricing Methods Tell About Valuation of Closely Held Firms?' *Business Valuation Review* (June).

Hayek, F. A. 1954 *Capitalism and the Historians.* Chicago: University of Chicago Press.

Helmkamp, J. 1982 *Principles of Accounting.* John Wiley & Sons.

Herzlinger R. E. & Nitterhouse D. 1994 *Financial Accounting and Managerial Control for Nonprofit Organisations.* Cincinnati: South-Western Publishing.

IMF Research Department. 2005 *World Economic Outlook.* IMF.

Johnson, R. 1990 *The 24 Hour Business Plan.* Century Business.

JSE Securities Exchange (South Africa) Listing Requirements, Section 21, 2003.

Leland Bach, G. 1968 *Economics* (6th ed.). Prentice-Hall, Inc.

Magliolo, J. 1995 *Share Analysis And Company Forecasting* Cape Town: Struik Zebra Press.

Magliolo, J. 1996 *The Business Plan: A Manual for South African Entrepreneurs* Cape Town: Struik Zebra Press.

Magliolo, J. 2002 *The Millionaire Portfolio* Cape Town: Struik Zebra Press.

Magliolo, J. 2002 *Jungle Tactics: Global Research, Investment & Portfolio Strategy* Heinemann.

Magliolo, J. 2004 *A Guide to AltX: Listing on South Africa's Alternative Exchange.* Cape Town: Struik Zebra Press.

Magliolo, J. 2005 *Become Your Own Stockbroker*. Cape Town: Struik Zebra Press.

McGregors. 1987 *Privatisation in South Africa*. Juta & Co.

Navarro, P. 2006 *The Well Timed Strategy: Managing the Business Cycle for Competitive Advantage*. Wharton School Publishing.

Orley, M. A. Jr. 1994 *A Pedestrian's Guide to Economics*. Oklahoma State University Press.

Owen F. 1998 *Understanding Exchange Rates*. Federal Reserve Bank of Cleveland.

Pacelle, M. 'Venture Firms Dethroning Buyout Kings'. *Wall Street Journal*, June 7 1999.

Peters, E. 1992 *Chaos and Order in the Capital Markets*. John Wiley & Sons.

Peters, E. 1994 *Fractal Market Analysis*. John Wiley & Sons.

Pithey, M.. 1993 *It's your Business!* Chameleon Press.

Reisman, G. 1996 *Capitalism - A Treatise On Economics*. Jameson Books.

Ricardo, D. 1962 *Principles of Political Economy and Taxation*. Cambridge: Cambridge University Press.

Richardson, J E 2005. *Annual Editions Marketing 06/07* McGraw-Hill.

Richardson, P. 1997 *Globalisation and Linkages: Macro-Structural Challenges and Opportunities*. OECD Economic Studies.

Robinson, G. 1986 *Strategic Management Techniques*. Canada: Butterworths.

Rosso, H. 1996 *Rosso on Fund Raising*. San Francisco: Jossey-Bass.

Sexton, D. & Kasarda, J. 1992 *The State of the Art of Entrepreneurship*. KWS-Kent.

Silver, D. A. 1980 *The Entrepreneurial Life: How to go for it and get it*. John Wiley & Sons.

Silver, David A. *Venture Capital: The Complete Guide for Investors*, John Wiley & Sons, 1985.

Sraffa, P. *The Works and Correspondence of David Ricardo*, Cambridge University Press, 1962.

Stern G. J. 1990 *Marketing Workbook for Nonprofit Organisations*, Vol. 1, Develop the Plan. Amherst.

Stuart Mill, J. 1976 *Principles of Political Economy*. Fairfield.

Sumariwalla, Russy D. 2000 *Unified Financial Reporting System for Not-for-Profit Organizations* San Francisco: Jossey-Bass.

The JSE Securities Exchange (South Africa) Listing Requirements, 2002 Butterworths.

Thompson, A. A. 1973 *Economics of the Firm* Prentice-Hall.

Timmons, J. A. 1994 *New Venture Creation: Entrepreneurship for the 21st Century*, Irwin Press.

Touche Ross. 1986 *A Guide to Business Growth*. Touche Ross & Co.

Van der Merwe, S. 1976 *The Environment of South African Business*, Maskew Miller.

Von Mises, L. 1969 *Bureaucracy*, Chicago Economic department, New Rochelle, NY.

Von Mises, L. 1966 *Human Action* (3rd ed.). Chicago: Henry Regnery Co.

Weiss, J. 1980 *A Framework for Strategic Planning to Support Strategic Management*. Chase Manhattan Bank.

INDEX

Note: Page numbers in italics refer to figures or tables.